Quality | Research Papers

Nancy Jean
Vyhmeister

Your Indispensable
GUIDE to Writing

Quality | **Research Papers**

For Students of
Religion and Theology

GRAND RAPIDS, MICHIGAN 49530

ZONDERVAN™

Quality Research Papers
Copyright © 2001 by Nancy Vyhmeister

Requests for information should be addressed to:

Zondervan, *Grand Rapids, Michigan 49530*

Library of Congress Cataloging-in-Publication Data
Vyhmeister, Nancy Jean.
    Quality research papers : for students of religion and theology / Nancy Jean Vyhmeister.
        p. cm.
    Includes bibliographical references.
    ISBN 0–310–23945–1
    1. Religion—Research. 2. Theology—Research. I. Title.
BL41.V94 2001
200'.72—dc21   2001017662

Interior design by Todd Sprague
Printed in the United States of America

02 03 04 05 06 07 /❖ DC/ 10 9 8 7 6 5 4

TABLE OF CONTENTS

LIST OF ILLUSTRATIONS

Tables

Figures

INTRODUCTION

Books giving instructions for doing student research in biblical, theological, and pastoral research tend to be somewhat one-sided, often concentrating on bibliography and sources. Possibly their authors assume that their target students have already taken a course in research methods and know how to organize a paper and give it a correct format. More often than not, this is not true. This handbook tries to put several aspects of research writing—bibliography, search techniques, organization, and form—into a balanced perspective.

Born of a great need at the Seminario Adventista Latinoamericano de Teologia, the original text was written in Spanish in 1980 for South American graduate students. The first English version (1989) was designed to meet the needs of students working in English as a second language at the Adventist International Institute of Advanced Studies in the Philippines. This revision incorporates my experience teaching research and dissertation writing to graduate students at the Seventh-day Adventist Theological Seminary, at Andrews University, Berrien Springs, Michigan, over the last decade. Especially significant in this book are the innovations in technology, especially those of the James White Library at Andrews University.

The ideas and techniques in this book are not original. They have been collected from many authors, as the bibliography will attest. Over the years, these instructions have been given, with slight variations, to students in the Americas and Asia. The students' reactions and concerns have, to a certain extent, helped to shape this handbook. Therefore, this book is the result of the combined efforts of many people. To all who have somehow contributed, many thanks!

Several different research formats exist. The one used in this text is based on Kate Turabian's work, commonly used for theology and religion. Matters of detail may be consulted in that book,[1] of which serious students should own a copy.

---

[1] Kate L. Turabian, *A Handbook for Writers of Term Papers, Theses, and Dissertations*, 6th ed., rev. John Grossman and Alice Bennett (Chicago: University of Chicago Press, 1996). *The Chicago Manual of Style*, 14th ed. (Chicago: University of Chicago Press, 1993), which has more detailed instructions on writing, agrees with Turabian and may be useful to researchers and professors of research.

Quality Research Papers has four purposes:

1. to stimulate and develop students' capacity for doing careful and fruitful research
2. to help students improve their ability to clearly express the results of their research
3. to assist theology students to meet the requirements of their educational programs
4. to allay students' fear of doing research by improving their skills and tools

Because most people learn better when they are shown than when they are told how to do things, models are provided to show how a paper should look. The margins, spacings, headings, footnotes, and bibliographical entries are all done according to the rules presented in this book.

The first twelve chapters present the steps and procedures of research. Chapters 13 through 17 describe specialized forms of research: exegesis, description, program development, the case study, and book reviews. Chapter 18 discusses statistics, graphs, and tables as used in research. Chapter 19 deals with theses and dissertations, while chapter 20 presents instructions for writing a Doctor of Ministry project. Together, these chapters give the basic guidelines for students in theological education who desire to achieve success in research.

May your research be fruitful, stimulating, and even enjoyable!

Nancy Jean Vyhmeister

I | WHAT IS RESEARCH?

What makes research different from other types of studying and writing? What are the specific objectives of research? What are the essential steps in doing research? What pitfalls are to be avoided? How can one tell research from other forms of communication? What are the values and benefits of student research? These are questions this chapter endeavors to answer.

Definition of Research

Research can be defined as a method of study that, through careful investigation of all evidence bearing on a definable problem, arrives at a solution. To research a topic is to collect, organize, evaluate, and present data. This process cannot take place without analysis and synthesis, for research is more than a compilation of information. The results of research must be presented in a clear and concise way so that anyone can follow the process, without having to repeat any of the steps, in order to see how you, the researcher, have arrived at your conclusions.

A four-part definition of research is given by Isaac Felipe Azofeifa: "Research is a (1) systematic search for (2) adequate information to reach (3) objective knowledge of a (4) specific topic." Each element deserves individual analysis.[1]

1. Systematic search. This requires effort. It does not just happen. A researcher must develop and use a clear method and a logical system. Research is not easy; it requires time, energy, thought, and effort.
2. Adequate information. Research does not look for someone's ideas about matters touching on the problem; it seeks precise answers to the questions being asked. The information presented must be from authoritative sources, speak to the problem, and be duly documented.
3. Objective knowledge. In order to reach objective knowledge, you must have prior knowledge of the topic. To this prior knowledge you

---

[1] *Guía para la investigación y desarrollo de un tema* (San Jose, Costa Rica: Dpto. Publicaciones de la Universidad de Costa Rica, 1975), 5.

will add facts, not suppositions or possibilities. Research is done with the head and not the heart. Research looks at facts, not conjectures, nor even possibilities, much less long-cherished pet ideas .

4. Specific topic. It is impossible to do adequate research on a large topic. The research paper is not an encyclopedia. A specific, clearly delineated problem is the only one that can be solved.

Research may be writing a ten-page paper on Nazareth in the time of Christ. Research is what the writer of an M.A. thesis does for weeks on end. Persistent research efforts—over long months—go into producing a dissertation. As used in this book, the term *research* applies to all scholarly studies at undergraduate, graduate, or postgraduate level. Some teachers may call it a *research essay,* others may label it a *term paper.* Most of what students write for classes involves research.

Research is the search for truth—for God is truth—whether it be historical, scientific, or theological—it is all God's truth, as Frank E. Gaebelein points out.[2] This makes research a very appropriate activity for believers. Yet, because God is ultimate truth and human beings are limited and finite, our arrival at truth must not be considered final. We may never be able to see the whole picture. Furthermore, what is "truth" today may be changed tomorrow by a new discovery. For this reason, even a careful researcher must be humble.

Even in the area of theology we should be open to truths not seen before. In *Counsels to Writers and Editors,* Ellen White wrote last century about the attitudes that should exist in those who study the Scriptures. "We have many lessons to learn, and many, many to unlearn. God and heaven alone are infallible. Those who think that they will never have to give up a cherished view . . . will be disappointed."[3] Discussing further the search for theological truth, White wrote: "Truth is eternal, and conflict with error will only make manifest its strength. . . . We must study the truth for ourselves. No living man should be relied upon to think for us. No matter who it is, or in what position he may be placed, we are not to look upon any man as a perfect criterion for us."[4] Thus, we research, in search of all truth, humbly using our God-given minds to accomplish our search.

The Research Process

Although the research process will be studied carefully in the following chapters, at this point a brief synthesis of this endeavor is useful. In addition, we will consider some of the hindrances to the successful completion of research.

In its simplest form, the process to be followed in research is to identify, collect, evaluate, and present. Once you have selected a topic, you must identify the

[2]Frank E. Gaebelein, *The Pattern of God's Truth* (Chicago: Moody, 1968), 20, 23.
[3]Ellen G. White, *Counsels to Writers* (Nashville, TN: Southern Publishing Association, 1946), 37.
[4]Ibid., 44–45.

problem or issue to be tackled. The issue must be specific, often expressed as a research question, not something vague and general. After you know exactly what the problem to be solved is, you can begin collecting data. Gather information carefully from many sources. Organize your data in a way that is clear and logical to you and others. After you have gathered all the information, you will need to analyze and evaluate it: Not all sources are equally valuable; not all opinions are of the same weight. Finally, after you have gathered the evidence, you must draw conclusions regarding the solution of the problem. You will have to write a research report that gives a clear view of the problem, of the information gathered, and of the solution reached.

Some of the most dangerous pitfalls for researchers are those that relate to a previous mindset. When a cherished idea is being defended, for example, it is extremely difficult to be objective, to take into account adverse evidence, to break out of a limited thinking pattern. The prejudices (meaning here "prejudged results") taken into a research project set the tone and often determine the answer to a question. People usually see what they want to see. It is impossible to do research without presuppositions. One must, then, recognize what these presuppositions are, state them in the introduction to the research, and proceed from there. For example, if you accept the Genesis 1:26 statement that human beings were made in the image of God, whatever conclusions you reach on the treatment of psychological problems in children will reflect that basic understanding.

Other errors are those of hurriedness, inaccuracy, or carelessness. It is easy to come to premature conclusions, without having finished the research because of lack of time or bibliography. It is also easy to miss an important detail or to write down an erroneous fact. Researchers do not mean to make this kind of mistake. But these errors do happen, especially to students who are scrambling to survive the term. Research demands extreme caution and care—and much time.

Kinds of Research

Many different types of papers are written as part of theological education. Here is a list of twelve different ones.

1. **Essay:** a short paper (1–10 pages) that explores a topic without the rigor of a research paper. While the opinions of the writer may be prominent, referenced footnotes are required for all quotations, citations, and allusions.
2. **Report:** a short paper (1–10 pages) that summarizes findings on an assigned topic. All quotations must be referenced.
3. **Sermon:** a paper written as the basis for a later oral presentation. While research may be needed, it is not reported in the same way as in other papers. However, quotations should be referenced.

4. **Term paper or research paper:** a major paper (15–30 pages) that investigates a specific issue. Such a paper needs a clear introduction, as well as a summary and conclusions. All quotations, citations, or allusions are referenced. (The rest of this book will dwell on this type of paper.)

5. **Book review:** a short (1–3 pages) paper that describes and briefly evaluates a book or article.

6. **Critical book review:** a somewhat longer (2–4 pages) review that emphasizes the evaluation of the book or article. See chapter 17.

7. **Project:** a paper, either for a class or a degree, which emphasizes planning and doing as much as reading and writing. Projects are common in applied theology, especially in the Doctor of Ministry program.

8. **Thesis:** a major paper required for the completion of some master's degree. Its length is usually 100–150 pages. A written proposal must be approved before the task is undertaken. Theses may have to be defended before an examination committee (see chapter 19).

9. **Pastoral theology paper:** a major paper (20–30 pages) that applies the findings of research to a pastoral situation (see chapter 17).

10. **Case study:** a major paper (15–30 pages) that presents a case, analyzes factors affecting it, interprets what happened theologically, and proposes pastoral action to resolve the situation. The case study is used in practical theology, especially in the Doctor of Ministry program (see chapter 16).

11. **D.Min. dissertation:** a paper that ends the Doctor of Ministry program. It tends to be practical, as is the degree. This kind of paper is considered in chapter 20.

12. **Ph.D./Th.D. dissertation:** a major study, similar to a thesis, but longer and more complex, often 250–300 pages long. It must be written on an issue not previously researched (chapter 19).

While all these papers are different and are measured and evaluated by different criteria, professors still expect to find the following general attributes in any one of them:

1. Correct English, including spelling, grammar, syntax, and paragraph construction
2. Clarity of expression
3. Logical organization
4. Appropriate introduction and summary
5. Conclusions naturally derived from evidence
6. Correct format (in most English-speaking seminaries, this format is Turabian)

What Research Is Not

Perhaps giving some ideas on what research is *not* will help to clarify what it is.

Research is not simply a compilation of quotations. True, quotations are used to document and clarify findings. But research is not the result of an afternoon spent with scissors, glue, and photocopies. A good research paper shows that you have assimilated and synthesized (digested, if you like) the material and drawn logical conclusions.

Research is not simply rewriting other people's words and ideas into a neat description. In secondary or high school, we wrote papers by summarizing what we found in the textbook and the encyclopedia. The paper we proudly handed in gave a nice description of Outer Mongolia or the migration of Canada geese. It might have qualified as research at that level; however, it no longer counts! At the tertiary level, students need to analyze—break ideas and facts into small parts—and organize their ideas and facts into the appropriate thought "boxes." Only then can they write the research report or essay.

Research is not a defense or apology of my own convictions. This type of writing too often ignores unfavorable evidence and tends to look at one's position through rose-colored glasses. Research seeks truth; it does not hide—for any reason—what may disagree with esteemed ideas. If the position being maintained is tenable, research can defend it; if the position is not based on truth, it is defended in vain. We cannot allow ourselves to use unsound arguments, even for a good cause.

Likewise, research is not polemical. Its objective is to clearly present truth, not to fight others' positions, even if those may be erroneous. In good research, truth is presented in such a logical and convincing way that there is no need for harsh language.

Research is not the presentation of one's own opinions. Research demands showing facts, data, information. Naturally, the conclusions we reach are somewhat modified by our personal opinions, but whoever reads the research report must be able to follow the logic and the evidence to see how we reached our conclusions.

Finally, especially for theology students, research is not a sermon. It is different in content, style, and language. Some research may be involved in the preparation of a sermon, but the main purpose of a sermon is to reach the heart and change people's lives. The language and the message are appropriate to this goal. Research, on the other hand, seeks to inform and convince the mind. Research vocabulary is neutral, free of superlatives and emotional language. Furthermore, a sermon becomes effective through the delivery, whereas in research writing, there is no dramatic rendition from the pulpit. What appears on paper must stand, just as it is written, without any further embellishment.

The Value of Research

No one doubts the importance of the research that made vaccinations against polio or smallpox available. Neither do most people worry about why some erudites sit at their desks and read, study, and write, day after day. But some students question the importance of doing research papers since they are not researchers and may not plan to become such. They should realize that going through the discipline of research is valuable beyond the information obtained in the course of preparing the paper.

Learning to do research teaches you how to recognize a problem and how to go about solving it. Evidently, even educated people will not know all the answers; they should, however, know where to find them. Doing a research paper helps you learn how to find answers, in a library or elsewhere.

Writing a research paper can teach you far more than a teacher could. On the topic of the research paper, you become an expert, sometimes knowing more about it than the professor who assigned the paper. Besides, when you learn by doing, you learn better.

Preparing a quality research paper teaches skills of observation, analysis, synthesis, and judgment. You will learn to think differently when you think research. The ability to think critically—and that does not mean criticism, but weighing carefully all the evidences—is enhanced by learning the research process. In addition, writing a research paper helps develop character. When the going is hard and the task becomes drudgery, sticking with the work is a discipline that enhances the worth of any student.

Finally, the preparation of a research paper gives opportunity for the development of good writing skills. Learning to write well takes hours of rewriting and correcting. But being able to write clearly is a worthy achievement, which will prove useful to you as a student and later to you as a professional.

Aside from these considerations, I should mention the satisfaction of a job accomplished and the joy of discovery as important outcomes of writing research papers. Most students agree that research done well is worth the time and effort it takes.

With this chapter as a basis for research, the following chapters will discuss, one by one, the steps and procedures of research. The first step is to explore the topic through reading.

II | FINDING SOURCES

The aspects of research described in chapters 2 through 10 often take place simultaneously. You do not find sources first and then choose a topic; both activities happen together. The same can be said for developing a bibliography and taking notes. The processes are detailed in separate chapters only to facilitate the organization of the book. The first activity described is finding sources for the research.

Choosing a research topic presupposes some knowledge of the field. This means reading. And to read, one must find sources. Using a library can be intimidating, especially for the first time and if it is large. Even more disconcerting can be one's first venture into cyberspace, with its World Wide Web and myriad sites. How does one find things? Some general instructions may help diminish the panic and increase efficiency.

Resources in the Library

A student's first task is to become acquainted with the library and all its parts. Read the library handbook, if there is one. Walk through the library, noting where different collections are housed—indexes, reference works, electronic media. Find out where the reference and circulation desks are located and what services are offered there. Do not forget such basic services as restrooms and drinking fountains! Sign up for whatever library orientation programs are offered, even if they are not required. Make sure you know and understand the loan policies of the library, including those for interlibrary loans.

General library orientation takes new library patrons through all the main library sections. These sessions are helpful, but may not answer all the questions. Since your main interest is theology/religion, you should meet the theological librarian or bibliographer (the person who chooses and orders books for the theology collection) and ask about orientation for the specific area.

Acquaintance with the library must begin at the catalog, whether real or virtual. It will then continue to departments such as periodicals, electronic media, and the rare book rooms.

The Catalog

One gains access to the materials in a library through the catalog, where all the holdings are listed. While there are differences between the old-fashioned card catalog and the newer electronic catalog, the search approach is similar in both.

Card Catalog

The first step in using a card catalog is knowing how it is organized. Card catalogs list materials alphabetically: by author, title, and subject headings. In "divided" card catalogs, books listed by author and title are in one section, whereas books listed by subject heading are in another. Some libraries have a "unified catalog," with one alphabetical listing, containing authors, titles, and subject headings.

Catalog cards contain all the information needed for a bibliographical entry: author, title, place of publication, date of publication, editor, illustrator, series to which the book belongs, and sometimes notes about the book. You will also find the call number, which tells you where to look for the item, and one or more subject headings at the bottom of the card.

When you know the author or title of a book, you can start with that information. Remember, however, that the author's last name comes first. In addition, the initial article, definite or indefinite, in whatever language does not count for alphabetization. Look under *Greek-English Lexicon*, rather than *A Greek-English Lexicon*. Yet, do remember that in the rest of the title, articles do count.

When you do not have an author or title, you must search by subject heading. Although this kind of search is the most fruitful, it can be confusing at first. Subject headings are predetermined. You cannot change them, neither can your local librarian. The trick is to find out what subject headings are used for your topic. You may ask for the classification book and study it, or you may get at your information through the "back door." For example, you want to research "church planting." Dead-end street: the Library of Congress system does not have such a subject heading. What might the heading be? You try "church work," but the subject area is too large, not specific enough. Then you remember that you just read a book on church planting by Russell Burrill. You check the author catalog, under Burrill, Russell. You find the book *Rekindling a Lost Passion: Recreating a Church Planting Movement*. At the bottom of the card you find the subject heading: "Church development, new." Now you can look under that heading and discover other sources for your research.

All subject headings for topics related to Scripture begin with "Bible." You will find the subheadings "Bible, NT" and "Bible, OT." You will then find sub-subheadings, "Bible, NT, Acts" and so on. Even in "Bible, NT, Acts" there are subdivisions: "Bible, NT, Acts 2, Commentaries" is an example. Something else to remember: Librarians did not expect everyone to know the books of the Bible in order, so they have arranged them alphabetically: Revelation comes before Thessalonians.

Not all books that touch on a given topic are classified under the same subject heading. If the author's approach is sociological, the classification will be different from that of a psychological or religious approach. That means that you need to think of many and diverse possibilities. Keep asking yourself: What other words could be used to describe my topic?

Call numbers in the library catalog cards tell you where to find a book. The call number is usually given in Dewey Decimal or Library of Congress numbering systems. Whichever system is used, the result is the same: a fingerprint of the book. The first line (in Dewey) or first two (in LC) give you the subject category. The second (or third) line, beginning with a letter of the alphabet, identifies the author. The third (or fourth) line gives the date of publication.

Mastering the card catalog may take an hour or two; nevertheless, the benefits far outweigh the effort.

Electronic Catalog

Electronic library catalogs are fast becoming the norm for academic libraries. Not only are they faster to use, they also permit transfer of information to a printer or to your own computer. Typing and computer skills make their use even more effective. (That is not the last time you will hear about the need for these skills in doing research.)

The information contained in the electronic catalog—the bibliographic information, subject headings, and call number—are the same as found in the card catalog. Only the delivery system is different. What was said above about the contents of the cards stands. Electronic catalogs vary from library to library. However, once you have learned to use one, you can quickly learn another.

When you enter an electronic catalog, you find several options for searching: keyword, author, title, subject heading, and author/title. Of these, the most fruitful is the keyword search. It looks for a word or words in the title or subject heading of a book. For example, at the James White Library, when I type in "planting," I get 170 entries. I soon realize that there is a lot of agriculture in them, so I want to limit my search to "planting *not* agriculture"; I still get 163 hits. I try "church *and* planting" and find 76 items containing both words. Then I wonder if by not having other forms of the verb "plant" included I am missing something, so I type "plant* and church" and I am informed that the library has 131 items that match my query. The asterisk I added tells the computer to look for words beginning with "plant," but that add other letters, such as "planter" or "planted." Perhaps, I wonder, authors are using other words for church planting, so I try "(plant* or start) and church." As a result I find 161 entries.

This search shows how Boolean operators work. When I use the operator *and*, I am asking for both words to appear in the title or in the subject heading. When I use the operator *or*, I am happy to have one or the other. The operator *not* asks that items containing the term following *not* be eliminated. The parentheses look much like those in algebra; they do the same thing.

In electronic catalogs, the second most effective search strategy is the subject heading. What was said before about subject headings in a card catalog still holds: You can only guess at the headings used in cataloging. However, those guesses can become educated. The system provides electronic help. I type "Acts"; I am immediately reminded to look under "Bible, NT, Acts." I click and find 126 different subheadings.

Once you find one book on your topic, you can search for others like it by clicking on the subject heading. You can also click on the call number to see what other books sit on the shelf near the one you have chosen.

Most electronic catalogs allow you to transfer information from its system to your notes. You may print the references you find on a printer near the computer where you are working. You can copy bibliographical information to your diskette. You may also email yourself any number of entries. The problem with printed pages is that you still have to copy them to your note cards—and mistakes can creep in. If you have an electronic version of your bibliographical entries, you can edit it without having to retype completely. If you are working in the library, you can use the physical diskette; working from home mandates email. You will need to experiment with transmission of data from your library's electronic catalog to find the most efficient transfer system.

Now that you are well acquainted with the catalog at your library and the location of items in the library, you are ready to explore other ways to find sources.

Other Library Sources

Indexes

Whether you use this now-accepted spelling or stick with the traditional "indices," these books or electronic media do for periodicals what the card catalog does for the library. In a printed index you can search by author and subject. The electronic media give more flexibility.

Printed indexes

General periodical indexes may not be very useful to theology students. Thus, my listing only notes the most important ones in religion.

Religion Index One, published under different names since 1949, is the most productive of the religion indexes, providing access to some 600 periodicals. In the early days it had three sections: subject index, author/abstract index, and book review index. As the book got fatter and fatter, the author index was dropped and the book reviews went into a separate volume, *Index to Book Reviews in Religion*. Published as a companion volume, *Religion Index Two* contains a subject index to multi-author books; it thus provides access to essays by different authors in books edited by someone else. The same producer, the American Theological Library Association, has an index of Doctor of Ministry projects: *Research in Ministry*. To find materials in these books, you will need to search each volume separately. The subject headings are those of the Library of Congress.

Three important publications index periodical articles and give abstracts (short summaries) as well. *Religious and Theological Abstracts* covers the areas indicated by its name, but abstracts only 400 journals. *Old Testament Abstracts* and *New Testament Abstracts* cover the two areas of biblical studies. Foreign language articles are abstracted in English.

Some denominational indexes may be helpful on subjects that deal with specific religious groups. The *Catholic Periodical Index* does just what its name says: It indexes articles in Catholic journals and magazines. A similar index, the *Christian Periodical Index*, notes articles in Protestant journals and magazines. The *Seventh-day Adventist Periodical Index* does the same for Adventist publications.

Advanced students will find *Elenchus of Biblica* useful. Its editors, at the Pontifical Biblical Institute in Rome, have a hard time keeping up; the index is usually two to three years behind. While *Elenchus* covers many of the same periodicals listed in *Religion Index One*, it includes additional items in biblical studies, especially in foreign languages. Doctoral students should not forget the *Internationale Zeitschriftenschau für Bibelwissenschaft und Grenzgebiete* [International Review of Biblical Studies], for it will contain additional materials.

At times other indexes may provide access to materials needed for research done by theology students. The Education Resource Information Center (ERIC) provides access to vast holdings in education, from 1966 onward. The *Education Index* covers articles in periodicals dealing with education. The *Philosopher's Index* deals with philosophy. *Psychological Abstracts* would lead you into the world of psychology. Your specific topic may require use of other indexes.

CD-ROM indexes

An amazing quantity of information fits on each CD-ROM. Furthermore, powerful search engines and increasingly rapid readers make the CD-ROM a major asset to the research process. While each CD-ROM has its own special features, most are user-friendly and require minimum instruction from a librarian. If your library has CD-ROM indexes, you will be able to perform a more efficient search than in printed indexes. Advantages to this format are finding all materials in one source, not having to search year by year, and being able to transfer information to a printed page or disk.

Searches are made by author, title, and subject. In addition, most CD-ROMs permit search by key words, which is probably the most effective way. For example, one could search for the words "bibliography" and "gospels" to find any item that has those two words in the author, title, series, or notes. Usually libraries facilitate printing a bibliographical entry from the CD-ROM to a disk or making a hard copy on an attached printer. CD-ROMs are usually updated at least once a year.

CD-ROM resources are increasingly dedicated to full-text resources rather than indexes. What was once in paper, became CD-ROM, but now is going to the Internet.

The *ATLA Index* is the electronic version of *Religion Index One*, *Religion Index Two*, *Research in Ministry*, and *Index to Book Reviews in Religion*. This is a veritable gold mine of information. *Religious and Theological Abstracts* is also available on CD-ROM.

Given the rule that dissertations must be done on topics not before researched, doctoral students will find *Dissertation Abstracts International* (*DAI*) indispensable. Published by University Microfilms (UMI) of Ann Arbor, Michigan, *DAI* contains the title of the dissertation, together with short, author-produced abstracts. The author, adviser, and school where the dissertation was written also appear. If the abstract suggests further reading, and the volume is not in your library, you can have your library request it on interlibrary loan from another library. If borrowing is not possible, the dissertation can be purchased, on microfiche or photocopied, from University Microfilms, Box 1764, Ann Arbor, Michigan 48106, U.S.A.

In addition, another valuable research tool is the *Thesaurus Linguae Graecae*, which covers Greek writings of some fifteen centuries. These writings are fully searchable, and this resource is also available online.

Reference Materials

Reference materials such as dictionaries, encyclopedias, and concordances are useful in the initial search for information. Later on, once the topic has been defined, these general works are less important. However, their bibliographies may have valuable references. A visual check of the call numbers that yielded sources in the stacks should be made in the reference section.

Bibliographies

In times past, books such as *Index to Periodical Literature on Christ and the Gospels*, compiled under the direction of Bruce M. Metzger, were tremendously helpful to students who had no access to electronic indexes. Bibliographies figured prominently in the search strategy of advanced students. Today topical bibliographies have become less important, at least for current materials; they are, however, very important to older materials. Some bibliographies are still being prepared, often using modern technology. An example is

Casurella, Anthony. *Bibliography of Literature on First Peter*. Leiden: Brill, 1996.

Bibliographies may be located in the Z section (LC classification) or in the appropriate subject area. Wherever they are physically, such items are first found in the library catalog.

Special Departments

Archives, rare book room, heritage center, manuscript center, media center, pamphlet files—these can be sources of precious information. Usually, materials held in these special departments appear in the library catalog. If these special materials do not appear in the general catalog, they certainly will be in some kind of departmental listing. You may need to visit each department to find out what it can offer to your topic.

Online Resources

As we enter the twenty-first century, online resources are becoming more and more abundant. They are also indispensable to the research process. Online resources come in different categories; the two most evident are those offered through a library and those for which one must surf on the World Wide Web.

Three important caveats on online resources: They do not always behave as they are supposed to; what I write about them today will be obsolete within six weeks; and finally, I take no responsibility for the time you spend surfing!

Online Resources Through the Library

Online services offered through the library vary from library to library. However, since these are the easiest and cheapest to use, whatever online resources the library offers should be the first ones to be explored.

The examples presented in this section come from JeWeL, the electronic catalog of the James White Library (and yes, someone got a prize for thinking up that cute name), at Andrews University. I have done so because it is impossible to write in the abstract.

The opening menu of JeWeL offers access to several electronic resources. Among these, the *ATLA Religion Database* and the *Seventh-day Adventist Periodical Index* have already been explained. Others are also interesting.

Academic Search EBSCO "provides full text for nearly 1,250 journals covering the social sciences, humanities, general science, multi-cultural studies, education, and much more." The search screen tells me to type in a keyword or words separated by "and," "not," "or"—the Boolean operators we already met. I type "theological AND education." The search turns up 298 hits. I refine the search by specifying that I want articles published between 1995 and 2000. The count comes down to 157. Some of the items are shown as available in "full text." I can read those on my computer and download them if I choose. While this database is not directly concerned with religion or biblical studies, some materials are available.

JSTOR provides access to full-text articles from journals in different disciplines. Not usually considered a premier source for religious and biblical research, it nevertheless provided more than 200 hits when I typed in "ministry," asking for a search in education, philosophy, and sociology journals. For articles related to mission, I would want to add the anthropological journals.

Back on the opening menu, I click on "Online Databases." I can explore these databases by subject area or by name. To get an idea of what links to cyberspace databases are available, I choose to look at the topics. A long list, in alphabetical order, appears. Scrolling down, I find "Religion/Theology/Philosophy." There I find another list, shorter this time. Clicking on one of them will open the door to cyberspace.

One of the most helpful online resources is WorldCat, the Online Computerized Library Catalog (OCLC). It includes the holdings of thousands of libraries in the United States. Here I find books that are not in my own library and request them by interlibrary loan. Searches can be simple or very complex. Finding too many sources can be helped by judiciously limiting the search by time or another key term. If you have trouble using this tool, ask the librarian at the reference desk for help.

Dissertation Abstracts International is included in the online resources. It is used in the same way as the CD-ROM.

JeWeL provides access to other libraries. For practical purposes, searching other libraries may not be too fruitful. WorldCat includes most of them anyway and is linked to interlibrary loan. However, a search in COPAC, the Consortium of Research Libraries of the United Kingdom, would provide information on materials not available in the United States. Out of curiosity, you could check on holdings in libraries from Hong Kong to Helsinki, but the information may not add much to your search.

Libraries have to pay for many of these services. For that reason you usually need to be a student or have some kind of pass to be able to use them. As distributed education becomes more common, the library of your school will probably have some way for you to access their services from many miles away, as long as you are a student.

Internet Resources

The number of resources for research in biblical studies, theology, and ministry may not be as large as the number of sources that provide information on entertainment and computers. However, the Web is worth exploring. To "surf the Net" you will need to have the appropriate equipment, a good and cheap telephone connection, and plenty of time.

An attempt to systematize information on cyberspace resources in religion was made by Patrick Durusau. That the second edition appeared only two years after the first shows the constant need for updating in this field, where change occurs almost daily.

Durusau, Patrick. *High Places in Cyberspace: A Guide to Biblical and Religious Studies, Classics, and Archaeological Resources on the Internet.* 2d ed. Atlanta: Scholars Press, 1998.

A list of Web sites that could be useful for research in religion and related areas has been provided by Terry Robertson, seminary librarian at the James White Library, Andrews University. Undoubtedly there are more, but these are some of the very best.

Comprehensive Megasites

These megasites provide access to multiple smaller sites where all types of material are available. Spend some time exploring!

Computer-Assisted Theology, Oxford University
http://info.ox.ac.uk/ctitext/theology/index.html

Hartford Institute for Religion Research
http://hirr.hartsem.edu

Not Just Bibles: A Guide to Christian Resources on the Internet
http://www.hclnet.ort/pub/resources/christian-resouces.html

Virtual Religion Index, Rutgers University
http://religion.rutgers.edu/vri/index.html

The Wabash Center Guide to Internet Resources for Teaching and Learning in Theology and Religion
http://www.wabashcenter.wabash.edu/Internet/front.htm

Special Interest Sites

ATLA World Christianity Website, Yale University
http://www.yale.edu/adhoc/research_resources/wcig.htm

Electronic Resources for Classicists, University of California (classical history and languages)
http://www.tlg.uci.edu/~tlg/index/resources.html

Mark Goodacre, Birmingham University (New Testament resources)
http://www.bham.ac.uk/theology/goodacre/

The Religious Movements Homepage, University of Virginia
http://cti.itc.virginia.edu/~jkh8x/soc257/

University of Chicago Oriental Institute
(includes a virtual museum tour)
http://www-oi.uchicago.edu/OI/default.html

Professional Interest Sites

Barna Research Online
(up-to-date research on religion in the United States)
http://www.barna.org/cgi-bin/Home.asp

Christian Missions Homepage
(emphasis on mission to non-Christian, non-Western people)
http://www.sim.org/index.html

World Religions Index
http://wri.leaderu.com/

Worship Place (information on contemporary worship)
http://www.worshipplace.com/

Research Tools

Theological Research Exchange Network
(theses, dissertations, and papers at a reasonable cost)
http://www.tren.com/

Religious and Theological Abstracts
(online access to RTA database for a modest fee)
http://www.rtabst.org/

Society of Biblical Literature
http://www.SBL-site.org

Society of Biblical Literature Book Reviews
http://www.bookreviews.org

Of course, you can do your own search. Using a good search engine (I like Metacrawler), type in the word or phrase you want to look for and see what you can find. You may want to try your search on several different engines. I searched for "historical Jesus" and had 29 hits.

The search for sources has only begun. If the research project is major—such as a dissertation—you will spend many, many hours in the library and online. The materials are there for you to find them. And now, on to the question of choosing a topic, presented in chapter 3.

III | CHOOSING A TOPIC

Topics come in many varieties: good and better and best, simple and complex, shallow and deep, interesting and boring, impossible and rewarding. Unless a teacher specifically demands a certain topic, students can make the most of a topic by choosing wisely. This chapter intends to help novice researchers make a good choice.

In high school, students do a "paper" on "The Amazon Rain Forest." Using an encyclopedia, a geography textbook, and two Web sites, they can construct a five-page description of the flora, fauna, economy, and human population of the area. For a college paper, they would need to concentrate on one of those aspects. At the graduate level, the paper would need to wrestle with an issue such as the "Global Effects of Deforestation of the Amazon Rain Forest." This is an example of how a topic goes from shallow to deep.

The same occurs in papers specific to the area of religion. A paper on "The Divinity of Christ in the New Testament" would be very general. You could make it more specific by limiting the study to "The Divinity of Christ in the Gospel of John." Even this might be too involved for anything less than a doctoral dissertation. Much better would be "Christ as the Bread from Heaven in John 6." Not only does the topic go from shallow to deep, it goes from impossible to feasible.

Important steps in choosing a topic are reading, asking questions, and narrowing the scope. These steps feed on each other. Reading raises questions; questions take you back to reading. Even when the topic is assigned, following these steps can result in a better topic and, hence, a better paper.

Reading

A topic cannot be chosen in a vacuum. You cannot research an island in the sea of your ignorance. General knowledge of the area is basic. Knowing how to find sources (see chapter 2), you are ready to comb the library for ideas for your topic.

Textbooks are a good place to start. Dictionaries and encyclopedias may also be helpful. The following list of sources is a starting place. The first two are good, however old, general religious encyclopedias. The third is more up to date.

Hastings, James, ed. *Encyclopaedia of Religion and Ethics*. 12 vols. and index. Edinburgh: T. & T. Clark; New York: Scribner's, 1908–1926.

The New Schaff-Herzog Encyclopedia of Religious Knowledge. 12 vols. and index. New York: Funk and Wagnalls, 1908–1912; reprint, Grand Rapids: Baker, 1955. Supplemented by *Twentieth Century Encyclopedia of Religious Knowledge*. 2 vols. Grand Rapids: Baker, 1955.

Eliade, Mircea, ed. *Encyclopedia of Religion*. 16 vols. New York: Macmillan, 1986.

These two encyclopedias give a specific slant to religious matters:

New Catholic Encyclopedia. 15 vols. New York: McGraw-Hill, 1967.

Encyclopedia Judaica. 16 vols. New York: Macmillan; Jerusalem: Encyclopedia Judaica, 1971–1972.

The following is an example of a denominational encyclopedia:

The Mennonite Encyclopedia: A Comprehensive Reference Work on the Anabaptist and Mennonite Movement. Hillsboro, KS: Mennonite Brethren Pub. House, 1955–1990.

Among the many Bible dictionaries, the following could prove useful:

Bromiley, Geoffrey, ed. *International Standard Bible Encyclopedia*. Rev. ed. 4 vols. Grand Rapids: Eerdmans, 1979–1987.

Freedman, David Noel, ed. *Anchor Bible Dictionary*. 6 vols. New York: Doubleday, 1992.

For general church history, the following may be consulted:

Oxford Dictionary of the Christian Church. 3d ed. New York: Oxford University Press, 1997.

On topics related to mission and mission history, consider:

Neill, Stephen, Gerald Anderson, and John Goodwin, eds. *Concise Dictionary of the Christian World Mission*. Nashville: Abingdon, 1971.

Barrett, David B., ed. *World Christian Encyclopedia*. 2d ed. New York: Oxford University Press, 2000.

As you read, take note of information on your sources. You will want to be able to find the items again. Also make notes on what you read. See chapters 5 and 7 for specifics on taking notes. Be especially attentive to questions your reading brings up.

Asking Questions

Asking questions—of yourself, of your peers, of your professors, of the books you read—can help you determine whether you have a good topic. Questions can also help you narrow the topic and focus on an issue to research. Questions concern content and feasibility.

Questions on Content

These are some important questions regarding the organization of the topic: What are its parts? Of what larger whole is this topic a part? You can find the parts of a topic in the subdivisions of an encyclopedia article or in the table of contents of a book. For example, the *New Schaff-Herzog Encyclopedia of Religious Knowledge* divides its article on sun worship in the following way:

I. Among the Hebrews	II. In Other Lands	Monumental Testimony
Names and Titles	1. In General	Arabs, Nabateans
General Conceptions	2. Babylonians	5. The Hittites
Worship	3. Egypt	6. India
Date of Introduction	4. Aramea, Syria	7. China and Japan
	Place Name	8. W. Indo-Europeans
	Personal Names	9. Primitive Peoples

This outline would indicate that one part would be enough, perhaps sun worship among the Hittites.

Another set of questions to ask regarding the history of the topic include: What has been written on this topic? Is this a controversial topic? Are lines clearly drawn between two opposing sides over this topic? What can I add to this history? For example, the discussion on Paul's intention when he informed Timothy that women should not teach (1 Tim 2:12) has a very long history. Positions have been taken—on both sides. Is there something new that I can add to this history?

Given the hours and hours you will spend researching and writing on this topic, ask yourself: Do I find this topic interesting? Can I get excited about it? To commit yourself to sixty hours (for a serious twenty-page paper) with a topic about which you could care less makes no sense.

The ultimate questions involve the usefulness of the topic. What good is this topic? How can I use the results of my research? Besides me, who else will benefit from my work?

Questions on Feasibility

While you might be inclined to make heroic efforts to research the topic of your choice, certain practical considerations must prevail. The following questions deal with the feasibility of a topic.

1. Do I have the necessary sources to do this research? If the topic chosen must be researched from original documents in Bombay, a student in Buenos Aires will be hard put to finish the task. If the chosen topic is a word study of the Hebrew word *niṣdaq*, the researcher must have access to Hebrew dictionaries, lexicons, and word studies already done on *niṣdaq*, as well as articles published in journals.

2. Am I qualified to do this research? A researcher who has chosen to study the word *niṣdaq* in Daniel 8 but knows no Hebrew will not be able to write a good research paper. Sometimes it is possible to acquire the skills needed to complete a research project—languages, statistical expertise, or thorough knowledge of a specific area in a discipline—but often there is not enough time to do this.

3. Do I have enough time to complete the research of this topic by the due date? This question is of prime importance to students, especially in intensive courses. If one needs to send halfway around the world to get information to write the paper, it may be impossible to finish by the end of the semester. Some students choose topics that require interviewing someone who lives at a distance. Interesting as that research might be, one must count the cost—in time or money—before embarking on the project.

4. Does this research demand finances I do not have? The cost of mailing questionnaires or traveling to complete research can become heavy. The expense of typing a paper (or worse, having it typed) must also be considered. Of course, it is not possible to escape all financial burdens, but one must take finances into consideration before settling on a topic.

In synthesis, one does well to ask Jesus' question recorded in Luke 14:28: "For which of you, desiring to build a tower, does not first sit down and count the cost, whether he has enough to complete it?"

Narrowing the Topic

Congratulations for having chosen a good topic! Now comes the narrowing, the task of making the topic even more specific.

The questions asked about feasibility point to limitations: reasons why something cannot be done properly or done at all, limits placed on the research by circumstances. In narrowing the topic, limitations no longer count. Now we speak of delimitations—self-imposed limits that make the topic better, clearer, more manageable.

Delimiting a study is indispensable because in doing good research, the researcher is responsible for turning up and examining every single piece of information on the chosen topic. It is as if one were putting a fence around a certain piece of land and agreeing to turn up every stone and investigate every plant enclosed in that fence. If the piece of ground is too large, the task cannot be completed. It is better to fence a small piece of ground and examine every pebble and blade of grass on it—not forgetting the small insects that might be hiding under the surface. In doing research one must become a specialist in the area.

One delimitation could be that of a time period. A research project studying the chronology of the kings of Judah would take several years to complete. It would be wiser to study the chronology of the reign of Josiah. Considering the chronological problems involved, it might even be better to study only the date of the death of Josiah. Because you set forth this time delimitation, no one will ask why you did not include other kings.

Another delimitation could have to do with sources you will use. Your topic could be an examination of the "kingdom of God" concept in the works of G. E. Ladd. Unless you are writing a dissertation, you will want to delimit the sources to one work by Ladd. In a paper comparing the divorce passages in Matthew 5 and Mark 10 you could appropriately delimit yourself to the biblical passages and commentaries on those passages. Thus you would protect yourself from accusations of not having taken into account the latest Christian book on divorce.

A paper could be delimited to include only certain aspects of a topic. For example, in writing a paper on the theology of worship you might choose to exclude the issue of whether or not contemporary music is appropriate for worship. The topic would not have room for that discussion. You could, for example, state that "the study is limited to the nine texts containing the same Hebrew verb form," or that "the research confines itself to a study of the general body of Rastafarians, ignoring the splinter groups," or that "only those members whose names are on the local church books are taken into account in this study."

You will often see the phrase, "this topic is beyond the scope of" this paper/thesis/dissertation. That simply means that the author has chosen certain parameters that do not include a topic. Of course, too many delimitations would suggest that your topic is too narrow. Choose your delimitations with care. Make sure they make as much sense to your readers as they do to you.

Selecting a Thesis or Dissertation Topic

Most of what has been said about selecting a research topic is as valid for a thesis as for an undergraduate term paper. However, a master's thesis is expected to cover more ground. The fenced-in area is larger and the student is expected to more carefully examine the soil turned over by the researcher's spade. Furthermore, a thesis should make an original contribution to knowledge. It cannot be simply a survey, no matter how well organized and presented, of what has already been written.

The selection of a topic for a thesis must be made in close communication with the adviser or committee. Naturally, the final choice is the student's, and the preliminary reading is his or her responsibility. Before seeing the professor about a topic, complete the initial pre-research and write down ideas on two or three possibilities. The professor can then help to focus on the research area, possibly by clarifying the delimitations. More information on theses will be found in chapter 19.

Just as the thesis is more complex than the term paper, the doctoral dissertation is deeper and broader than the thesis. The dissertation in theology or religion may have a practical or theoretical orientation, depending on the degree pursued. Dissertations are discussed in chapters 19 and 20.

Once a viable topic has been chosen and approved, the research plan can be implemented. The development of the research plan is the topic of chapter 4.

IV | PLANNING RESEARCH

Writing a research paper takes time. Some scholars find that for every finished, double-space typewritten page, with its appropriate footnotes, they need at least two hours; most need three hours. On that basis, a twenty-page paper would take some forty to sixty hours to complete—from choosing the topic to handing the paper in. A dissertation may take as much as five hours for every page written. If the professor requires rewriting, even more time must be allotted. Of the total time, about two-thirds is research time; one-third is writing time.

Already in the selection and narrowing of the topic, some time has been consumed. Before the bibliography list is made or the actual note-taking process begins, a student should define the problem to be studied, write a short proposal, and prepare a tentative outline. Some professors require these even for a term paper; others only want a proposal for a thesis or dissertation. Even if the proposal is not required, the time spent in preparing it is amply repaid because the proposal brings the whole project into focus and saves time in the long run. A proposal is always required for a thesis or dissertation.

Chapter 4 explains three basic steps: problem, purpose, and methodology. Having accomplished these steps, you will be able to write the proposal and outline the contents of your paper. These activities are also explained.

Basic Steps
Step 1: Define the Problem

Once you have a research topic in hand, you must define the problem. The problem should point to a gap in knowledge, an unclear situation, an unresolved question, a lack of information, an unknown, a specific question to be investigated and answered, or a problem to be researched and solved. It is important to state the problem because this statement guides the research. It also helps the professor give appropriate guidance. Those who do not like the term *problem* because of its negative connotations could just as easily think of the problem as an issue or even a research question.

Some problems are simple; others are complicated. In either case, the problem must be clearly stated: Exactly what is to be researched? The following are statements of simple problems: There is disagreement regarding the exact date of the death of Josiah. Or, there is only scattered information on the beginning of the Methodist mission in the Solomon Islands. Or, lay members are frequently uninformed concerning their function in the church.

Often the problem can be expressed in a question to which a direct answer may be given. For example, What is the relation between tithing and the receiving of God's blessings? Or, Which kind of Christian mission has won the most converts among the Muslims of Mindanao? Regarding the transmission of religious heritage in the Jewish faith, the problem could be expressed: What is the role of the Jewish family in the transmission of the religious heritage from one generation to the next?

A student, writing on the history of the Guadalajara Sanitarium in Mexico, the first Adventist medical institution outside the United States, stated his problem in the following terms: "In 1897 Seventh-day Adventist leaders declared that this sanitarium was the 'most important and the most promising enterprise of the sort to have been undertaken in modern times.'[1] However, by 1907 it had been closed. Why did the Guadalajara Sanitarium fail?" (The footnote reads: [1]J. H. Kellogg, "An Appeal for Mexico," *Review and Herald*, 29 June 1897, 408.)

A 1999 dissertation proposal listed the following problem: "Few terms in the Old Testament have caused as many differing opinions and misunderstandings, which have been so disturbing and controversial as to lead scholars to fierce polemic, as the Hebrew word *sheol*. In spite of valuable contributions by many scholars, there is no consensus in regard to the nature, function, and purpose of the term."

Another problem, elaborated for the written dissertation proposal, reads:

Evangelicals have assumed that while methods of evangelism may be changed, the evangelical salvation formula is the essential message of the gospel and therefore must remain the same. Thus when a spiritual seeker asks, "What must I do to be saved?" an evangelical Christian is likely to respond with terminology and concepts that have remained relatively unchanged for decades. Evangelistic presentations may now be accompanied by multimedia pyrotechnics and contemporary Christian music, but when a seeker wants to know how to cross over from death to life, the message is likely the same one the seeker's parents heard years before. This traditional way of describing the way of salvation, however, no longer elicits the positive response it once did. It seems to fail to communicate to the postmodern mind with clarity and impact.

Only half in jest, it has been said that a research problem that can be written on the back of one's business card is the most apt to be solved. If the question is clear, the answer will also be clear. Time spent on clarifying the statement of the problem is not wasted.

Step 2: Determine the Purpose

At this point you must determine what to do with the problem. Are you going to analyze? Compare? Reconstruct? Synthesize? Design a program? Any of these may be a valid option, depending on the problem and what you want to accomplish.

The purpose follows on the heels of the problem. It tells the reader (and the professor) what you are going to do about the problem. If the problem is that there is no information, the purpose will be to find that information. If the problem states that there seems to be disagreement between two of Jesus' sayings on peace, the purpose could be to try to bring harmony or understand the difference. Some examples of purposes: to reconstruct the events of a given historical period, to compare two theories, to organize certain information, to determine the relation between two events, to synthesize, to discover, or to formulate.

The purpose for the dissertation on the evangelical presentation of the gospel was described as follows: "The purpose of this dissertation is to critique the typical evangelical response to the question, 'What do I need to do to be saved?'"

The purpose of the *sheol* dissertation is straightforward: "To examine the sixty-six occurrences of the Hebrew word *sheol* in the Old Testament in order to discover the nature, function, and purpose of this term."

Suppose the problem is that the Christian church is not growing in the Czech Republic as it did in the first years after the fall of the Communist regime. The purpose might be to describe the growth patterns of the church or even to consider the factors affecting church growth. It might be to compare the growth of the church in the Czech Republic with the growth of the church in another post-Communist country. In a recent dissertation, a student proposed "to explore the contextual and institutional factors of the current Czech situation in order to develop a strategy for revitalization of local congregations, rooted in Czech culture."

After completing this step, two things are settled: What the issue is and what is being done about it. The next question is how to go about solving the problem.

Step 3: Design a Methodology

Why the "method" of solving a problem is called "methodology" is not quite certain. In any case, "methodology" is the way you go about achieving the purpose already stated. You must ask: "How am I going to do this?" In a class paper, you need only convince the professor. In a thesis or dissertation, the adviser and/or committee need to be convinced that the route chosen will lead to a successful resolution of the problem.

In theological, biblical, or ministerial research, methodology is not so clearly set out as in social science research. In fact, scholars on that side of the campus may look at the "method" used in seminary research and find only "madness." Various methods are used in seminary research. Note the difference between the method to uncover the meaning and function of *sheol* and the method to develop a premarital seminar as part of a D.Min. dissertation. Yet, any good research must have a clear and logical method: A way to get from here to there.

If your research is to be done in the library, decide where you are going to start and where you will go next. Will you trace the history first? Or will you do the exegesis of your text first? You will also need to tell your professor how you plan to use your sources. Will they be outlined? Compared? Analyzed? If the research is other than bibliographical, the methodology of the survey or experiment to be used must be even more clearly spelled out. The instrument you plan to use to gather data also needs to be described or prepared. All steps of the research must be clearly enunciated. In some cases, the section on methodology may become an entire chapter.

Some examples: The method of the dissertation on the presentation of the gospel can be summarized as follows: The study will begin by surveying crucial terms and central concepts in the typical gospel presentation. Two basic questions will then be asked: Does the evangelical response employ sound communicational principles? Does the evangelical response present a balanced New Testament teaching on how one can be saved? To answer the first question, the principles of receptor-based communications will be studied. The second question will be answered on the basis of an analysis of New Testament responses to the question "What must I do to be saved?" The last step is to "summarize the results of my study and suggest biblical modifications to the traditional evangelical salvation formula that may communicate with more clarity and impact in North America at the turn of the millennium."

A church growth study of an inner-city church could have the following methodology: (1) review current literature on inner-city church growth, including theory and practical examples; (2) analyze the community in which the church functions; (3) study the church, its growth history, its activities, its climate, its membership; and (4) design a suggested church growth strategy for this church, based on the three previous points.

Before writing the methodology in beautiful prose, simply list the different steps. What will you do first? Second? Third? Make sure the steps are completely logical for the problem as presented and the purpose as intended. Consultation with your professor or adviser is indispensable. Additional reading may also help clarify the steps you must take.

The Proposal

As noted above, the preparation of a project or paper proposal, even though not required by the professor, is a valuable exercise. Not only does the proposal provide a clear guide for the research process, it also becomes the basis for the introduction to the paper.

The proposal described here is appropriate for a class or term paper. A thesis proposal will, of necessity, be more complex and extensive. Proposals for theses and dissertations are described in chapters 19 and 20.

Generally speaking, the research proposal needs to include the following items. (In this outline, items that have been described in the first part of this chapter are merely enumerated.)

1. An introduction giving the background for the problem; it may also show the scope or extension of the problem.
2. Statement of the problem.
3. Purpose of the research.
4. Significance of the research. Although a student paper may not have far-reaching consequences, any well-prepared research paper should be useful to someone. In this section the following questions should be answered: Who will benefit from having this problem solved? How will they benefit? How important is it to answer this question? What is the value of this research to a given discipline? Why is doing this research important? No rule prohibits the writer from being one of the beneficiaries. One value or objective of a research on Christian work for cripples might be its "use by the writer as a basis for ministry among the handicapped."
5. Definition of terms. An author should clearly indicate the use of certain terms to mean specific ideas. In writing about "young adults" the researcher might define them as "persons of either gender between the ages of 20 and 25." Thus the reader is informed of the exact meaning of terms used. It is important for everyone—writer, professor, and readers—to be exactly sure of meanings. When a paper is to be read by those not familiar with denominational or local terms, it is imperative for these to be clearly defined. A precise definition of theological terms characteristic of one's own tradition may be needed for noninitiated readers.

6. Limitations of the study. Here the researcher honestly states the limits imposed by shortness of time, lack of library facilities, or language limitation. However, too many of these limitations may suggest that a wrong topic has been chosen or poor research is under way.
7. Delimitations of the study. Not to be confused with "limitations" (see above), delimitations are parameters chosen by the researcher.
8. Methodology. The researcher must clearly show what steps are to be followed to complete the research.
9. Presuppositions or assumptions. Any researcher has presuppositions. The reader deserves to know what they are. One assumption may be that the readers are familiar with the history of the period under study, the general outline of theological development in a given denomination, or any other item considered by the author to be common knowledge of the readers, not needing further elaboration. See more about presuppositions in chapter 6, "Research Thinking."
10. Working bibliography. This is a list of sources already consulted and found useful to the topic. This list will grow as the research progresses. The tentative bibliography helps the professor gauge the student's familiarity with the topic.

Another item may or may not enter into the proposal of a bibliographical research, but is usually present in other kinds of research: the hypothesis. A hypothesis is the researcher's tentative solution to the problem, an indication of the expected result of the study. Sometimes called a "thesis," it is the proposed solution to the problem. If a hypothesis is clearly going to direct the research, it must be stated. For example, in a study of the history of the early change from Sabbath to Sunday observance, the hypothesis could be the following: "Second-century Christians replaced Sabbath observance with Sunday observance because they did not wish to look like Jews." The research would then present all the information to substantiate that position—without neglecting evidences to the contrary. The hypothesis could be proved or disproved by the evidence accumulated. The danger in blindly following one's hypothesis is that one might fail to see adverse evidence in the pursuit of a solution one has already decided on. If the hypothesis keeps the research on track but does not dominate it, it can be very useful. See chapter 6, "Research Thinking."

Sometimes a section on the need for the study is appropriate; it may be used as background material to the statement of the problem. On the other hand, a researcher may choose to write about the need as a separate item. Need may also be put together with the significance.

A proposal for a class paper can be written in one or two pages. A thesis proposal will be much longer and will reflect a great deal of study and research already completed. Some graduates have indicated that they had spent at least one-fourth of the total time employed in preparing their theses by the time they completed their proposals. This document usually includes a review of literature or equivalent evidence that the student has already read amply on the topic. A working bibliography will also document the sources one plans to use. On thesis and dissertation proposals, see chapters 19 and 20.

Tentative Outline

Some professors ask for a tentative outline early in the research process. Even if they do not, you should prepare one before proceeding with the research. Naturally, as you read, new information may change details or even sections of the outline, but the foundation will usually remain the same. A final outline will be prepared once the research is complete and you are about to write.

The outline is the backbone of the paper. It provides the basic organization for the research report. It is also the basis for the table of contents. Each chapter must be so well outlined that both student and professor can clearly follow the development of the topic. Outlines can be written using complete sentences or only phrases. The model given is of the second kind. Parallelism in form is important. Each item must have at least two subdivisions. All subdivisions of a topic must clearly relate to the overall heading.

Before preparing an outline, you will have completed a great deal of preliminary reading. The following outlines, of a research paper on the Bhakti way of philosophical Hinduism, show the researcher already has a good knowledge of the topic.

The first outline is done in the traditional form, using a sequence of Roman numerals, capital letters, Arabic numerals, and lower-case letters. The second outline uses Arabic numerals and the decimal system, in a style employed in many areas of the world. Both forms are correct and acceptable since they give a detailed outline of the study. Either model should be followed precisely, including all items, such as indentations, sequence of letters and numbers, and alignment of periods. Do not mix the two systems.

   I. Introduction
  II. Bhakti Yoga
      A. Definition of Bhakti
      B. Ninefold Bhakti

       1. Passive Bhakti
          a. Sravanam
          b. Kirtanam
          c. Smarmam
       2. Active Bhakti
          a. Padasevanam
          b. Archanam
          c. Vandanam
       3. Relational Bhakti
          a. Dasyam
          b. Sakhyam
          c. Atmanivedanam
    C. Madura Bhakti
       1. Symbolic Nature
       2. Allegorical Interpretation
III. Barriers to Bhakti
    A. Women
    B. Wealth
    C. Wrong Company
    D. Wrong Emotions
       1. Lust
       2. Anger
       3. Greed
       4. Attachment
IV. Summary, Conclusions, and Reflections

The second form is as follows:

1 Introduction
2 Bhakti Yoga
2.1 Definition of Bhakti
2.2 Ninefold Bhakti
2.2.1 Passive Bhakti
2.2.1.1 Sravanam
2.2.1.2 Kirtanam
2.2.1.3 Smarmam
2.2.2 Active Bhakti
2.2.2.1 Padasevanam
2.2.2.2 Archanam
2.2.2.3 Vandanam

2.2.3 Relational Bhakti
2.2.3.1 Dasyam
2.2.3.2 Sakhyam
2.2.3.3 Atmanivedanam
2.3 Madura Bhakti
2.3.1 Symbolic Nature
2.3.2 Allegorical Interpretation
3 Barriers to Bhakti
3.1 Women
3.2 Wealth
3.3 Wrong Company
3.4 Wrong Emotions
3.4.1 Lust
3.4.2 Anger
3.4.3 Greed
3.4.4 Attachment
4 Summary, Conclusions, and Reflections

Although the formulation of a research plan—including the writing of a proposal and the preparation of an outline—follows on the heels of choosing a viable topic, this activity takes place at the same time as the initial bibliographic search. Given the importance of correctly recording the findings of the bibliographic search, chapter 5 addresses the issue of keeping record of the books, articles, and other sources that form the bibliography.

V | PREPARING BIBLIOGRAPHIES

The search for bibliography begins at the same time as the selection and narrowing of a research topic. In research, the word "bibliography" has two different meanings. It can be the sum of sources used for a research project, or it can be the list of items consulted, which generally appears at the end of the paper. Chapter 2 considered the matter of finding sources. This chapter deals with the process of keeping track of these sources during the research process and presenting them in final form in a bibliography.

Bibliographic Records

The traditional way of keeping track of the bibliography for a paper was to make "bib cards." Today most bibliographic records are kept electronically. Both ways work; both must be done carefully, making sure no errors creep in.

"Bib Cards"

Bibliography cards, usually called "bib cards," but also "source cards," can be made on three-by-five-inch (or four-by-six-inch) note cards, purchased at a bookstore. However, slips of paper cut to approximately that size work just as well—one-fourth of a typing page is also a good size. In fact, notes may be taken on paper that has already been used on one side. As long as the slips of paper are cut to the same size and are not too thin, any paper will work. Although there are expensive little note-card boxes for sale, rubber bands or elastics are usually enough to keep the notes together. If you are writing a thesis, a shoe box makes a good place to keep notes.

Start making bibliography cards at the very beginning of the preliminary search. Doing this saves time later when you wish to find a certain book, but cannot quite remember what the title was and therefore cannot find it. Bib cards (or slips of paper) must contain all the information needed in order to find the item again—without returning to the library catalog—or to make up the bibliography for the paper without having to see the book again.

Each bibliography card must have the following information: author(s), title, number of volumes, editor, translator, edition, place of publication, publisher, date of publication, and the exact location of the book (call number and library). In addition, you should record information about the book or article, about the part of the topic it deals with, specific pages to look at, references found in it, and other matters of interest.

If the bibliographic cards are carefully made, that is, if they contain all the information and are totally legible, they will not need to be recopied before the final typing. They will be referred to throughout the research process and then will form the basis for the final bibliography. All you will need to do is alphabetize the cards and type out the bibliography.

The sample bibliography cards, which look something like the author card in the card catalog, contain all the information you will need. Note the location of each item. Note also the punctuation; this is the same that will be used in the final bibliography. The author (or editor) is first, followed by a period or full stop. Then comes the title of the book, underlined, and followed by a period. Next is the place of publication, followed by a colon and the name of the publisher. After this, a comma precedes the date of publication, which is followed by a period or full stop.

You will find information for a bibliographic entry on the title page of a book and on its verso. Missing information can be obtained from the library catalog. In order to save time later, these cards must be made correctly from the beginning.

```
REF
BS
1830
A3
      Charlesworth, James H., ed. The Old Testament
      Pseudepigrapha. Vol. 1, Apocalyptic Literature
      and Testaments. Garden City, NY: Doubleday,
      1983.

      Pp. 707-719: Apocalypse of Adam, 1st to 4th cent.
      From Nag Hammadi, in Sahidic Coptic.
      Prophecy of the flood, chap. 3.
      Chap. 7 alludes to virgin birth.
      Bibl., 710.
```

P

> Collins, John J. "Daniel and his Social World."
> Interpretation 39 (April 1985): 131-143.
>
> Collins sets Daniel's life in the Maccabbean
> period and considers chaps. 1-6 as legendary
> (135). See reference to Collins' other works on
> Daniel.
> Basic idea: The book reflects the sitz im leben
> of the author—in the time of Antiochus Epiphanes.

If your library system allows you to print bibliographical records as you do your search, you may want to use these printouts as the bibliographical record of your search. Simply cut the page into strips, one for each source, and put them in alphabetical order. These strips may be somewhat unwieldy, but they contain all the bibliographical data, free from possible copy errors. You can write additional information on the back of each strip. This system is a cross between the old-fashioned "bib cards" and electronic bibliographies.

And now, let us consider a "better way": the electronic record.

Electronic Record

The starting place for developing an electronic record of the bibliographic search is an electronic catalog of some sort: a library catalog, the *ATLA Index*, a WorldCat search. The process is as follows:

1. Find an item that you want for your bibliography.
2. Following the protocol of your electronic source, save it to a list.
3. Following the protocol, download the list to a floppy disk or e-mail it to yourself.
4. Retrieve the list and clean up the format so that the entries look like items on a bibliography.
5. Alphabetize the list, as if you were preparing the bibliography. (Use the sort feature of your word processing program.)
6. Add notes to your items, being careful not to insert a hard return between the bibliographical entry and the added note. (These notes will be deleted when you prepare your final bibliography.)

7. If you wish, print this list (and cut it up by individual items, if you like) and use it for your search in the library.

When I begin to write, I will keep the bibliography as a second document on my word processor. When I need to do a footnote, I will switch to that document and cut and paste the information into the paper, making the changes needed to transform the information from bibliography to footnote style.

Two helpful software packages can make the process faster: Biblioscape (www.biblioscape.com offers a free trial download) and Endnote (a free trial download is available at www.niles.com). Once your information is in the program (either typed in or imported electronically), you can make footnotes and bibliography entries almost automatically. If you become clever, you will not even need this handbook.

Whatever way you keep record of your bibliography, be meticulous. Do not allow yourself any mistakes!

Format of Bibliographic Entries

As is customary in theological education, the format used is that of Kate Turabian and the *Chicago Manual of Style*. The most common types of materials used in theological studies are given here; additional forms are given in chapter 9, where footnotes and bibliographical entries are compared.

In bibliographical entries for all kinds of materials, periods or full stops follow each segment: author, title, series, publication data. Accents and diacritical marks from foreign languages must be included.

Books

Several items must be considered: author, title, edition, and publication data. In addition, there are special rules for multivolume works and series.

Author

Normally, the order of the author or editor statement is surname, comma, given names (or name and initial), period or full stop. Honorific or academic titles are not used.

When a book has more than one author, all names are given. However, only the first is inverted (surname first). Subsequent authors appear with given name first and surname last. Commas separate the names. In a reference note, an item with three or more authors appears "Smith and others"; all names appear in the bibliography. Fortunately, books that have many authors usually have a principal author or editor. Only that one needs listing.

Hunter, George H., III. *Church for the Unchurched*. Nashville: Abingdon, 1996.

Anderson, Gerald H., Robert T. Coote, Norman A. Horner, and James M. Phillips. *Mission Legacies: Biographical Studies of Leaders of the Modern Missionary Movement*. Maryknoll, NY: Orbis, 1994.

Editor in place of author

McGavran, Donald, ed. *The Conciliar-Evangelical Debate: The Crucial Documents, 1964–1976*. South Pasadena, CA: William Carey, 1977.

Corporate author

When the item has been prepared by a committee or a corporate entity, that name is used in place of an author's name:

United Nations. *Yearbook of the United Nations*. New York: Department of Public Information, United Nations, 1992.

No author given

If no author or editor is given, the bibliographical entry begins with the title of the book:

The Illustrated Bible Dictionary. 3 vols. Wheaton, IL: Tyndale, 1980.

Title

The title comes one space after the period (full stop) following the author's name. The title of a book, pamphlet, or journal must appear in italics or be underlined. If there is a subtitle, it appears after a colon and is underlined. Titles in English have first and last and all important words capitalized. Titles in German have capitals on the first word and on all the nouns. French, Spanish, and Latin titles have capitals only on the first word. Titles of books in non-Latin scripts may be transliterated; a translation into English should appear in parentheses, not underlined but capitalized in sentence style immediately following the title.

Schweitzer, Albert. *Das Abendmahlsproblem auf Grund der wissenschaftlichen Forschung des 19. Jahrhunderts und der historischen Berichte*. Tübingen: J. C. B. Mohr (Paul Siebeck), 1929.

Stam, Juan B. *Apocalipsis y profecía: Las señales de los tiempos y el tercer milenio*. Buenos Aires : Kairós, 1998.

Tak, Myung-hwan. *Hankuk ui Shinheung Jonggyo* (New religions in Korea). Seoul: Song Chong Sa, 1972.

Edition

If the item is of any edition other than the first, this must be indicated. Printings do not count, for a book is only changed when a new edition is made. Give the number of the edition or the exact wording (such as Amer. ed.). Note the period and one space between title and edition. A period comes after the edition, before the place of publication.

Ferguson, Everett. *Backgrounds of Early Christianity.* 2d ed. Grand Rapids: Eerdmans, 1993.

Multivolume Works

If the source is made up of several volumes, this information is given after the title. For bibliographical entries of multivolume works with individual titles, see examples in chapter 9.

Balz, Horst, and Gerhard Schneider, eds. *Exegetical Dictionary of the New Testament.* 3 vols. Grand Rapids: Eerdmans, 1990–1993.

Series

The series to which a book belongs follows the title and is not underlined. The series statement ends with a period. A volume within the series is recorded as it appears on the title page.

Overholt, Thomas W. *Prophecy in Cross-cultural Perspective.* SBL Sources for Biblical Study, 17. Atlanta: Scholars, 1986.

Facts of Publication
Place of publication

If the city where the item was published is well known, give the name of the city alone: New York, Manila, Hong Kong. If the town is obscure, give also the state or the country. If two or more places are given, use only the first. Abbreviations may be used, but always consistently. For the states in the United States, use consistently **only** one option: (a) postal codes, (b) abbreviations, (c) full names. In this book we use postal codes; however, not all schools accept postal codes. If there is no place of publication, either in the book or in the library catalog, use N.p. for "no place" (capitalized following the period).

Healdsburg College. *Eleventh Annual Calendar.* N.p.: Healdsburg College, 1894.

Publisher

The publisher is separated from the place of publication by a colon and one space. Parts of the publisher's name, such as "limited" and "incorporated" should be omitted. An abbreviated form may be used if done so consistently (as in this *Handbook*): Zondervan instead of Zondervan Publishing House. However, university publishers cannot be abbreviated: Chicago University Press. If no publisher information is found, either in the book or in the library catalog, use n.p. for "no publisher."

Avondale School for Christian Workers. *Twelfth Annual Announcement.* Cooranbong, Australia: n.p., 1908.

Date of publication

The date of publication is separated from the publisher by a comma and one space. If there is no date, either in the book or in any catalog, use n.d. for "no date." The date given should be that of the edition, not of the printing. For reprint editions, give as much information as you have, in the following form.

Magil, Joseph. *The Englishman's Hebrew-English Old Testament: Genesis–2 Samuel*. New York: Hebrew Publishing, 1905; reprint, Grand Rapids: Zondervan, 1974.

If a multivolume source has different dates of publication, the beginning and end dates are given in a full bibliographical entry. If the work has not been completed, give only the beginning date: 1964–.

Charlesworth, James H., ed. *The Old Testament Pseudepigrapha*. 2 vols. Garden City, NY: Doubleday, 1983–1985.

When the material used is only a part of the multivolume set, this may be indicated as follows:

Robertson, A. T. *Word Pictures in the New Testament*. 6 vols. Nashville: Broadman, 1930–1933. 6:137–180.

Magazines and Journals

Magazines are usually general in nature, addressed to a lay population. Examples are *Moody Monthly, National Geographic, Time, Christianity Today,* and *Adventist Review.* Journals are academic and generally focused on one discipline. *Missiology, Journal of Biblical Literature, Theology Today,* and *Review of Religious Studies* are considered journals. The first bibliography example is for a magazine article; the second, for a journal article:

Bass, Dorothy. "Receiving the Day the Lord Has Made." *Christianity Today,* 6 March 2000, 63–67.
Costas, Orlando E. "The Mission of Ministry." *Missiology* 14 (1986): 463–471.

The simplest way to give the date for a magazine is day-month-year, to avoid using an extra comma; however, the date may also be written March 6, 2000. Only one form can be used in any one paper. The year of the journal is added in parentheses to make finding the item easier. If paging is continuous throughout the volume, the year is enough. If each issue starts with page 1, a month or season must be included: 15 (Spring 1991): 35. Note the space between the colon and the page(s) in a journal reference. When no month or season is given, the number of the issue follows the volume:

Merling, David. "The Search for Noah's Ark." *College and University Dialogue* 11, no. 3 (1999): 5–8.

Additional Materials

The entry for a chapter written by one author in a book edited by another is tricky. Note the *total* number of pages *before* the facts of publication. According to Turabian, this kind of entry should read as follows:

Larson, Donald N. "The Viable Missionary: Learner, Trader, Story Teller." In *Perspectives on the World Christian Movement: A Reader*, ed. Ralph D. Winter and Steven C. Hawthorne, 444–451. Pasadena, CA: William Carey Library, 1992.

Signed articles in specialized dictionaries or encyclopedias also deserve special attention:

Jepsen, Alfred. "אָמַן." *Theological Dictionary of the Old Testament.* Edited by G. Johannes Botterweck and Helmer Ringren. Translated by John T. Willis. Grand Rapids: Eerdmans, 1974–. 1:292–323.

Given the use of dissertations as research sources, an example should be included:

Gane, Roy Edwin. "Ritual Dynamic Structure: Systems Theory and Ritual Syntax Applied to Selected Ancient Israelite, Babylonian, and Hittite Festival Days." University of California, Berkeley, 1992.

Examples given in this section correspond to normal entries. More examples, especially of problem bibliographical entries, are found in chapter 9.

Final Bibliography

As you put together the final bibliography of your paper, you will carefully follow the rules of form. You will also have to decide on how you will organize your bibliography. Sometimes you will be asked to prepare an annotated bibliography. Instructions regarding these three topics occupy our attention now.

Form

The order of each entry is the same: author (or editor), title, number of volumes, edition, series, place of publication, publisher, date of publication. The punctuation is also standard; you have seen it in the instructions just given.

Because the typing of bibliographies demands total precision in matters of spacing, as well as punctuation and contents, be very careful. Word processing software will not place the spaces in their correct location when full justification is used; therefore, use left justification when entering a bibliography.

The bibliography always begins on a separate page. It is the last section in the paper or thesis. The title (in caps) is centered two inches from the upper edge of the paper (on the thirteenth line). Each bibliographical entry is single spaced; a blank line is left between entries. The first line (beginning with the author's surname) reaches the left margin; thereafter, the lines are indented five spaces (.5 inch in twelve-point font and .4 inch in ten-point font). Some schools may allow you to use the default indentation of your word processor.

If there are two or more items by exactly the same author (not in one as author and another as editor), the author's name is only written the first time. Thereafter, it is replaced by an eight-space line (underlined). The works of each author may be arranged alphabetically or chronologically. Your readers will prefer the alphabetic order.

Dybdahl, Jon. *Exodus: God Creates a People*. Abundant Life Amplifier. Boise, ID: Pacific Press, 1994.

_____. *Old Testament Grace*. Boise, ID: Pacific Press, 1990.

A sample typed bibliography is presented in chapter 12. The bibliography of this textbook may also be used as a model.

Organization

The simplest and most effective way to organize a bibliography is to put all entries in alphabetical order, by author. Well-made bibliography cards are simply alphabetized and typed. If you kept an electronic list, your bibliography only needs checking for details.

For some types of research, however, or to please certain professors, bibliographies may be divided into parts. Common divisions of a bibliography are books and journals; published and unpublished materials; primary and secondary sources. When dividing bibliographical entries by category, consult the preferences of the professor or thesis committee. However, remember that a reader may become frustrated at not finding sources listed under the heading where he or she thinks they should appear and having to check six different lists of sources. The alphabetical approach is the most user friendly.

Annotated Bibliography

An annotated bibliography contains the usual bibliographical information. In addition, it gives a brief description or summary of the book. At early stages of the research, professors may require an annotated bibliography to ascertain that you have read, or at least scanned, the items listed. The annotation should be between three and twelve lines, usually single spaced. Two examples show format and content.

Rouse, Ruth, and Stephen C. Neill, eds. *A History of the Ecumenical Movement.* 2d ed. with rev. bibliography. 2 vols. Philadelphia: Westminster Press, 1967–1970.

> A survey covering the period from the Reformation to 1968, this is an authoritative work with essays by many scholars in the field. Each volume includes an extensive classified bibliography, an analytical subject index, and an author index. Vol. 1 covers 1517–1948; vol. 2 covers 1948–1968. Vol. 2 was edited by Harold Fey.

Spencer, Donald H. *Hymn and Scripture Selection Guide.* Valley Forge, PA: Judson, 1977.

> Section 1 lists 380 hymns arranged by title. Under each hymn, brief phrases identify its subject and selected relevant Scripture passages are listed. Section 2 is a listing of Scripture passages in canonical order. Under each passage, the numbers of the more appropriate hymns are listed. This is useful for selecting hymns to go with a sermon on a particular text.

This chapter has given pointers for keeping records of the developing bibliography. It has also described the organization and formatting of the final bibliography. Chapter 6 takes us from form to philosophy—how we think when we do research.

VI | RESEARCH THINKING

Research has a special way of thinking attached to it. Or perhaps it would be better to say that research is built on a particular way of thinking. This includes a specific mindset, certain thinking processes, and the asking of many questions.

Research Mindset

Researchers start their work from the premise that knowledge is attainable and that finding truth is possible. The quest may be long and difficult, but results are assured. Without this optimistic mindset, little research would take place. The research mindset is characterized by objectivity, focus, clearly set-forth presuppositions, logical organization, and intellectual honesty. In a more biblical frame, it is adorned by humility.

Objectivity

A much-touted component of the scientific method of research is "total" objectivity: Researchers should be able to detach themselves from their preferences and convictions, and dispassionately consider the evidence. Today we realize that total objectivity is a myth. It is not possible to put aside all cherished ideas—even in research. Furthermore, we recognize that some aspects of life on planet Earth are not subject to disinterested appraisal and total objectivity. Just as a baby is perfect to his or her mother, a researcher's "brain child" cannot be improved on.

While one might have to admit that total objectivity is not probable, a researcher's goal is to be as objective as possible. This means that one must place preferences and prejudices in abeyance. One must consider all the evidence—pro and con. When defending our own ideas, we find it easy to weight the evidence in their favor. Objectivity demands that we look also at the other side of the coin. Once I asked a student why he had not included a certain author in his paper. The answer was quick: "Oh, but he does not agree with me, so I could not use him." His objectivity score was very low, below passing.

Objectivity requires me to consider negative evidence, to analyze ideas that are foreign or different, to look at arguments that might upset my position. Being objective requires courage and humility; it demands putting pet ideas on hold while examining all the evidence; it insists on developing wisdom to consider every facet of a topic.

Focus

With Paul, a researcher must say: "One thing I do" (Phil 3:13). Just as Paul did (v. 14), we focus on the problem and its solution. Research thinking must fly straight as an arrow, without deviating from the goal. For that reason you cannot begin researching until you have determined your problem and purpose—what needs fixing and how you are going to do it.

Some cultures (and languages) enjoy a way of thinking that repeats itself. Take, for instance, the stories of the Hebrew Bible. In Genesis 24, the phrase "Drink, and I will also draw for your camels" appears three times: when Abraham's servant prayed (v. 14), when Rebekah said the words (v. 19), and when Eliezer told her family about it (v. 44). Repetition is natural and normal. However, in research there is no space for saying the same thing twice. "Say it well, say it once" is good advice.

Another way of thinking allows for digressions, going off on tangents. You may find fascinating information, but if it does not further your argumentation, you will have to leave it aside. Keep focused on your goal! As Deuteronomy 5:32 admonishes, "You shall not turn aside to the right hand or to the left."

Clear Presuppositions

A presupposition is a basic understanding that undergirds our thinking on a given topic. Sometimes presuppositions are also called "assumptions," in other words, what we take for granted. Such a presupposition appears in Hebrews 11:6, "Whoever would draw near to God must believe that he exists." Attempting to approach God without believing in God's existence makes no sense!

Presuppositions are the givens, the things we do not need to explain—at least not to ourselves. When we write a paper on Paul's understanding of baptism in Romans 6, we may take for granted that our readers accept that Paul existed and know him as an influential writer and apostle of the first century. Additionally, we might take for granted that they consider his opinion important (as we do) and that the inclusion of Romans in the canon makes it authoritative. On the other hand, readers who do not share our "givens" may not be able to follow our thinking, unless we set out our assumptions.

My understanding—of life, of what I read, of what I judge—depends to a great extent on my presuppositions. If I believe in a recent creation, this basic understanding colors everything I read about theistic evolution. If I am convinced of the depraved nature of human beings, Rogerian counseling, with its emphasis on the neutral or good nature of human beings, makes me nervous. In both cases, the opposite is equally true.

At times authors do not state their presuppositions. They may, however, give hints through their choice of sources, their way of organizing information, or their commendation of ideas or authors. If they do not state them, the reader spends unnecessary energy wondering: "Does she or doesn't she?" "Is he or isn't he?"

In the area of religious studies and theological education, presuppositions are usually strong, often considered matters of life and death, vitally important to who I am and what I say. To sweep presuppositions under the rug and pretend they do not exist is unwise as well as impossible. On the other hand, it may be difficult even to admit having presuppositions.

An important task in research thinking is to ask the question: "Which of my presuppositions affect the way I think and write?" Simple propositions deal with assuming that readers are familiar with the topic. For example, I assume that my reader can understand the Greek words I put into my paper. At a somewhat deeper level, I accept Paul as a historical figure, an apostle, and writer of several canonical New Testament books; I assume my readers do likewise. Even more influential on my research outcome would be the acceptance of Romans as an inspired and authoritative book. These convictions will set the tone for my analysis of Paul's death-and-resurrection motif in Romans 6. To let my readers know what my basic assumptions are is not merely courteous, it insures that they will understand what I say.

To understand someone, we need to know "where she is coming from," to use a popular phrase. To know what my writing truly means, my reader must know where I am coming from and what my presuppositions are. Thus it becomes my duty to explain to my reader the presuppositions that underlie my research. Before doing that, I will first have to bring my presuppositions into the open, list them, and decide which ones I must describe for my readers. My statement of presuppositions must be written in a way that explains my writing without making the reader feel that I consider her a heretic or a fool if she does not share my presuppositions.

To summarize, presuppositions are neither bad nor good—they simply are. And readers have a right to know which ones are guiding an author's research and writing.

Organization

When my mother spied my messy room, she would remind me of Pope's assertion: "Order is Heaven's first law." Whether order is the first or second law matters not; beyond doubt in research thinking, order and organization come near the top of the list.

Organized thinking puts similar ideas and concepts in the same category: Everything has its own place. For example, a paper describing a target unreached people would describe various characteristics of these people: socio-cultural, religious, politico-economic. You would not expect to find their history or the plans laid by mission societies to reach them under these categories. Neither would you expect to find a description of their diet under the heading "Religion."

Organized thinking also places ideas, phrases, and words in a logical order, allowing the reader and hearer to immediately guess the criteria used to organize them. In other words, the order makes sense. For example, the organization could go from small to large, from deep to shallow, from important to inconsequential, from old to new—or any number of logical sequences. In history, for example, we expect to proceed chronologically.

Yes, order should prevail in my research thinking and writing—not only in my messy room. Samuel Smiles was right to urge: "A place for everything and everything in its place."

Intellectual Honesty

Honesty and dishonesty are defined in different ways by different peoples. Intellectual honesty and dishonesty are also differently defined in different cultures. In some cultures, to repeat the words of the masters only shows how much one respects their wisdom. Borrowing from their writings is the only way to write. Quotation marks or footnotes add nothing to that reverence. In other cultures, the flow and beauty of the words is far more important than my admission that so-and-so wrote them; besides, that author would be delighted to have me use her words and ideas! If a sick baby keeps me up all night just before a difficult examination, my friend is quite happy to allow me to share his learning. As an act of compassion, he may even place his paper deliberately so that I can see and copy what he has written. Cheating is a non-issue.

Without evaluating the honesty of the practices just described, we Westerners underline that none of these fit in our research culture. Here I must recognize that whoever wrote before me opened the way. Her work made mine easier. Therefore, I owe her a debt of gratitude. I must acknowledge this debt by inserting a reference to her work. In a similar vein, the writer who said what he did in words so much better than mine (compelling me to use them) produced those words; they are his work, his art. I have no business taking what is not mine, using it as if it were mine. Consequently, I must put these wonderful words in quotation marks, recognizing the author's unique claim to that phrase.

Obviously, this concept of research honesty precludes my putting my name to a paper taken from the Internet, whether I paid for it or not. It entirely forbids using my name as the author of a paper when the piece is actually an article in an obscure journal. It would be equally dishonest for me to quote an author in such a way as to distort her meaning. The epitome of such dishonest usage would be to say that a reviewer found a book "magnificent," not quoting the whole sentence, which reads: "The study is a magnificent exercise in futility." All these usages fall under condemnation in the commandments: "Thou shalt not steal" and "Thou shalt not bear false witness."

Intellectual honesty at times may require me to admit that I do not know something, or even that someone else has a better answer than mine. An admission of this kind is not dishonorable. In fact, it will be applauded as honesty.

Most schools have a "Plagiarism Policy" that states just how seriously the institution takes using another person's materials as one's own. Punishment may range from a zero on the paper, to a failing grade in the class, to dismissal from school. While the outcomes of intellectual dishonesty may be fearful—after all, those that love and make lies are left outside the pearly gates (Rev 22:15)—the results of following an honesty-best-policy attitude bring their own reward. Doing right for right's sake is always right. It is always best. See chapter 8 on footnotes for specific instructions on being honest in your papers.

Humility

Humility is a basic Christian virtue. Christ presented himself as "humble" (Matt 11:29) and indicated that those who humbled themselves would be exalted (Matt 23:12). Paul and Peter appealed for humility in the dealings of one Christian with another (Phil 2:3; 1 Pet 3:8; 5:5). James tied research and humility together by stating that "humility . . . comes from wisdom" (Jas 3:13 NIV).

When a book or an article exude arrogance—the know-it-all, better-than-everyone-else attitude—readers soon lose interest. A wiser path is to write in a way that is humble, tentative, willing to learn. This kind of writing makes room for dialogue, for reaching solutions.

Above all, conclusions should be stated in language that shows humility—willingness to learn, to accept other possibilities. After all, few researchers, especially students, would be willing to lay down their lives for the results of their research.

Thinking Processes

According to Bloom's taxonomy of the cognitive domain of learning, knowing and thinking take place at different levels. Knowledge is the simplest. Thinking about knowledge is more complex: for example, analysis and synthesis, evaluation and application, require more complex thinking skills. The process of making deductions and inferences is also important to research thinking.

Analysis and Synthesis

Both processes are indispensable to good research. Analysis could be exemplified by a small boy taking an alarm clock apart to find out what makes it tick. Synthesis is putting parts of three clocks together to make one functioning alarm piece.

Analysis is examining the evidence piece by piece. Analysis requires description and classification of each aspect of a topic, each piece of a history. Analysis demands considering what each piece is, what it does, and how it fits the other pieces. Before deciding how to teach a history class, the new professor carefully analyzes the syllabi of his predecessor and of two colleagues who teach the same course in other universities. He looks at all the parts, all the details, and sees what each part is and how it fits with the rest.

Synthesis, on the other hand, begins with two or more ideas or systems. After studying how each one works, you put parts of the old together to form a new one. Our new history professor takes pieces and parts of the three syllabi, adds his own ideas, and creates a new syllabus for his course. While it may be built on previous work, his course syllabus is a new creation, a wise combination of several sources, a synthesis.

Analysis and synthesis are mental activities. They may appear in writing, but they first take place in the researcher's thinking. In a paper, analysis usually appears in the body of the paper, while synthesis is more evident in the development of a model or a program, or in the conclusions at the end of the paper.

Application and Evaluation

Application and evaluation are at the deepest level of Bloom's taxonomy. These are not lightweight activities.

Application refers to using information. One applies rules of Greek orthography to write Greek correctly. One applies exegetical principles to derive a coherent meaning from the text. One applies church growth procedures to a church in order to add new members. Application of information requires thought and insight. It answers the questions, So what? How can this be used?

What can I do with this information? Knowing without applying could make for useless knowledge.

Evaluation does not use information to do something, it uses information to decide whether something is of value. Evaluation requires setting up criteria by which to measure. One must not only answer the question, How good is this? but also, How do I know this is good?

Research must constantly evaluate. Is this quotation good? Appropriate? Is there a better one? Does this idea fit well here? Are these the best words to use? Does this author's work deserve further attention? Finally, researchers should be able to evaluate their own work: Have I done a commendable job? Where could I do better?

Inductive and Deductive Reasoning

Both inductive and deductive reasoning are used in research; both may be needed in the same paper. Yet, if I use faulty procedures, both can yield invalid results.

Induction has been defined as the process by which people discover and prove general propositions. Starting from the particulars, we formulate conclusions, laws, principles. Inductive reasoning is at the heart of the scientific method. Inductive reasoning undergirds surveys, polls, and advertising.

We are acquainted with "inductive" Bible study. We might carefully study the Sermon on the Mount (Matt 5–7) and then state the principles of the kingdom that Jesus taught in that sermon. In a similar vein, I could taste apples from a hundred different trees, noticing the color, the texture, the flavor of the fruit. From my research I could induce that apples are a sweet-tasting fruit, with white flesh and seeds in the center.

As useful as inductive reasoning is for research, it has evident pitfalls. One of the most serious is using limited observations. If I only taste red apples, I could conclude that all apples are red. Recently I saw a poll of students' favorite drinks on a certain campus. I was interested until I found that the report was based on the preference of fifty-five students on a campus of more than three thousand students. Furthermore, there was no information on how these students were chosen. Were they buddies of the researcher? Were they all women? What was their age? Did they really represent the whole student body? How could I be sure that a certain cola drink was truly the favorite?

Inductions will be more accurate the more thorough the study of the phenomena. To find out what Paul says about church elders, I need to study all the passages in his writings that even touch on what elders should be and do. I need to analyze and compare them, especially where I see discrepancies. Only then will I be able to induce and then synthesize what Paul says about elders.

Another important issue is the way I state my conclusions. Apples are sweet. Always? Could I have missed a variety that is sour? Perhaps, then, I need to state that apples are generally sweet. I leave room for further conclusions, technically called *inductions*, derived from studying particulars.

While inductive reasoning goes from the particulars to the principle, deductive reasoning starts from the general, the universal. Merriam Webster's *Collegiate Dictionary* defines deduction as "the deriving of a conclusion by reasoning; *specifically*: inference in which the conclusion about particulars follows necessarily from general or universal premises"; and "a conclusion reached by logical deduction."

In philosophy and theology deductive reasoning is more common than in scientific research. After all, we work from grand and everlasting principles. For example, God is love. Because God is love, we deduce that everything God does is loving. So we look at God's activities to understand what it means for God to be love. It is easy to see that this manner of thinking can lead to circular reasoning.

Asking Questions

Doubt is considered by some as basic to research. Others call the same principle *criticism*. Neither term sounds good to godly ears. However, asking questions is acceptable. Research asks hard questions, questions about the source of information, as well as about the content and meaning of that source. See chapter 7, "Reading and Taking Notes," for further suggestions on asking questions.

My father-in-law read his Bible and the *Reader's Digest*. Whatever he read, in either source, was true. For many, what is printed is to be believed. Research thinking demands that I question the source of information. I am especially interested in the author and publisher. Questions about the author include: Who wrote this? Is he an expert in his field? Is she a recognized scholar? Who funded this research? Questions about the publication in which the material appears are also important: Is what I am reading published in a reputable journal? Is the book from a creditable publisher? Just as important, does this publisher have an "angle"?

As I read critically, I need to query the content. What exactly is the author saying? Is it the same thing throughout the piece I am reading? Is the author consistent with himself throughout the piece? How does this compare with other items she has written? I will also ask what presuppositions undergird the argument, what research techniques the author is using. The answers to these questions will help me discern meaning.

I will also ask what the writer wants me to know and believe after reading this piece. Is she trying to inform me or convince me? What is her intention? Obviously, if I sense that there is an attempt to coerce my thinking, I will rebel.

In my freshman English class I read an article about the importance of an open mind. The author posited that the mind is something like a can. If it is closed, nothing comes in or goes out. If it is open on one end, ideas come in and go out. If the lid is used as a strainer, ideas coming in or out can be evaluated, straining out the bad, leaving in the good. Finally, a can that is open at both ends is of absolutely no use, for ideas flow in and out with no evaluation. Research thinking demands a mind like the can with a strainer lid.

At first, the research mindset may feel uncomfortable. As you read, think, and write, you will become more and more comfortable in this way of thinking. Your professors will notice the improvement in your writing. Learning to think research is worth the effort.

So, with your mind in research gear, you can go on to reading and taking notes. These topics are discussed in chapter 7.

VII | READING, EVALUATING, AND TAKING NOTES

Reading for a research paper takes time. To get the most benefit from this major part of the research activity, you will have to constantly evaluate or weigh what you are reading. You will also need to make notes of what you read. This chapter gives suggestions for reading, evaluating, and taking notes.

Reading

Reading is one of the most profitable of all intellectual activities. In reading, ideas and facts go from one brain to another through the printed page. However, not all books have the same effect on the reader. Francis Bacon, English philosopher and writer of the sixteenth century, said that some books should be tasted, others swallowed; only a few might be chewed and digested.[1] Some books are light reading and can be finished in one evening. Most of those needed for research are heavy and must be chewed and digested. Research reading—beyond the early exploratory reading—takes time and thought. The search for information and concepts demands concentration, determination, and time—much time.

Research reading demands the understanding of (1) words—look up ones you do not know in the dictionary; (2) phrases and sentences; (3) paragraphs—try summarizing the contents of each paragraph in one sentence; (4) the chapter—summarize each in a maximum of three sentences; and (5) the book—summarize it in one paragraph. Making these summaries, mentally or on paper, fixes the content in your mind.

Research reading begins with finding information about the author, possibly on the back cover or the dust jacket of the book. It continues with the title page and its verso, where there is information regarding the publisher and date of publication. After carefully examining the table of contents, you should examine the introduction, where you find information about the author's purpose, the recognized limitations of the work, the audience for whom it is intended, and the

---

[1] "Of Studies," in *Harvard Classics,* ed. Charles W. Eliot (New York: Colliers, 1909), 3:128.

organization of the book. Next, read—or at least browse—the concluding chapter, in which the author summarizes and draws conclusions. Only after all this work are you prepared to read the body of the book. By then, you may have decided to put the book aside as not useful to the study.

Some suggestions for successful reading:

1. Read in an appropriate place. You will need good light and ventilation. You need a place to write, for you will be taking notes. Find a quiet place without distractions. Be prepared with pencils, cards, and other materials—not least of which may be your computer—so you do not need to interrupt your study.

2. Read when you are most apt to be awake and alert. Some people do best in the morning; others at night. Find your own best time and use it well.

3. Alternate periods of study with moments of relaxation and physical exercise. Although some people can sit for hours, most tend to lose their power of concentration after an hour or so. Some scholars say they like to study hard for about fifty minutes, then get up for a drink and five minutes of exercise before returning to their desks. If you cannot sit still that long, build up your resistance by five minutes at a time. Start by forcing yourself to sit and concentrate for fifteen minutes. Eventually you will be able to endure an hour. To work efficiently, keep your body in top condition with proper rest, diet, and exercise.

4. Take notes of what you read. The intellectual exercise of putting information on paper or into your computer helps your brain absorb the materials you read. Only if you assimilate your reading can you organize, analyze, and synthesize it.

5. Do not wait until you feel like reading or studying. Make yourself a schedule and stick to it. Do not let yourself be distracted by other matters, interesting as they may be.

Evaluating Sources

You could read for years—in books, journals, or online—for there is much written on almost every topic. However, not all written materials are of the same value, even if they deal with the subject you are researching. While the fourteen questions that follow can help you weigh anything you read, Question 15 deals specifically with the evaluation of websites.

1. Who is the author? Information about the author may be found on the back cover, on the dust jacket, or in the preface. You will find the author's qualifications and a list of other books she has written. Some libraries keep the dust jackets and other materials in a special author file; ask the librarian. If you cannot find information about an author, ask your professor, who knows most of the important people in his or her area. To find information about authors the following sources are helpful: *Who's Who in Religion,* which gives brief biographical data about living scholars, and the fourth volume of *Directory of American Scholars,* which lists scholars in the areas of religion and philosophy. Check the *ATLA Index* and WorldCat for items this person has written. These sources will show you the author's areas of expertise, and what journals and publishers carry his or her work.

2. Who is the publisher? Not all publishers are equally serious. Some specialize in learned books; others publish popular works. Whether the book was published by a Protestant or Catholic publisher makes a difference, if you are interested in a certain approach to your topic. If a book was published by the author or has no imprint at all, it is appropriate to question whether a publisher was unwilling to take the manuscript. Serious publishing companies are careful to have their imprint only on quality books. Ask the librarian or a professor about publishers.

3. If the source in question is an article, is the journal in which it appeared recognized as a specialized and serious journal? An article about an archeological finding in *Time* is not worthy of as much confidence as one on the same finding in *Biblica* (from the Pontifical Biblical Institute in Rome) or *Biblical Archaeologist* (from the American Schools of Oriental Research). Somewhere between the two extremes would be an article in *Biblical Archaeology Review,* which admits its purpose is the popularization of biblical archaeology. Popular magazines, such as *Reader's Digest, Newsweek, Christian Woman,* or even the *National Geographic* are not usually good research sources—unless your research is unique. You need to take the time to become acquainted with the specialized journals in your field.

4. What is the date of publication? If you are looking for a source that includes the latest research on a Hebrew-language problem, the date needs to be recent. A 1907 book may be useful to know what authors wrote then, but will only be of value to the history of your problem.

On the other hand, if the research concerns the history of Presbyterians in Korea, a book written in Korea in 1907 about Presbyterian mission activity would be valuable. The date that counts is that of the copyright or edition, not that of a printing, when no changes are made to the book.

5. What is the author's purpose? Generally the introduction to a serious book will give the author's basic philosophy, the purpose for writing the book, the audience to which it is directed, and maybe even a hint on the conclusions reached. You can safely judge a serious book on the basis of its introduction (written by the author, not to be confused with a preface written by someone else). After reading the introduction to some books you may decide to drop them from the list of potential sources!

6. Is the style of writing popular or serious? This question is answered by reading a little here and there. If the answer is "popular," the source may not be valuable for serious study. That does not mean that research writing is all dry. It does mean that books written for entertainment may sacrifice content to readability. Items written with quoted conversations, colorful language, or abundant contractions are suspect.

7. Is there a bibliography? How extensive is it? Are there footnotes? Are they complete? The presence of these items indicates the writer has done a serious piece of work. Notes and bibliography show that the author took the time to look at other people's work and was honest enough to note what was borrowed.

8. Are there tables? Graphs? Maps? Not all sources need these items, but a book that contains well-made graphs and tables, together with the source and date for the information presented therein, usually can be considered a serious work. A map can say something about the book: If it is sloppily made, or a copy from a lesser atlas, it may indicate carelessness. On the other hand, pictures in a book—unless the topic is archaeology or something of that sort—do not enhance the research value of a source.

9. Is the table of contents detailed? Is there an index? Much information may be obtained by reading the table of contents. A very sketchy one may suggest lack of precision and care for detail—unforgivable flaws in research. In modern English-language books, the index is often a mark of a good research source. The same cannot be said for other languages. Certainly, an index facilitates research and is to be considered a plus.

10. In the footnotes and bibliography, are the works recent and the authors specialists in their fields? Sometimes a fairly recent work quotes rather old sources. This would indicate that the research was done some time ago and the author did not take the trouble to update the material. If authors quoted or consulted are not specialists, it is fair to wonder if the writer knew who the specialists in the field were.

11. What is the tone of the writing? Is it sober and objective? Or is it emotional? How are adjectives used? Are epithets applied to people? Some authors are not able to convince their readers by the information they give nor by their logic, so they use emotional phrases that appeal more to the heart than the mind. When the language is strong, the content may be weak. If an author needs to tear down an opponent in order to build up his or her work, there is a problem. The best research sources are clearly written, in an objective style.

12. Is the style of writing clear and easy to read? Is the phrasing concise? Is the vocabulary as simple as the topic will permit? There is no virtue in using long sentences and unnecessarily difficult words; in fact, such writing may suggest the author is hiding ignorance behind fancy language. Good research writing is simple and straightforward.

13. Has this source been translated from another language? How many editions has it had? An item translated from another language has been considered important enough to receive wider dissemination. A book that has been re-edited has evidently been deemed significant. Thus, a positive answer to both questions suggests a good research source. In choosing between the original and the translation—if you can read both—choose the original.

14. Is this a primary source? A primary source on Vatican Council II would be the documents put out by the council. A secondary source would be a book that comments or interprets those documents. In the secondary source the author can interject his or her ideas and thus color your understanding of the original. Likewise, what the Latter-day Saints say about themselves is a primary document; what someone else says about them is secondary, and liable to bias or distortion. Using primary sources minimizes the danger of misinterpretation.

15. What about this website? Each website you visit is a potential source of information for your research. But not all websites are created equal. You must evaluate by asking questions. Some of the most valuable are the following: What is the purpose of this site? Entertainment, information, or research? Who sponsors the site? A credible

organization, such as a university? A professional society? An advocacy group? A company trying to sell something? An individual interested in the topic? Obviously, the first is better than the last! Use your good judgment and ask questions to determine the value of a site. Then, ask questions about the author. Is the author named? If so, is he or she an authority? Use approaches described under Question 1 to answer this question. In addition, refer to the Internet Directory of Published Writers (http://www.writers.net). When was this material written or published? If no date is given for the piece you are interested in, when was the last time the site was updated? What is the tone of the piece? Is someone trying to get you to buy something? Or convince you of some ideological stance? To what kind of sources do the hyperlinks (if there are any) lead you? Consider the company your website keeps. Exercise utmost caution!

Asking these questions is literary criticism. It is not finding fault with authors, but deciding which works are most trustworthy and appropriate for your research. Mistakes in judging can happen, but experience sharpens your skills and makes the process easier. These queries are similar to those answered in a book review. Although the critical review of books or articles is not usually considered research, such work demands critical thinking and good writing. Critical reviews of books and journal articles are dealt with in chapter 17.

Taking Good Notes

The making of bibliographic notes has already been discussed. Notes considered here are those we take to remember what we read. These notes must be complete and painstakingly detailed. Time spent taking proper notes is time saved in the total process. There is no way to do good research without taking good notes, either manually or on a computer.

A Method for Manual Notetaking

Notes for research can be taken in a notebook or on large sheets of paper. However, the most effective method uses note cards or slips of paper. These slips or cards are easy to organize; they can then be arranged and rearranged to suit changes in outline or approach. Cards may be added or deleted without affecting the total scheme. Finally, when put in order, they almost write the paper by themselves.

Note Cards

All the cards should be of the same size, usually 3 by 5 or 4 by 6 inches. Typing paper cut in four equal parts may also be used. Some researchers prefer a larger card, but the small one is a reminder of a basic rule of note-taking: only one item on a card. Since bibliography cards are used at the same time as note cards, it is helpful to use a different type or color of paper, or slips of a slightly different size so the two kinds are not confused.

Filing System

Before beginning to read and take notes, it is a good idea to prepare one card—a little larger, stiffer, and of a different color than the note cards—for each of the sections of the paper as envisioned in the tentative outline. These index cards are labeled to serve as dividers for a simple filing system. Rubber bands or elastics may be used to keep each packet of notes together, or a small box may be used as a file cabinet.

As you do your reading, take notes as needed. At the end of your reading session, put your notes in the appropriate section of your file. This system is simple, yet effective.

Parts of the Note Card

Each note card has three indispensable parts: (1) heading, (2) text, and (3) source. Notes may be written in ink or pencil; the first looks messy when corrections are made, but the second tends to dim with time and use. Some library research rooms only allow the use of pencils; in that case, pencil will have to do.

Heading

The headings on the cards correspond to sections of the paper. A paper on the history of Nestorianism in China would include a section on Rabban Sauma. Thus, one heading would be RABBAN SAUMA. There would also be several subheadings under the main heading: biographical data, relation with Rabban Mark, travels in Europe, return to Mongolia, and so on. Sub-subheadings may also be used. As you review your cards, especially if you change your outline, you may need to revise your headings. For starters, however, give the information a place where it can belong.

Headings may be written in a different color; however, changing pens every few minutes may be a nuisance. Whatever the color, write clearly. The heading must always be located in the same place on the note card. The upper right corner is quite handy.

Text

The text of a note card may be a direct quotation, a summary of what has been read, or the researcher's reaction to the reading.

Direct quotations. A quotation card must say exactly what the source said. No spelling or punctuation differences are allowed. Even if there is an evident error, it must be copied. But immediately following the error, place the bracketed word [*sic*], which is the Latin for "thus" and means that, right or wrong, this was what appeared in the source. If you omit anything the author wrote, use ellipsis marks. For an omission . . . within a sentence, three double-spaced dots are used. If the omission includes a break between sentences, four dots are used. . . . If the quoted sentences or phrases are from two different paragraphs, ellipsis marks are not permitted; you must record two quotations. If a quotation comes from two pages (80, 81), mark the page break // so that if you use only part of the quotation, you can tell whether it is from page 80 or 81. Put quotation marks around all quoted material.

Summaries. It is not always necessary to copy an author's actual words. A summary or synthesis may be sufficient. However, when you do this, be careful not to change the sense or thrust of the author's thought. Make sure that summary cards tell you they are summaries, not quotations.

Comments. I can easily forget my reactions to a certain reading. Thus I need to jot down my comments and impressions. These may be notes on the reading, ideas about possible sources, or suggested modifications to any part of the paper. They may be doubts or questions, sometimes only tangentially related to the topic. However, I need to write them down and give them a heading—possibly that of the item that triggered them—so that later I can retrieve my brilliant idea. A date on the comment card can help me reconstruct my intellectual pilgrimage. I initial these cards to identify them as comments or queries

Source

Each note card must record the source from which the material was quoted or summarized. The page(s) and the author's last name are usually enough, except when an author has two books or there are two authors with the same last name. In the first case, an abbreviated form of the title must be used: Bruce, *Acts*, 24. In the second case, an initial with the surname is enough: L. Smith, 78.

Computer Notetaking

Those of us who are computer addicts cannot write any other way. Taking notes on the computer not only saves time but insures accuracy and readability. Whether I take a laptop to the library or bring the books to my desk, I can easily take notes on the computer. The problem is sorting the cards. Even if you use a database to sort them, you cannot see more than two or four at a time on the monitor! Let me share instructions for a system that works well for me.

1. Make your page margins as small as the printer will allow; then sub-divide your 8.5 by 11 page into 4 or 6 pages. Number your subpages in small font (bottom center).

2. Take notes as described in the manual system. Be sure to put in appropriate headings and subheadings. Do not forget to write down the source. If you have a two-page note, be sure to indicate the number of the first page on the second one so you can put them together (something like "follows 35").

3. Use two files simultaneously—one for bib cards, one for content notes. Make an alphabetical listing of bib entries on one; take notes on the other file. Save often.

4. Print out your note cards, cut the pages up, and sort as you would manually. You will be able to see what you are doing and arrange and rearrange your piles.

5. When you input your paper into the computer, using your piles of notes, have three files open. One has the bibliography (from where you will take the sources for your footnotes); another holds the notes; the third, the developing paper. When you come to a quotation, simply paste it in place from the note file, without retyping it. Cut and paste bibliographical information from the bib file (remembering, of course, to change bibliography form into footnote form).

Useful Advice

The most useful note card is the short one, which contains only one idea, one reference, or one precise piece of information. It is written only on one side of the card or slip. The note system here described—whether manual or computerized—is efficient precisely because any card or slip may be moved without disturbing the whole. When there is only one idea on a card, moving it is simple. If two ideas are copied on one card, organization may later demand they be separated—which will require recopying. Obviously, when only one idea is written on each card, there will be many cards, but the ease of organization makes up for having to deal with many cards. Model note cards are shown on page 61.

When to quote and when to summarize? When dealing with ideas, you can summarize, but always take care not to distort the meaning or emphasis of the original. When an author expresses an idea with lucidity or in picturesque words, better than any other way to express that idea, you probably should quote. In any case, when in doubt, copy the actual quotation. Later you can choose to quote or summarize. You will be happy to have the full information when you are writing your paper late the night before it is due.

The system of taking notes described in this chapter may be new to some students—and even to some professors guiding research. However, there is little doubt that it works well. The first attempt may take some time, but the ease and precision gained should make the time spent worthwhile. By using this system conscientiously, you will avoid returning to the source once you have done your reading.

Finish all your reading on a given topic (or section of your topic) and sort your notes before sitting down to write. This will give you a full picture of your topic. It will also allow you to write seamless prose, blending different authors into their correct position in your writing.

Here are ten tips for better notetaking:

1. Use cards or slips of paper of uniform size; do this manually or on the computer. Make heading cards for each section of the paper and keep slips organized, in a box or using rubber bands.
2. Write clearly (or type) on one side only.
3. Put only one idea, one thought, one piece of information on each card to facilitate the organization of the paper.
4. Make short notes (remember number 3), but if you do need a second card, make it evident that this is a second card of a set.
5. Put a heading and a subheading (and even a sub-subheading) on each card.
6. Indicate clearly (yet in abbreviated form) the source of information.
7. Indicate clearly whether you have quoted or summarized. Be very consistent in your system.
8. Summarize as often as possible; only quote when the author's words are impossible to improve on.
9. When quoting, copy material exactly as it appears. Use ellipsis marks for omission. Use [*sic*] to show the error is copied.
10. Make your notes so clear and understandable that anyone else could take over your incomplete work.

This chapter has discussed reading, evaluating, and taking the notes. These notes will be the building blocks of the paper. They will also supply the information you need for preparing footnotes, which are presented in chapter 8.

Sample Note Cards

These samples illustrate what has been explained. Use your own creativity—always within an organized system—to produce useful notecards for your paper.

Codices-Earliest Christian-Egypt

The existence of Christian codices in Egypt "was historically plausible if not downright necessary." There are no historical or technical arguments against their existence.

Tiede, 7

R. Sauma—Report on Mongols

Asked by the cardinals in Rome about his religion, Sauma said: "Know ye, O our Fathers, that many of our Fathers have gone into the countries of the Mongols, and Turks, and Chinese and have taught them the Gospel, and at the present time there are many Mongols who are Christians. For many of the sons of the Mongol kings and queens have been baptized and confess Christ. And they have established churches in their military campus and they pay honour to the Christians, and there are many among them who are believers."

Budge, 174.

VIII | FOOTNOTES: WHY, WHEN, AND HOW

Student researchers are often in doubt concerning whether or not they should footnote a given item. Once they have decided they should, they wonder how to do it. This chapter seeks to elucidate both aspects of the problematic footnote. A comparison of footnotes and bibliographical entries appears in chapter 9.

One should really speak of *notes*, for this term includes content and reference notes, whether they be located at the bottom of the page (footnotes) or at the end of a chapter (endnotes). Endnotes are considered appropriate for short papers and are always numbered consecutively through the chapter or paper. Footnotes are normally required in theses and dissertations; they can be numbered consecutively through the chapter (as in this book) or page by page.

Why Footnotes?

At times, writers employ footnotes to impress the reader by using foreign languages and difficult words. Some footnotes seem to convey false modesty: "I don't want to parade my learning, but I've read a lot of books." Some seem to be trying to sell: "See my book on this topic." Others suggest the writer had a piece of information which did not fit in anywhere, and put it in the footnote in order to get it in somehow. At times footnotes are used to show snobbery: "In an interview with the author, the celebrated artist XX said." A "see above" note may suggest the reader has a very poor memory or is not intelligent enough to look for herself. And finally, "there is the flattery footnote: 'The reader will naturally recall. . . .' (And if the reader does remember, he is pleased; if he does not, he is happy the author thought he might.)"[1] These uses are not appropriate to research and should be avoided.

There are, however, legitimate uses for footnotes. Reference notes (collectively called documentation; designated as footnotes if placed at the bottom of a

---

[1]Taken from Carter V. Good, *Essentials of Educational Research* (New York: Appleton Century-Crofts, 1966), 401.

page, or endnotes at the end of a chapter or paper) are provided to show where information was obtained. They serve a triple purpose: (1) to indicate that there is authority behind statements made, in order to strengthen the researcher's assertions; (2) to help the scholar who is looking for information on the topic to easily find the material referred to; (3) to honestly admit intellectual indebtedness to another author.

Content notes provide information that could disrupt or unnecessarily complicate the text. The content footnote may point out a contrast or discrepancy, give further explanations, or indicate sources for further study. These notes are more usual in theses and dissertations than in short research papers. They are also more varied in style than reference notes. Since many readers do not read footnotes, the text should make sense without the content footnotes. Obviously, if a content note quotes or cites, it must give a source.

When to Footnote

Content notes are used at the discretion of the writer—any time the addition of a note would enrich or enhance the elaboration of ideas. Reference notes are used whenever materials from another author are cited or quoted.

A reference note is used to indicate the source of a quotation—whether it be three words or three lines. It is also used to show the source of an idea, even though that idea may be expressed in the researcher's own words. Failure to use quotation marks for quoted materials or give due credit to a source by using a reference note is considered a major flaw in research. Plagiarism, as such illegitimate copying is called, is considered a dishonest use of other's property—intellectual thievery. Therefore, a writer must give references for all quoted or cited words or ideas, and remember to use quotation marks for every borrowed phrase or sentence.

No footnotes are needed when the ideas and words in the paper are yours or are common knowledge. If you present a paper with no footnotes, your reader would surmise that you did everything by yourself, that you are not indebted to anyone. Such a paper would contain only your opinions or be superficial, consisting exclusively of general knowledge; it would not qualify as research. Of course, facts that everyone knows—such as A.D. 79 for the eruption of Mount Vesuvius—need no footnote. For an idea or a piece of information to qualify as common knowledge, it must appear in several places. On the other hand, if eighteen authors say one thing, and two say something different, you will want to note the dissenters in a footnote.

How to Footnote

Since content notes are varied in structure and form, what is asked of them is that they be clear, logical, and as short as possible. The reference appears after the content, as is shown in footnote 1 on this page, given simply as an example of a content footnote.[2] Reference notes, on the other hand, follow fairly strict rules.

Format of the Reference Note

Since the purpose of a reference note is to permit a reader to find the original source, you must provide sufficient information to make locating it easy. Using a uniform format helps the reader and impresses your professor.

In the text the footnote appears only as an Arabic number one-half space above the line (superscript) at the end of the quotation, citation, or allusion. The text of the footnote appears at the bottom of the page. One space below the last line of text, use the underlining to draw a 2-inch line (20 or 24 spaces, depending on whether you use pica or elite type), beginning at the left margin. Place the superscript number 1.5 spaces below this line, at eight spaces from the left margin. Begin the note one-half space below the superscript number (two spaces below the line). The first line of the note is indented eight spaces; following lines reach the margin. Single space foot or endnotes, but leave two spaces between notes.

Now that you have waded through the old explanation, let me assure you that Microsoft Word™ and WordPerfect™ do it perfectly, automatically! Some quick pointers, however, will help you. Set the margins of your page at 1.5 inches and your paragraph indent at 0.6 before you start typing at all. Also place the footnote below the text, not at the bottom of the page (in footnote options). Other settings should be left as default. Do this to save yourself the grief of fixing margins and indents for footnotes after you have typed them. See more on format in chapter 12.

In reference notes, abbreviations are commonly used. Be sure to use them consistently. In current usage, the abbreviation for page or pages is omitted. In indicating pages, 2–4 means pages 2 through 4, including page 3; using 2, 4 means only pages 2 and 4. The publication data are in parentheses, and the only full stop is the final one.

Full Reference Notes

The following are examples of full reference notes, given the first time an item is mentioned. They are the basic models: a book, a journal article, a magazine article, a chapter in a multi-author book, a thesis, and a signed dictionary article. Use the bibliographical entry as the basis for your footnote (chapter 5). Chapter 9 shows the relation between bibliography and footnote format.

---

[2]If the note contains a first reference, the citation is given in full (Kate L. Turabian, *A Manual for Writers*, 6th ed. [Chicago: University of Chicago Press, 1993], 163). Notice that parentheses within parentheses become square brackets. An alternative calls for a period after the content note, as in this example. Kate L. Turabian, *A Manual for Writers*, 6th ed. (Chicago: University of Chicago Press, 1993), 163. Use the style you choose consistently throughout the paper. If the note refers to an already-quoted source, the second reference form is used (Turabian, 163); if the source is already clear, you may use only the page number in parentheses (163).

Book

Author's name in normal order, title in italics (or underlined) with first and last and all important words capitalized, publication data in parentheses, page (or pages) used at the end of the note. For a city that may not be well known, you must give the state or the country. The state may be written in full (Illinois), abbreviated (Ill.), or identified by postal code (IL). Whichever system you choose, use it consistently. (Make sure your school allows you to choose.) Another choice shows in my use of InterVarsity for InterVarsity Press. If I use a short form for one publisher, I must use the short form of all other publishers: Zondervan, Hendrickson, Orbis. However, I cannot shorten the name of university presses: University of Chicago Press, Andrews University Press.

¹Grant R. Osborne, *The Hermeneutical Spiral: A Comprehensive Introduction to Biblical Interpretation* (Downers Grove, IL: InterVarsity, 1991), 25.

Journal article

Title of article in quotation marks (in American style, commas go *within* the quotation marks!), title of journal in italics (or underlined), no comma before or after volume number, date of issue in parentheses, colon, one space, page number. If paging is continuous in each volume (as in this example), the year is enough. If paging is not continuous, month or season should be given.

²Stephen Thompson, "The End of Satan," *Andrews University Seminary Studies* 37 (1999): 257–261.

Magazine article

Do not give volume number; the date is enough. The date may be expressed in library or European style, as here, or in the traditional American style: April 24, 2000 (note the extra comma). Use one style or the other, but do so consistently.

³Loren Wilkinson, "Saving Celtic Christianity," *Christianity Today*, 24 April 2000, 80.

Chapter in a multi-author book

Note the "in," showing this is a part of a book. Note also the editor *after* the title of the book. Here "ed." means "edited by"; it is not pluralized. Since this is a note, you can use "and others" for the three other editors. In the bibliography, you need to give all the names.

⁴Dana L. Robert, "Adoniram Judson Gordon, 1836–1895," in *Mission Legacies: Biographical Studies of Leaders of the Modern Missionary Movement,* ed. Gerald Anderson and others (Maryknoll, NY: Orbis, 1994), 23.

Dissertation

A dissertation is not considered a published book; its title is presented in quotation marks. The specific degree, the university, and date are in parentheses. If the institution is not well known, its location is given.

⁵Trust Ndlovu, "The Church as an Agent of Reconciliation in the Thought of Desmond Tutu" (Ph.D. dissertation, Andrews University, Berrien Springs, MI, 1999), 57.

Signed dictionary article

Start with the author of the article. Then give the name of the article in quotation marks, followed by the dictionary or encyclopedia, the editors, publication data in parentheses, and exact location of the quotation: here, volume 1, page 165. By placing the abbreviation for the title in parentheses, I can use it for a later reference to the same book.

⁶Sverre Aalen, "*Ôr*," *Theological Dictionary of the Old Testament* (*TDOT*), ed. G. Johannes Botterweck and Helmer Ringren (Grand Rapids: Eerdmans, 1974), 1:165.

A footnote (or endnote) differs from a bibliographical entry in three main ways: (1) The author's name is in normal order, (2) publication data appear in parentheses, and (3) there is only one period in the entire note.

Second or Later References

If reference is made to the same source twice, consecutively, the second reference is given as "ibid." (for the Latin *ibidem*, "in the same place"). If the same page is quoted, ibid. is enough. If a different page is used, the note will read: Ibid., 3. Here the word is capped at the beginning of a note; otherwise it is in lowercase.

If reference is made to the same source more than once, but not consecutively, the second time only the author's surname is given, together with the page number. However, if there are two authors by the same surname, distinction must be made by using at least an initial. If more than one work of an author is used, a shortened form of the title is used to distinguish one from the other.

⁷Laird R. Harris, Gleason L. Archer, and Bruce K. Waltke, *Theological Wordbook of the Old Testament* (*TWOT*), 2 vols. (Chicago: Moody, 1980), 1:103.
⁸*TWOT*, 1:157.

If two or more items by one author appear following each other in the same note, the second time, the author's name is replaced by the word "idem" (not italicized), Latin for "the same." For example:

⁹Turabian, *A Manual*, 46; idem, *Student's Guide*, 68.

Two or more short footnotes may be typed on the same line, with a minimum of six spaces between them. A note beginning on a line with two entries may not continue on a second line. This is for typing only; word-processing programs do not allow this. Automatic footnoting is well worth this limitation.

The following sequence of footnotes illustrates:

¹⁰Richard N. Soulen, *Handbook of Biblical Criticism* (Atlanta: John Knox, 1976), 24.
¹¹Ibid.
¹²William D. Mounce, *Basics of Biblical Greek*, vol. 1, *Textbook* (Grand Rapids: Zondervan, 1993), 201.

[13]Soulen, 28.

[14]William D. Mounce, *The Morphology of Biblical Greek: A Theology for Infant Baptism* (Grand Rapids: Zondervan, 1994), 302.

[15]Walter C. Kaiser Jr., "What Commentaries Can (and Can't) Do," *Christianity Today*, 2 October 1981, 26.

[16]Mounce, *Basics*, 1:52.

[17]Otto Kaiser, "David und Jonathan: Tradition, Redaktion und Geschichte in I Sam 16–20: Ein Versuch.," *EphemeridesTheologicael Lovanienses* 66 (1990): 291.

[18]W. Kaiser, 24.   [19]Ibid., 27.

Bible References

In a research paper on a nonbiblical topic, the biblical references will probably appear as footnotes or endnotes. However, in a biblical or theological paper, the Bible references are commonly placed in parentheses directly in the text. In English it has been accepted practice that no version is indicated when one uses the King James Version (KJV). Any version other than the KJV must be indicated. This is usually done in a footnote (see next examples).

[20]Unless otherwise indicated all Bible references in this paper are to the *New American Standard Bible* (NASB) (La Habra, CA: The Lockman Foundation, 1973).

[21]All Greek references are from *The Greek New Testament*, 3d ed. corrected (Stuttgart: United Bible Societies), 1983.

Although you could use several versions in one paper, this practice is frowned on. When you write a serious research paper, choose one version of the Bible and use it continuously throughout. Jumping from one version to another, choosing the wording that suits your purposes, suggests that you are trying to make the Bible say what you want it to say.

In modern usage the abbreviations of the books of the Bible are not followed by periods. The list of appropriate abbreviations is given below:[3]

Gen	1 Kgs	Prov	Amos	Matt	Phil	1 Pet
Exod	2 Kgs	Eccl	Obad	Mark	Col	2 Pet
Lev	1 Chr	Cant	Jonah	Luke	1 Thess	1 John
Num	2 Chr	Isa	Mic	John	2 Thess	2 John
Deut	Ezra	Jer	Nah	Acts	1 Tim	3 John
Josh	Neh	Lam	Hab	Rom	2 Tim	Jude
Judg	Esth	Ezek	Zeph	1 Cor	Titus	Rev
Ruth	Job	Dan	Hag	2 Cor	Phlm	
1 Sam	Ps	Hos	Zac	Gal	Heb	
2 Sam	(Pss)	Joel	Mal	Eph	Jas	

[3]This list was taken from the *SBL Handbook of Style for Ancient Near Eastern, Biblical, and Early Christian Studies* (Peabody, MA: Hendrickson, 1999), 73–74. Except for the absence of the period, these abbreviations are the same as those given in the *Chicago Manual of Style*, 14th ed. (Chicago: University of Chicago Press, 1993), 474–475.

This chapter has given the rationale for the use of reference notes and the basic guidelines for their format. Chapter 9 presents examples of reference notes (footnotes) and bibliographical entries for different—and difficult—types of materials.

American Psychological Association Style of In-text Citations

If your school uses the in-text citation method advocated by the American Psychological Association, see Appendix A.

IX | REFERENCE NOTES AND BIBLIOGRAPHICAL ENTRIES COMPARED

Reference notes and bibliographical entries are similar, yet different. This chapter compares the two. The format of the entries presented here—including spaces, indentation, and punctuation—is proper Turabian academic paper style and should be carefully followed. Italics may be replaced by underlining, but do not use both underlining and italics in the same paper. If you use the APA style, see appendix A.

In preparing notes and bibliographical entries that do not seem to fit into any category, follow the rules as closely as possible, using common sense to make modifications as needed. References should make it easy for a reader to locate any source. Refer to chapters 5 and 8 for more details on bibliography and note format. For further information, consult Turabian, *The Chicago Manual of Style*, and *The SBL Handbook of Style*.[1]

The examples use the following abbreviations:

N (for Note) shows the format of a full reference note.

B (for Bibliography) gives the format for a common, uncomplicated bibliographical entry.

BP (for Bibliography Partial) indicates the format to use when only a part of the source has been consulted.

BA (for Bibliography All) indicates the format to use for the whole source (in contrast with BP).

---

[1] Kate L. Turabian, *A Manual for Writers of Term Papers, Theses, and Dissertations*, 6th ed., rev. John Grossman and Alice Bennett (Chicago: University of Chicago Press, 1996). This is based on *The Chicago Manual of Style*, 14th ed. (Chicago: University of Chicago Press, 1993). For ancient Near Eastern, biblical, and early Christian studies, you will find additional information in *The SBL Handbook of Style*, ed. Patrick H. Alexander and others (Peabody, MA: Hendrickson, 1999). The main difference between SBL and Turabian styles is that SBL puts editors, translators, and series within the parentheses around the publication data (*SBL Handbook of Style*, 48–51).

Published Materials

Published materials include books (specialized and general), pamphlets, and periodicals (journals and magazines). Facts of publication must be given in full form in the first reference. For the format of second references, see chapter 8.

Abbreviations can be used for often-repeated titles or series. If there are only a few, give the abbreviation the first time the item is mentioned. If you use many abbreviations, put a list of them in the paper or thesis, usually between the introduction and first chapter (see Appendix D for a list of accepted abbreviations). Abbreviations may be used in the notes, but not in the bibliography. When they represent books or journals, they should be underlined or italicized.

General Books

Under this heading, several issues are addressed. First, and most abundant, are those related to authorship. Next come examples of how to handle multivolume works. Finally, entries showing how to deal with series, reprints, and secondary sources are presented.

Authorship
One author

N   [1]Lewis Drummond, *Miss Bertha: Woman of Revival* (Nashville: Broadman & Holman, 1996), 151.

B   Drummond, Lewis. *Miss Bertha: Woman of Revival.* Nashville: Broadman & Holman, 1996.

Two or three authors

N   [2]Bruce Malina and Jerome H. Neyrey, *Portraits of Paul: An Archaeology of Ancient Personality* (Louisville, KY: John Knox, 1996), 134.

B   Malina, Bruce, and Jerome H. Neyrey. *Portraits of Paul: An Archaeology of Ancient Personality.* Louisville, KY: John Knox, 1996.

More than three authors

N   [3]Willem A. VanGemeren and others, *The Law, the Gospel, and the Modern Christian* (Grand Rapids: Zondervan, 1993), 78.

B   VanGemeren, Willem A., Greg L. Bahnsen, Walter C. Kaiser Jr., Wayne G. Strickland, and Douglas Moo. *The Law, the Gospel, and the Modern Christian.* Grand Rapids: Zondervan, 1993.

Corporate author

N   [4]Southern Baptist Convention, *Annual of the Southern Baptist Convention* (Nashville: Southern Baptist Convention, 1975), 25.

B   Southern Baptist Convention. *Annual of the Southern Baptist Convention.* Nashville: Southern Baptist Convention, 1975.

No author, edition other than first, with translator

N   [5]*Bhagavad-Gita as It Is*, abr. ed., trans. A. C. Bhaktivedanta Swami Prabhupada (New York: Bhaktivedanta Book Trust, 1972), 74.

B   *Bhagavad-Gita as It Is*. Abridged edition. Translated by A. C. Bhaktivedanta Swami Prabhupada. New York: Bhaktivedanta Book Trust, 1972.

Editor instead of author; joint publication

N   [6]James C. VanderKam and William Adler, eds., *The Jewish Apocalyptic Heritage in Early Christianity* (Assen, Netherlands: Van Gorcum; Minneapolis: Fortress, 1996), 35.

B   VanderKam, James C., and William Adler, eds. *The Jewish Apocalyptic Heritage in Early Christianity*. Assen, Netherlands: Van Gorcum; Minneapolis: Fortress, 1996.

Component part by one author in a work edited by another

N   [7]Richard M. Davidson, "Headship, Submission, and Equality in Scripture," in *Women in Ministry: Biblical and Historical Perspectives*, ed. Nancy Vyhmeister (Berrien Springs, MI: Andrews University Press, 1998), 266.

B   Davidson, Richard M. "Headship, Submission, and Equality in Scripture." In *Women in Ministry: Biblical and Historical Perspectives*, ed. Nancy Vyhmeister, 259–295. Berrien Springs, MI: Andrews University Press, 1998.

Multivolume Works

Several different types—from simple to complex—are presented:

N   [8]Justo González, *A History of Christian Thought*, 3 vols. (Nashville: Abingdon, 1970–1975), 1:176.

B   González, Justo. *A History of Christian Thought*. 3 vols. Nashville: Abingdon, 1970–1975.

Multivolume work—one author, different titles:

N   [9]Kenneth Scott Latourette, *A History of the Expansion of Christianity*, vol. 3, *Three Centuries of Advance* (Grand Rapids: Zondervan, 1970), 17.

BA   Latourette, Kenneth Scott. *A History of the Expansion of Christianity*. 7 vols. Grand Rapids: Zondervan, 1970.

BP   Latourette, Kenneth Scott. A *History of the Expansion of Christianity*. Vol. 3, *Three Centuries of Advance*. Grand Rapids: Zondervan, 1970.

Multivolume work—several authors:

N   [10]Bruce W. Winter, gen. ed., *The Book of Acts in Its First Century Setting*, 6 vols. (Carlisle, UK: Paternoster, 1994), vol. 3, *The Book of Acts and Paul in Roman Custody*, by Brian Rapske, 38.

B   Winter, Bruce W., gen. ed. *The Book of Acts in Its First Century Setting*. 6 vols. Carlisle, UK: Paternoster, 1994. Vol. 3, *The Book of Acts and Paul in Roman Custody*, by Brian Rapske.

If for some reason the author of the book you are citing or quoting is more important than the multi-volume source, you may use the following format:

N   [10]Brian Rapske, *The Book of Acts and Paul in Roman Custody*, vol. 3, *The Book of Acts in Its First Century Setting*, ed. Bruce W. Winter (Carlisle, UK: Paternoster, 1994), 38.

B Rapske, Brian. *The Book of Acts and Paul in Roman Custody*. Vol. 3, *The Book of Acts in Its First Century Setting*, ed. Bruce W. Winter. Carlisle, UK: Paternoster, 1994.

Part of a Series

N   [11]Wayne C. Booth, Gregory G. Colomb, and Joseph M. Williams, *The Craft of Research*, Chicago Guides to Writing, Editing, and Publishing (Chicago: University of Chicago Press, 1995), 155.

B Booth, Wayne C., Gregory G. Colomb, and Joseph M. Williams. *The Craft of Research*. Chicago Guides to Writing, Editing, and Publishing. Chicago: University of Chicago Press, 1995.

Reprint

N   [12]John L. Nevius, *Demon Possession* (New York: Fleming H. Revell, 1894; reprint, Grand Rapids: Kregel, 1968), 274, 275.

B Nevius, John L. *Demon Possession*. New York: Fleming H. Revell, 1894; reprint, Grand Rapids: Kregel, 1968.

N   [13]H. R. Reynolds, "Introduction to the Gospel of St. John," in *The Pulpit Commentary*, ed. H. O. M. Spense and Joseph S. Excell (Grand Rapids: Eerdmans, reprint 1977), 17:v.

B Reynolds, H. R. "Introduction to the Gospel of St. John." In *The Pulpit Commentary*, ed. H. O. M. Spense and Joseph S. Excell, 17:iv-clxi. Grand Rapids: Eerdmans, reprint 1977.

Secondary Source

N   [14]Pontius the Deacon *The Life and Passion of Cyprian, Bishop and Martyr* 1.3, quoted in Roger E. Olson, *The Story of Christian Theology* (Downers Grove, IL: InterVarsity, 1999), 116.

B Pontius the Deacon *The Life and Passion of Cyprian, Bishop and Martyr* 1.3. Quoted in Roger E. Olson, *The Story of Christian Theology*, 116. Downers Grove, IL: InterVarsity, 1999.

Periodicals

Magazines

N   [15]Michael D. Lemonick and Andrea Dorfman, "The Amazing Vikings," *Time*, 8 May 2000, 70.

B Lemonick, Michael D., and Andrea Dorfman. "The Amazing Vikings." *Time*, 8 May 2000, 69–74.

Journals

N   [16]David Shank, "Mission Relations with Independent Churches in Africa," *Missiology* 13 (1985): 27.

B Shank, David. "Mission Relations with Independent Churches in Africa." *Missiology* 13 (1985): 23–44.

If the pagination of a periodical is successive throughout the different issues of the volume (as in *Missiology*), use only the year. If pagination begins with each issue, use a month or season. When no month or season is given for a journal that begins each issue with page 1, give the number of the issue with the volume: *Newsletter* 4, no. 1 (1980): 9. Use Arabic numerals for volume numbers.

Specialized Books

Classical Authors and Church Fathers

Generally it is enough to give the author, title, book, and section of a work of one of the classical authors or of a church father. Whatever the edition, these works, somewhat like the Bible, are always divided the same way. However, it is a courtesy to the reader to give the place where you found the work.

N   [17]Irenaeus *Against Heresies* 2.2.3.

or

[17]Irenaeus *Against Heresies* 2.2.3, *ANF* 1:421.

BP   Irenaeus *Against Heresies. The Ante-Nicene Fathers*. Grand Rapids: Eerdmans, n.d. 1:315–567.

BA   Roberts, Alexander, and James Donaldson, eds. *The Ante-Nicene Fathers*. Grand Rapids: Eerdmans, n.d.

N   [18]John Chrysostom *The Priesthood* 3.17, Migne, *Patrologia Graeca*, vol. 48, col. 656.

BP   Chrysostom, John. *The Priesthood. Patrologia Graeca*. Edited by Jean Paul Migne. Paris: Apud Garnier Fratres, 1862. Vol. 48, cols. 623–692.

BA   Migne, Jean Paul, ed. *Patrologia Graeca*. Paris: Apud Garnier Fratres, 1862.

N   [19]Josephus *Jewish War* 2.14.5.

B Josephus, Flavius. *The Works of Josephus*. Edited by William Whiston. 4 vols. New York: Oakley, Mason & Co., 1869.

Rabbinical Works

The Mishnah, which is the basic authority of rabbinic halakah, is divided into 63 tractates, which in turn are divided into *perakim* and *mishnayyoth*. This division is analogous to that of the Bible into books, chapters, and verses. Refer to the Mishnah by name of tractate, number of *perek*, and number of *mishnah*, thus:

N   [20]Mishnah *Sanhedrin* 10:3.

B *The Mishnah*. Translated by Herbert Danby. London: Oxford University Press, 1933.

The Talmud is an expansion of the Mishnah and is arranged as a commentary on the Mishnah. Therefore, it is divided into the same 63 tractates. But references to the Babylonian Talmud are customarily made in terms of the folio number and the side (a or b) of the folio in the most ancient Hebrew version. Because this system is unique to the Babylonian Talmud, and different from that used in the identification of the parts of the Mishnah or the Jerusalem Talmud, many times the word Talmud is omitted in the reference. Thus, *Sanhedrin* 10:3 is a clear reference to the Mishnah, while *Sanhedrin* 97a is a reference to the Babylonian Talmud.

N   [21]B. T. *Sanhedrin* 97a.

   or

     [21]B. Talmud *Sanhedrin* 97a.

B   *The Babylonian Talmud*. Edited by I. Epstein. London: Soncino, 1935.

The Jerusalem Talmud is referred to by the same system used for the Mishnah. Care must be taken to add the letter "J" to distinguish from the Mishnah.

N   [22]J. *Berakoth* 3:5.

   or

     [22]J. T. *Berakoth* 3:5.

Bible Commentaries and Concordances

References to commentaries can be complicated. Some have one author for the whole commentary; others have one author for each book in a series, which may or may not have numbered volumes. Some have several authors for each book. Yet others have no known authors, only an editor. These variations show in the references.

Commentaries—author given

N   [23]John B. Polhill, *Acts*, New American Commentary (Nashville: Broadman, 1992), 175.

B Polhill, John B. Acts. *New American Commentary*. Nashville: Broadman, 1992.

N   [24]Edward R. Campbell, *Ruth*, Anchor Bible, 7 (Garden City, NY: Doubleday, 1975), 27.

B Campbell, Edward R. Ruth. *Anchor Bible, 7*. Garden City, NY: Doubleday, 1975.

N   [25]F. Delitzsch, *Biblical Commentary on the Book of Job*, 2 vols., Biblical Commentary on the Old Testament (Grand Rapids: Eerdmans, 1949), 2:115.

B Delitzsch, F. *Biblical Commentary on the Book of Job*. 2 vols. Biblical Commentary on the Old Testament. Grand Rapids: Eerdmans, 1949.

N   [26]Fred B. Craddock, "The Letter to the Hebrews: Introduction, Commentary, and Reflections," *New Interpreter's Bible*, 12 vols. (Nashville: Abingdon, 1998), 12:75.

B Craddock, Fred B. "The Letter to the Hebrews: Introduction, Commentary, and Reflections." *New Interpreter's Bible*. 12 vols. Nashville: Abingdon, 1998. 12:3–173.

N   [27]G. Ernest Wright, "Exegesis of the Book of Deuteronomy," *Interpreter's Bible* (New York: Abingdon, 1954), 2:331.

BP   Wright, G. Ernest. "Exegesis of the Book of Deuteronomy." *Interpreter's Bible*. New York: Abingdon, 1954. 2:331–540.

BA   Buttrick, G. A., ed. *Interpreter's Bible*. 12 vols. New York: Abingdon, 1954.

Commentaries—no author given

N   [28]Edward Hastings, ed., *The Speaker's Bible*, 18 vols. (Grand Rapids: Baker, 1971), 17:159.

To point out the exact phrase commented on, the following entry may be used:

N   [29]"The Blood of Christ" [Heb 9:13–14], *The Speaker's Bible*, ed. Edward Hastings (Grand Rapids: Baker, 1971), 17:159.

BP   "The Blood of Christ" [Heb 9:13–14]. *The Speaker's Bible*. Edited by Edward Hastings. Grand Rapids: Baker, 1971. 17:159.

BA   Hastings, Edward, ed. *The Speaker's Bible*. 18 vols. Grand Rapids: Baker Book House, 1971.

Concordances

N   [30]Robert Young, *Analytical Concordance to the Bible*, 22d Amer. ed. (Grand Rapids: Eerdmans, n.d.), s.v. "soul."

B   Young, Robert. *Analytical Concordance to the Bible*. 22d American ed. Grand Rapids: Eerdmans, n.d. S.v. "soul."

Dictionaries and Encyclopedias

Dictionaries and encyclopedias come in many stripes. Some deal with modern languages: Webster's and Larousse, for example. Some deal with themes: *Theological Dictionary of the New Testament* and *The Anchor Bible Dictionary*. Most of the first category have unsigned articles, while most of the second have signed articles. These variations must be taken into account in notes and bibliographies.

Dictionaries and encyclopedias with unsigned articles

Reference to a modern-language dictionary appears in a footnote but not normally in the bibliography. While publication data are not considered important, the number of the edition or the year of edition is important.

N   [31]*Merriam Webster College Dictionary*, 10th ed., s.v. "sin."

On well-known dictionaries and encyclopedias, omit the place and publisher in the note and omit the whole entry from the bibliography.

N   [32]*Columbia Encyclopedia*, 4th ed., s.v. "war."

Specialized dictionaries and encyclopedias with unsigned articles do not need the place or publisher in the note, but they do need an edition or date. Note the format for the date rather than edition. This type of source goes in the bibliography, with complete publication data.

N   [33] *Nelson's New Illustrated Bible Dictionary* (1995), s.v. "angel."

BP   *Nelson's New Illustrated Bible Dictionary.* Rev. ed. Edited by Ronald F. Youngblood. Nashville: Nelson, 1995. S.v. "angel."

BA   *Nelson's New Illustrated Bible Dictionary.* Rev. ed. Edited by Ronald F. Youngblood. Nashville: Nelson, 1995.

N   [34] *Seventh-day Adventist Encyclopedia* (1996), s.v. "Kingsway College."

BP   *Seventh-day Adventist Encyclopedia.* Revised edition. 2 vols. Hagerstown, MD: Review and Herald, 1996. S.v. "Kingsway College."

BA   *Seventh-day Adventist Encyclopedia.* Revised edition. 2 vols. Hagerstown, MD: Review and Herald, 1996.

Dictionaries and encyclopedias with signed articles

Full information must be given for this kind of source, both in the note and the bibliography. The only exception is the use of abbreviations when the item appears in a list of abbreviations at the beginning of the paper. The first example presupposes the existence of such a list.

N   [35] Hayim Lapin, "Rabbi," ABD, 5:601.
           or
N   [35] Hayim Lapin, "Rabbi," *Anchor Bible Dictionary*, 6 vols., ed. David Noel Freedman (New York: Doubleday, 1992), 5:601.

BP   Lapin, Hayim. "Rabbi." *Anchor Bible Dictionary.* 6 vols. Edited by David Noel Freedman. New York: Doubleday, 1992. 5:600–602.

BA   Freedman, David Noel, ed. *Anchor Bible Dictionary.* 6 vols. New York: Doubleday, 1992.

The Greek or Hebrew title may be transliterated and underlined or italicized, or typed in the original script. Handwritten script is not acceptable. An acceptable transliteration scheme is given in Appendix B.

N   [36] Rudolf Bultmann, "*Aidōs*," *Theological Dictionary of the New Testament* (Grand Rapids: Eerdmans, 1964–1976), 1:169.

BP   Bultmann, Rudolf. "*Aidōs*." *Theological Dictionary of the New Testament.* Grand Rapids: Eerdmans, 1964–1976. 1:169.

BA   Kittel, Gerhard, and Gerhard Friedrich, eds. *Theological Dictionary of the New Testament.* 10 vols. Translated by Geoffrey Bromiley. Grand Rapids: Eerdmans, 1964–1976.

N   [37] Aaron Demsky, "Education: In the Biblical Period," *EJ*, 6:384.
           or
N   [37] Aaron Demsky, "Education: In the Biblical Period," *Encyclopaedia Judaica* (Jerusalem: Encyclopaedia Judaica, 1971–1972), 6:384.

BP   Demsky, Aaron. "Education: In the Biblical Period." *Encyclopaedia Judaica*. Jerusalem: Encyclopaedia Judaica, 1971–1972. 6:382–398.

BA   *Encyclopaedia Judaica*. 16 vols. Jerusalem: Encyclopaedia Judaica, 1971–1972.

Collected Works of Individual Authors

A great deal of variation is observed in references to collected works of well-known authors. When in doubt, use common sense. Be consistent in whatever you do.

N   [38]Karl Barth, *Church Dogmatics*, III/3 (Edinburgh: T. & T. Clark, 1960), 82.

BP   Barth, Karl. *Church Dogmatics*. Edinburgh: T. & T. Clark, 1960. III/3.

N   [39]Martin Luther, *Sermon on the Sum of Christian Life*, *Luther's Works* (*LW*), Amer. ed. (Saint Louis: Concordia, 1955–1976), 51:260.

BP   Luther, Martin. *Sermon on the Sum of Christian Life*. *Luther's Works*. American edition. Saint Louis: Concordia, 1955–1976. 51:259–287.

BA   Luther, Martin. *Luther's Works*. American edition. 55 vols. Saint Louis: Concordia, 1955–1976.

A second reference could read:

N   [40]Luther, *On the Sum of Christian Life*, *LW*, 51:259.

Book Reviews

N   [41]Carol Meyers, review of *The Archaeology of Israel: Constructing the Past, Interpreting the Present*, ed. Asher Silberman and David Small, *Journal of Biblical Literature* 118 (1999): 530–531.

B   Meyers, Carol. Review of *The Archaeology of Israel: Constructing the Past, Interpreting the Present*, ed. Asher Silberman and David Small. *Journal of Biblical Literature* 118 (1999): 530–531.

Video and Sound Recordings

Information for this type of source may be lacking. Use whatever you can find. Follow the same organization as for other materials.

N   [42]*Hudson Taylor*, 85 min, Ken Anderson Films, 1989, videocassette.

B   *Hudson Taylor*. 85 min. Ken Anderson Films, 1989. Videocassette.

N   [43]Luis Landriscina, "Judío en el Vaticano," in *Mano a mano con el país*, vol. 5, Phillips 64232, 1985, sound cassette.

B   Landriscina, Luis. "Judío en el Vaticano." In *Mano a mano con el país*, vol. 5. Phillips 64232, 1985. Sound cassette.

Unpublished Materials

The search for information should not be limited to published materials. Theses and dissertations, interviews and voice recordings, as well as manuscripts—

all of these academic or nonacademic unpublished materials can contribute worthwhile data to a research project.

Academic Sources

Theses and dissertations are the most commonly cited unpublished academic papers. Other miscellaneous academic papers may also be used.

Theses and Dissertations

N   [44]Phuichun Richard Choi, "Abraham Our Father: Paul's Voice in the Covenantal Debate of the Second Temple Period" (Ph.D. dissertation, Fuller Theological Seminary, School of Theology, 1997), 189.

B Choi, Phuichun Richard. "Abraham Our Father: Paul's Voice in the Covenantal Debate of the Second Temple Period." Ph.D. dissertation, Fuller Theological Seminary, School of Theology, 1997.

N   [45]Hotma Silitonga, "Christological Implications of Leviticus 16:11–23: A Study from an Indonesian Perspective" (M.Th. thesis, Adventist International Institute of Advanced Studies, Silang, Cavite, Philippines, October 1988), 35.

B Silitonga, Hotma. "Christological Implications of Leviticus 16:11–23: A Study from an Indonesian Perspective." M.Th. thesis, Adventist International Institute of Advanced Studies, Silang, Cavite, Philippines, October 1988.

Miscellaneous Academic Papers

Class papers

N   [46]Teresa Reeve, "The 'Just Man' in the Writings of Philo," a paper presented for THEO 611 Philo Seminar, University of Notre Dame, December 1997, 13.

B Reeve, Teresa. "The 'Just Man' in the Writings of Philo." A paper presented for THEO 611 Philo Seminar, University of Notre Dame, December 1997.

N   [47]Wann Marbud Fanwar, "He Who Created the Heavens and the Earth: Contributions of Isaiah to Rev 14:7c," seminar paper for GSEM 920 Religious Studies Seminar, Andrews University, May 1999, 19.

B Fanwar, Wann Marbud. "He Who Created the Heavens and the Earth: Contributions of Isaiah to Rev 14:7c." Seminar paper for GSEM 920 Religious Studies Seminar, Andrews University, May 1999.

Syllabi

N   [48]Nancy Vyhmeister, Course outline for GSEM 854 Ph.D. Proposal Seminar, Theological Seminary, Andrews University, Berrien Springs, Michigan, 1999, 7.

B Vyhmeister, Nancy. Course outline for GSEM 854 Ph.D. Proposal Seminar, Theological Seminary, Andrews University, Berrien Springs, Michigan, 1999.

Class notes

N   [49]Class notes, Program in Language Acquisition Techniques, Missionary Internship, Farmington, Michigan, September 1980.

B Class notes. Program in Language Acquisition Techniques. Missionary Internship, Farmington, Michigan, September 1980.

Miscellaneous Unpublished Sources

Footnotes and bibliographical entries for miscellaneous unpublished materials can be difficult. To make them useful, clarity and consistency are vital. A good dose of common sense is also essential. Examples for reports, speeches, manuscripts, letters, and interviews are provided.

Reports

N   [50]Seventh-day Adventist Theological Seminary, Far East, "Financial Statement of Graduate Apartments," 31 August 1985, 4.

B Seventh-day Adventist Theological Seminary, Far East. "Financial Statement of Graduate Apartments." 31 August 1985.

N   [51]Association of Theological Institutions in Eastern Africa, "1978/79 Bachelor of Divinity Degree Syllabus," 3.

B Association of Theological Institutions in Eastern Africa. "1978/79 Bachelor of Divinity Degree Syllabus."

Speeches and Presentations

N   [52]C. Mervyn Maxwell, "Which Sacrifice, Lord?" Seminary Chapel sermon, Andrews University, 20 October 1976, 10, typewritten.

B Maxwell, C. Mervyn. "Which Sacrifice, Lord?" Seminary Chapel sermon. Andrews University, 20 October 1976. Typewritten.

N   [53]Jon Paulien, "The Lion/Lamb King: Reading Revelation from Popular Culture," a paper presented at the annual meeting of the Society of Biblical Literature, 24 November 1996, New Orleans.

B Paulien, Jon. "The Lion/Lamb King: Reading Revelation from Popular Culture." A paper presented at the annual meeting of the Society of Biblical Literature, 24 November 1996, New Orleans.

Manuscripts

References to manuscripts must permit readers to know exactly what the item is and where it is found. The name of the collection and its location must be clear.

N   [54]Peter L. Benoit, 1875 diary, Archives, University of Notre Dame.

B Benoit, Peter L. 1875 diary. Photocopy of typewritten transcript of Canon Benoit's diary of a trip to America, 6 January to 8 June 1875, including descriptions of Josephite missions among freed slaves. Archives, University of Notre Dame.

N [55]Ellen G. White, Manuscript 154, 1902, Ellen G. White Research Center, Silang, Cavite, Philippines (hereafter abbreviated EGWRC).

B White, Ellen G. Manuscript 154, 1902. Ellen G. White Research Center, Silang, Cavite, Philippines.

Letters

A letter addressed to the author of the paper is assumed to be in the author's files. If the letter referred to is addressed to someone else, information should be given regarding its location. Quotations from letters should be as easy to verify as those from published sources.

N   [56]Bryan Ball, editor of *The Essential Jesus*, to Nancy Vyhmeister, 13 March 2000.

B Ball, Bryan, editor of *The Essential Jesus*, to Nancy Vyhmeister, 13 March 2000.

N   [57]Ellen G. White to Dr. Patience Bourdeau, 8 June 1905, Letter 177, 1905, Ellen White Research Center, Newbold College, Bracknell, England.

B White, Ellen G., to Dr. Patience Bourdeau, 8 June 1905. Letter 177, 1905. Ellen White Research Center, Newbold College, Bracknell, England.

Interviews

N   [58]Choo Lak Yeow, Executive Director of the Association for Theological Education in Southeast Asia, interview by author, Singapore, 15 July 1985.

B Yeow, Choo Lak, Executive Director of Association for Theological Education in Southeast Asia. Interview by author. Singapore. Interview, 15 July 1985.

Electronic Media

Here are several suggestions on referencing electronic sources. Refer to electronic sources only when items are not published elsewhere. Make sure the electronic address is accurate, even to the spaces and dots. Enclose electronic address in angle brackets. If you must write the URL on two lines, divide only immediately before a dot. Place the date you retrieved the item in parentheses. By all means, retain copies of downloaded material until your paper or dissertation has been approved. Finally, "Love your neighbor as yourself" (Matt 22:39). Make it easy for the budding scholar who follows in your footsteps to find exactly what you found.

CD-ROM

N   [59]John Bunyan, *Pilgrim's Progress*, stage 2, Logos Library System, 1998.
B Bunyan, John. *Pilgrim's Progress*, stage 2. Logos Library System, 1998.

World Wide Web

N   [60]"About Electronic Sources," *Writer's Handbook* (Madison: University of Wisconsin-Madison Writing Center, 2001), available <http://www.wisc.edu/writing/Handbook/DocChicago.html#electronic> (31 October 2001).

B "About Electronic Sources." *Writer's Handbook*. Madison: University of Wisconsin-Madison Writing Center, 2001. <http://www.wisc.edu/writing/Handbook/DocChicago.html#electronic> (31 October 2001).

N   [61]Peter J. Bryant, "History of Life on Earth," in *Biodiversity and Conservation*, April 1999, <http://darwin.bio.uci.edu/~sustain/bio65/lec01/b65lec01.htm> (31 January 2001).

B   Bryant, Peter J. "History of Life on Earth." In *Biodiversity and Conservation*, April 1999. <http://darwin.bio.uci.edu/~sustain/bio65/lec01/b65lec01.htm> (31 January 2001).

N   [62]Kenneth Wade, "A Fresh Look at Jesus, #144," Recent discussions, 13 January 2001, <http://www.sdanet.org/archive/2001/Jan22001/0064.html> (30 January 2001).

B   Wade, Kenneth. "A Fresh Look at Jesus, #144." Recent discussions, 13 January 2001. <http://www.sdanet.org/archive/2001/Jan22001/0064.html> (30 January 2001).

For further information on the citation of online materials, consult <www.bedfordstmartins .com/online/cite7.html> or <www.people.memphis.edu/%7Emcrouse/elcite.html>.

Now that you have a clearer understanding of footnote and bibliographic entry forms, you may confidently prepare these in accurate and acceptable form. Chapter 10 turns from the minute, detailed work described above to a study of the overall organization of the paper.

X | ORGANIZING THE PAPER

Organizational decisions take place from the moment you choose a topic until that last change just before you hand the paper in. You will deal with macro-organization as well as micro-organization. This chapter speaks to both issues. The larger picture deals with the organization of the parts of the paper, especially the body of the report. Micro-organization deals with smaller items, including the visible organization of headings and enumerations.

Parts of the Paper

A well written research paper should have five main parts: the preliminary pages, the introduction, the body, the summary and conclusions, and the bibliography. If needed, appendixes may be added.

The principal parts of the paper—introduction, body, and conclusion—must harmonize. That is, they must integrate into one whole. The introduction sets the stage, preparing the reader to understand the purpose, nature, and direction of the research. The main body of the text gives a clear report of the findings. The conclusion summarizes and evaluates the results of the investigation. The bibliography documents what has been presented.

To achieve the overall harmony of the paper, take your proposal very seriously. Then begin writing with the first content chapter (chapter 1 in a paper, chapter 2 in a dissertation), leaving the introduction for later. Write all the rest of the body, chapter after chapter. Then summarize and draw conclusions. After all that, you will be ready to smooth the proposal into an introduction. Then prepare the bibliography and appendixes before going to the preliminary pages, which include the table of contents.

Preliminary Pages

In a class paper at the graduate level, the preliminary pages include the title page, the table of contents, and, if needed, lists of figures, tables, or illustrations.

A thesis may include a dedication and/or acknowledgment. In a short class paper, the preliminary pages are not numbered; the introduction is page 1. In a thesis or dissertation, the preliminary pages are numbered from the title page (no number typed here!) with lowercase roman numerals, at the bottom center of the page.

Title Page

The title page includes the name of the institution where the paper is being presented, the title of the paper, the name of the class or program for which the paper is written, the name of the writer, and the date. The professor's name is not included. A thesis or dissertation also requires an approval sheet (see chapter 19). A model title page appears in chapter 12.

Table of Contents

The table of contents lists everything that comes after it, starting with lists of abbreviations and tables, and continuing through the bibliography. Chapter titles, as well as headings and subheadings to the third level, are listed. Examples of the format of a table of contents are given in chapter 12.

List of Illustrations

If tables, figures, or illustrations are used, these should be listed. The format to follow is shown in the list of illustrations for this book. If there are only a few of each, these lists may be on the same page.

List of Abbreviations

To avoid writing out the titles of books and journals you use repeatedly, you may insert a list of abbreviations just before the introduction and then use only the abbreviations. Some schools require that the abbreviated sources be spelled out the first time they are used, even if they are in a list; others consider that the list takes the place of the first reference. Make sure you know what your school requires. Include in this list only items used in the paper or dissertation. This list does not take the place of a bibliography. Abbreviations of titles of books and journals should be underlined or italicized. Other abbreviations, such as PW for Pauly-Wissowa, *Real Encyclopädie der classischen Altertumswissenschaft*, are not underlined or italicized. A short list of acceptable abbreviations in correct format appears in appendix C.[1]

---

[1]For a much longer list of abbreviations, especially in biblical and Near Eastern studies, see *SBL Handbook of Style* (Peabody, MA: Hendrickson, 1999), 89-121. The ultimate list of abbreviations is available in *Theologisches Realencyklopädie Abkurzungsverzeichnis*, 2d ed. (Berlin: De Gruyter, 1993).

Introduction

A carefully written proposal is the basis for a clear and effective introduction, which should contain the same parts suggested for the proposal (see chapter 4). The introduction is a reader's guide to the paper. It tells the reader what the problem studied (and solved) was, how the researcher went about finding the answers, and may even suggest the solution to the problem.

Whereas the proposal usually simply lists the items included (statement of the problem, purpose of the research, significance of the research, definition of terms, limitations and delimitations, methodology, and presuppositions), the introduction polishes the writing and smoothes the transition from one to another. It often adds a paragraph or more on the background of the problem. Additionally, the future tense of the proposal becomes past tense, since the research is now done.

The length of the introduction varies. An introduction to a class paper may be only one page long. An introduction to a thesis may contain twenty or more pages. What is important is that all parts are included and the paper is correctly introduced.

Page one of the introduction is the first page of the paper. In class papers the title, INTRODUCTION, is given chapter standing (on the 13th line or 2 inches from the top edge of the page), but not a chapter number. In a thesis or dissertation, the introduction usually is chapter 1. A model introduction for short papers appears in chapter 12.

Main Body of the Paper

In this part of the paper you report the findings of the research. The body is evidently the longest part of the paper. It is divided into chapters (or major sections, in a short paper), each with its own divisions and subdivisions. Since the organization of the main body of the paper is so important, this topic will be covered in a separate section.

Summary and Conclusions

As the title indicates, this part of the paper summarizes the findings and draws conclusions. No new evidence is brought in. The presentation of data has been done in the main body. The summary should be brief—only as long as needed to bring the issues into focus. The conclusions are then drawn from the summary. Remember that many paper/dissertation readers never read more than the introduction and summary/conclusions. Everything you want readers to know about your research must be in those two places.

Take the time needed to craft your concluding section with care. The conclusion or conclusions must match the problem or research question declared in the introduction of the paper. It would make no sense to ask one question and answer another. Conclusions presented may be firm or tentative. Sometimes the research only "suggests" a solution to a problem. At times the research may turn up areas that need to be investigated and could be a topic for further study. It is proper to note such instances in the conclusions.

The status of the summary and conclusions must match that of the introduction. If the introduction was given a chapter number, the summary and conclusions must be considered a chapter. If the introduction was not a chapter, the summary and conclusion will not be a chapter either.

Appendixes

A paper may have one or more appendixes. These are added sections that contain materials not indispensable for reading and understanding the paper, but useful in gaining deeper insight, or for validating and documenting what has been stated. Appendixes may include raw numerical data, statistical information, photocopied materials, or whatever else the researcher needs to present. Appendixes are much more common in dissertations than in papers. When there are several appendixes, as in this book, each has a title and is listed in the table of contents.

Bibliography

The bibliography documents and gives weight to the research. It tells the reader how serious the study was. It also leads readers to sources for further study on the topic. Instructions on preparing bibliographies appeared in chapter 5. Model bibliographies are those at the end of this book and in chapter 12.

A general overview of the organization of the paper may suffice. But organizing the body of a paper demands special attention. The next section deals with this specifically.

Organizing the Body of the Paper

There are no firm and exact rules about the way the body of a paper should be organized. Whatever system you choose must be clear and logical—to you and to your adviser, as well as to your readers. Ask your adviser and your peers for a critique of your suggested outline. Be able to defend your organization: Why does it make sense for you to start where you do and follow the thought path you do? Reread the section on "Organization" in chapter 6.

Each chapter must be a self-contained unit. That is, everything on one topic should be in the same chapter. Everything in one section should be related to the same matter; no extraneous material should be allowed. The same topic should not be discussed in several sections. Naturally, there may be references from one section to another, but good organization demands dividing the topic into independent units, tied to each other in some logical manner, but not repeating the same information.

The outline made and approved by the professor or adviser when the proposal was presented was a good starting point; it served as the skeleton for your paper in its initial stages. However, after reading and studying, you may feel the need for changing that outline. Remember, though, to talk to your adviser before you write on the basis of a new outline.

Two sample outlines were given in chapter 4. One important rule of outlining is that a section that is subdivided must have at least two subsections. You cannot cut an apple into one piece! Likewise, you cannot have a section A (or 1 or a) without a corresponding section B (or 2 or b). Another rule is to make subsections parallel to each other, in form and content.

Since there is no one accepted method of organizing a paper, this section presents a sampling of possibilities. Again, consultation with the advising professor is indispensable.

Historical topics lend themselves to a chronological method: What happened first is narrated first. The biography of Hudson Taylor, missionary to China, can be divided into sections: childhood, youth, early mission, death of wife, founding of the China Inland Mission, and so on.

The spatial (geographical) method might be used in reporting the research on an ancient city. The New Testament city of Ephesus could be described part by part: the port, the theater, the library, the Temple of Diana, the market place, and so forth.

A comparative method could be used in comparing the Buddhist and Hindu beliefs concerning death. First, each would have to be described fully; then they could be compared.

For some studies a cause-to-effect method is appropriate. A study of the rapid growth of Christianity in Korea could use this method. The different factors leading to this phenomenon would be studied, one by one. Then, the effect (the growth of the Christian church) would be delineated.

Some topics do well with an unfolding method. Here one idea needs to be clearly explained so that it can lead to another. For example, an understanding of the ceremonies of the Israelite tabernacle would need to be established before progressing to an analysis of the way the author of Hebrews deals with these ceremonies.

A Doctor of Ministry project or dissertation normally has a theoretical basis and a practical application. That means the work is organized into two basic parts. The theoretical foundation may be divided into biblical, theological, and sociological parts. The practical part may well be chronological—what happened first, what next. On D.Min. projects, see chapter 20.

The starting point for research need not be the same in every case. One may begin from the specifics and arrive at general conclusions—inductive reasoning. Or one may begin with general facts and arrive at specific conclusions—deductive reasoning. What is important is that the research process is so designed and executed as to make sense to the readers and to the professor.

Someone has suggested that writing a research report is like building a temple. One must lay the foundation, then erect each of the pillars. Finally, the roof is placed on the structure. As happens with all parables, this one, too, falls short. However, it does illustrate the need for balance and careful building so that a clear and convincing result may be achieved. It also suggests that each research paper is a unique construction and, to some extent, a work of art.

Specific guidelines for the organization of literary and bibliographic research are scarce. More is said about descriptive and program-development research in chapters 14 and 15. Specific schemes for organizing biblical-theological-pastoral research must be designed by the student, preferably in collaboration with the professor or committee for whom the paper or thesis is written.

Practical Helps for Organizing the Paper

The final organization of the topic takes place once all the research is finished. The task is difficult and important. This section gives practical suggestions for dividing up the topic and arranging its sections, and for planning the visible organization of the written report.

Organizing the Note Cards

Since the note cards or slips have headings and subheadings on them, they can easily be separated into piles. Use a table—or the floor—and separate the slips by headings and subheadings and sub-subheadings, if there are any. Then look through each pile, reading the notes as you do so. Organize each pile into a logical sequence. If there are notes that do not belong, take them out; put them where they do belong or discard them. Do not be surprised if the tentative outline no longer seems to fit. Once all the cards are distributed, a better outline may suggest itself.

When all the small piles are organized within themselves and put in a logical sequence with the other small piles that belong with them in a larger topic, the order and organization of each section or chapter of the paper is easily seen. Put an elastic or rubber band around each section to keep it separate and organized (if yours is a long paper, try using boxes). Then confirm your decision regarding the sequence of chapters.

Now, read the note cards in sequence, trying to feel (or see or hear) how these bits of information fall into place. If you are not satisfied with the way the cards fit together, you may start your sorting over again. It may take three sortings to organize the cards—and your paper. But the time will be well spent, for you will write with greater ease and speed for having gone through this process.

Visible Organization in the Written Report

Using different levels of headings and enumerations helps to visibly organize the contents of a paper. How to do it is discussed in the following paragraphs.

Headings

Throughout this book different kinds or levels of headings have been used. These headings show how a topic is divided and subdivided and what belongs with what. The headings and subheadings represent the different parts of the outline. Once more, a heading must have two subheadings, or not be divided at all.

A first-level heading indicates a main division of the chapter. In this chapter, **"Practical Helps for Organizing the Paper"** is a first-level heading. It is centered and bolded (in your paper it could also be underlined).

The second-level heading indicates a subdivision of that main division. In this chapter "Visible Organization in the Written Report" is a second-level heading. It is centered but not bolded or underlined. Its "twin" is "Organizing the Note Cards." The graphic presentation shows it is a part of **"Practical Helps for Organizing the Paper."**

The third-level heading indicates a part of the second-level subdivision. In this chapter **"Headings"** and **"Enumerations"** are third-level headings. These headings are placed flush with the left margin and bolded (they could also be underlined). In the three kinds of headings already listed the first, last, and principal words are capitalized.

The fourth-level heading indicates a division of a third-level heading. It is flush with the left margin, using the same font as second level but smaller typesize—and not bolded. Only the first word is capitalized. "Within the paragraph" is an example of fourth-level heading in this chapter.

The fifth-level heading, the smallest organizational subdivision in a paper, shows that what follows is a part of a fourth-level heading. This heading is usually reserved for a small segment, often only a paragraph. This heading is part of the paragraph; it is indented eight spaces, bolded (or underlined), and followed by a period or full stop. Only its first word is capitalized. Below, **"With short sentences"** and **"With longer sentences"** are examples.

If the organization of a paper does not need so many levels of headings, you may choose to use only three, for example, those that are underlined. However, you cannot use one scheme (complete sequence) in one chapter and the incomplete scheme (underlined only) in another chapter. Consistency is indispensable.

Following the outline scheme (see chapter 4), the chapter title corresponds to the Roman numeral; the first-level heading, to the capital letter; the second-level heading, to the Arabic numeral; the third-level heading to the lowercase letter. However, the letters and numbers that you use in an outline do not appear in headings or table of contents of a paper or dissertation.

Enumerations

Enumerations help to visibly organize materials in the written report. They can be used within a paragraph and within a sentence. Instructions follow.

Within the paragraph

Enumerations within a paragraph can be done in two ways. In both cases, periods after numbers must be aligned.

With short sentences. If most of the sentences are shorter than one line, place the numbers at the left margin. When one does run over, start the second line under the first letter of text in the first line. Final periods are needed only for complete sentences. For example:

1. The linguistic context must be accounted for.
2. The historical context must be considered.
3. The purpose of the author must be noted.

With longer sentences. The second style is used when the sentences in the listing are long, or each number has more than one sentence. In this case the number is indented as are the paragraphs and followed by a period. Arabic or Roman numerals may be used. Following lines reach the left margin. Dots after numbers are aligned. For example:

1. The number (usually Arabic) is typed after the same indentation as the paragraph and followed by a period or full stop. Two spaces are left before the beginning of the text.
2. Double spacing is used as in the rest of the paper.
3. A period or full stop follows each item. There may be several sentences after each number.

4. If double-digit numbers are used, the indentation must be modified so that all the periods are aligned.

Within the sentence

An enumeration within a sentence may use letters or numbers, set in parentheses. Numbers usually represent a larger division; letters, a smaller one. The items are set off by commas unless they have punctuation within them, in which case they are set off by semicolons. For example:

> He gave three reasons for his resignation: (1) age, (2) gradually failing eyesight, and (3) desire to live under less pressure.

> His failing eyesight is due to: (a) age, now 65 years; (b) a congenital, worsening disease; (c) stress, caused by the responsibilities of the job.

This chapter has explained the general organization of the paper and given suggestions, both theoretical and practical, for organizing the material in the research report. Chapter 11 gives instruction on good research writing.

XI | WRITING THE PAPER

Your research is now complete. You have consulted all relevant sources. Your note cards, organized according to the final outline, are ready to be transformed into a written report. The time to write has come. You have already put in about two-thirds of the total time needed to complete the paper; writing and rewriting will take another third. For many, this last third is the hardest part of all. If you do not write the report, however, your well-done research will pass unnoticed. Therefore, you need to write a clear, concise, readable report.

This chapter describes research English, makes suggestions on how to write coherent and interesting paragraphs, and instructs on the use of transitional and introductory phrases. It also outlines the stages of the writing process and lists helps for the novice writer.

Research English

English research writing uses simple, concise, and clear language. Other words to describe it are impersonal, objective, formal, dignified, factual, and unbiased. One author has said: "Research writing is exact writing, featuring well-planned sentences with proper subordination of minor elements and at the same time employing concrete, specific words."[1]

Impersonal language minimizes the importance of "me" and "I." Generally speaking, the first person singular does not appear in research writing. A modern trend does allow for its use in the introduction and conclusions; even then, the emphasis must not be on the writer but on the research topic. Some writers refer to themselves as "the writer" or "the researcher" to avoid use of the first person pronoun. Others use the first person plural, "we." None of these devices is desirable. While the passive voice ("the cake was eaten by the boy") can be employed to avoid the first-person pronoun, its use makes sentences heavy. As often as possible, use the active voice. Keep your writing alive! Write naturally, directly. While

[1]James D. Lester, *Writing Research Papers: A Complete Guide*, 2d ed. (Glenview, IL: Scott Foresman, 1976), 57.

minimizing yourself, avoid the impersonal passive as much as you can. For example, instead of saying in the introduction, "I decided to limit this paper . . . ," write "The natural limits of the topic determined the shape of the paper." Be sure to consult the preferences of your school and adviser on the matter of impersonal language.

A paper or thesis is not the place to use fancy words, metaphors, and similes. Imaginative phrases and comparisons, as well as superlatives (best, finest, largest) are to be shunned. Idiomatic expressions are out of place. Exclamation marks do not fit.

Research language is modest and tentative. Instead of definite and dogmatic words such as "never," "all," or "none," use "some," "somewhat," or "often." Even when you have evidence for what you write, do not overstate your case.

A well-written research paper will not contain as many adverbs and adjectives as nouns and verbs. Adverbs such as "marvelously" do not fit. Unfortunately, in research language no one is going to be "an outstanding success." On the other hand, research language should not be boring. Instead of a general noun such as "man," use a more specific one: "youth," "gentleman," or "scholar." Instead of a verb such as "go," use "amble," "stride," "ride," or "fly." To find these more specific and colorful synonyms, use a dictionary or thesaurus—the ones that come with Microsoft Word™ and WordPerfect™ are most helpful.

Research language is standard, not colloquial; it never uses slang. The contracted forms of the negative (can't, won't, didn't) are out of place. The full form must be used. Of the following four levels of English, the proper research language is the standard:

Formal	Standard	Colloquial	Slang
superlative	excellent	first-rate	cool
exacerbating	irritating	aggravating	burns me up
deranged	irrational	crazy	nuts

The greatest temptation of theology students is to use sermonic instead of research language. The language of the pulpit is not the language of the thesis. Phrases such as "souls won to the truth" should be replaced with something understandable to the general public: "people baptized into the church."

Another aspect of writing demands attention: inclusive language. The times require sensitivity to gender issues. Without syntactical errors ("everyone did their homework") or excessive recourse to "he or she" (or worse, he/she), write in ways that include both genders and do not stereotype sex roles. "Mankind" becomes "humanity"; singular "he" is changed into plural "they," or alternates with "she."

Excellent writing takes time and effort. Mediocre writing is faster and easier. However, it does not usually merit the professor's approval, a reader's interest, or your own satisfaction.

The Paragraph: Smallest Unit of the Paper

The smallest unit of the paper, the paragraph is somewhat like a link in a chain. And, as in the case of the chain, the paper is only as strong as its weakest paragraph. Therefore, time spent learning how to write strong paragraphs is time well spent.

A paragraph should be all about one topic. Its length is determined by how much has to be said about the matter. If it is too long, it probably includes ideas that do not belong to the main topic. Rule of thumb: If your paragraph fills more than one computer screen, it is suspect. Here short is better than long. On the other hand, a paragraph cannot be extremely short—one sentence is never a true paragraph—because it cannot cover the topic.

Many types of effective and interesting paragraphs can be designed. However, certain elements are found in all paragraphs that communicate well and please the reader. Specific elements discussed in this section are unity and coherence. A sampling of paragraphs is also presented.

Paragraph Unity

A good paragraph puts in one place all the material that belongs together and keeps it apart from other items that do not belong. Every well-constructed paragraph has some unifying thought. All the materials included are somehow related to that thought. This precludes the inclusion of extraneous ideas and comments.

One device that fosters paragraph unity is the use of the topic sentence. This sentence, which states the main idea of the paragraph, may come at the beginning, in the middle, or at the end of the sentence. Its purpose is not only to give the chief idea of the paragraph, but also to provide an anchor, so to speak, for the rest of the sentences in the paragraph. It does so by providing a center to which the rest of the paragraph can relate. Examples of the use of the topic sentence are found in this paragraph and in the majority of paragraphs of this book.

Paragraph Coherence

Even when all the sentences are closely related to the central thought, the paragraph may fail to convey the intended information in an effective manner. A strong paragraph hangs together, it coheres. Paragraph coherence is concerned with the order in which the information is presented and with the clear and logical relationship of one statement to the next in the development of ideas. Omitting a vital part of the chain of ideas may mislead or confuse the reader.

In the following paragraph, coherence depends on the repeated references to the hypothetical man being described and on the movement from the small, personal, and material, to the intangible and universal.[2]

> The civilized man has built a coach, but has lost the use of his feet. He is supported on crutches, but lacks so much support of muscle. He has a fine Geneva watch, but he fails of the skill to tell the hour by the sun. A Greenwich nautical almanac he has, and so being sure of the information when he wants it, the man in the street does not know a star in the sky. The solstice he does not observe; the equinox he knows as little, and the whole bright calendar of the year is without a dial in his mind.

> *R. W. Emerson, Self-reliance*

Sample Expository Paragraphs

As a sampling of effective expository paragraphs, four types are presented: definition, enumeration or classification, comparison, and cause and effect. Other types, such as reiteration, question and answer, and analogy, could also be cited.

Definition

The term *leitourgia* in classical Greek described the performance of a special honorific service for the state, such as, for instance, outfitting a warship or providing a choir for a theatrical performance at a major ceremony. The honor dimension was important to the term. By the second century B.C. the word was used in popular language for priestly service in the worship of the gods. In the Septuagint it was used for the Hebrew *sharath* to designate participation in the divine worship, either as an officiant or as a worshiper. While in the New Testament the more common term for serving is *diakonia*, by Hippolytus' time *leitourgia* and *munus* were the accepted terms for the performance of Christian worship, especially the Eucharist. These words conveyed the idea of the prestige of the one who could officiate in the church service.[3]

Enumeration or Classification

Women [in the nineteenth century] were not accorded what the twentieth century considers basic human rights. Politically, women were virtual nonentities. Their contributions were confined largely to the domestic

---

[2]Paragraph taken from Shirley Welch Mulkern, Teaching Notebook for GREL 610, Methods in Research, Andrews University, Berrien Springs, MI, 1979.

[3]Daniel Augsburger, "Clerical Authority and Ordination," in *Women in Ministry: Biblical and Historical Perspectives*, ed. Nancy J. Vyhmeister (Berrien Springs, MI: Andrews University Press, 1998), 83. (Hereafter referred to as *WIM*.)

realm. They could not secure employment in the occupation of their choice, and higher education was practically closed to them. In addition, they were not only denied the right to vote; they were, socially and individually, perceived as being under the jurisdiction of men. Once married, a woman lost all claim to any property she had previously owned; it was transferred to her husband. She had legal claims neither to her own body nor to her children in the event of divorce.[4]

Comparison/Contrast

In the evangelical Christian community, the issue of headship/submission/equality lies at the hear of the fundamental differences between the two major proactive groups in the ordination debate. The Council on Biblical Manhood and Womanhood, representing those who oppose women's ordination, ultimately basies its biblical argument on the premise that the divine plan in creation affirmed equality of the sexes in spiritual status but included role distinctions involving the headship of man over woman. . . . Those holding this position have been referred to as "patriarchalists," "hierarchalists," or (their preferred self-designation) "complementarians." The second group, Christians for Biblical Equality, representing evangelicals who support women's ordination, argue that the divine plan at Creation affirmed full equality of the sexes without any male headship or female submission. . . . Those holding this view have been referred to as "Christian feminists" or (their preferred self-designation) "egalitarians."[5]

Cause and Effect

Even in the religious arena, [nineteenth-century] women were limited. Most churches did not ordain women and either prohibited or frowned upon women speaking in public. Because a large sector of society perceived the church as responsible for the denigration of women, many elements in the women's movement became hostile to it. For example, powerful crusader Elizabeth Gage called the church the bulwark of women's slavery. For her, no entity was more offensive than organized religion. For this reason, freedom from religious orthodoxy became crucial to feminist leadership.[6]

These samples illustrate good writing. They also show different ways of constructing paragraphs.

---

[4]Alicia Worley, "Ellen White and Women's Rights," *WIM*, 357.

[5]Richard M. Davidson, "Headship, Submission, and Equality in Scripture," *WIM*, 259.

[6]Worley, 357.

Transitions and Introductions

Student writers often have trouble finding an appropriate word to make the transition from one idea or sentence to another. A further difficulty is finding words to introduce quotations. This section suggests some terms for both purposes.

Transitional Words

Following is a list of transitional words and phrases that may be useful in relating sentences and ideas one to another.[7] Using these words can *further* improve your research writing style.

accordingly	finally	likewise
again	first	meanwhile
also	further	moreover
thus	and	hence
next	so	at the same time
however	nor	besides
in like manner	but	in addition
on the whole	too	consequently
last	on the other hand	or
then	to sum up	to conclude
second	therefore	similarly
third		

To sum up, words and phrases such as these can be used effectively to smooth transitions and *thus* make for easier reading. *However*, make sure you are certain what the word means and choose the one that best fits your writing. *Finally*, use a variety of these transition words.

Introducing Quotations

Quotations are the words and ideas of another author; we borrow them to enhance a position or strengthen an argument. These quotations need to be introduced. Readers are jolted when a quotation comes out of the blue and upset when they have to look at the footnote to find who said such a thing. However, constantly introducing quotations with the phrase "So-and-so wrote that" bores the reader. Here is a list of different verbs that can be used to introduce quotations:

---

[7]Kate L. Turabian, *Student's Guide for Writing College Papers*, 3d ed. (Chicago: University of Chicago Press, 1976), 71.

accepts	asks	denies	mentions	proposes	stipulates
adds	believes	describes	objects	recalls	submits
admits	combats	discusses	opposes	recommends	suggests
affirms	confirms	expresses	points out	reports	thinks
agrees	declares	indicates	points to	reveals	verifies
argues	defends	labels	portrays	states	writes

Tense usage is important. To refer to an event of the past, use the past: "John Wesley argued that..." or "Manalo defended...." When referring to stated views and beliefs of present or past writers, the present tense may be used. The idea still stands! In a discussion of the theological understanding of Bultmann, it is correct to say: "Bultmann admits..., but points out that...." One could even write: "Luther accepts that... and confirms...," even when Luther has been dead for centuries. However, you should avoid changing back and forth between past and present. The simplest solution to the tense dilemma is to consistently use the past tense for whatever happened or was written in the past. Whatever the choice, consistency is mandatory; the rationale for using one verb tense over the other should be clear.

Formal quotations may be preceded by a colon or a comma. The setting will determine your choice. This type of quotation remains identical to the source, with only the possibility of changing the initial cap for a lowercase letter after the comma. For example, Paul wrote the Corinthians: "Make love your aim" (1 Cor 14:1). The quotation remains intact.

A quotation may also be woven into my sentence. In that case the initial cap can be changed to a lower case. The syntax of my sentence is the one that counts. For example, if my sentence began "Paul wrote to the Corinthians that," I would need to change the quotation. I could write: Paul wrote to the Corinthians that they should make love their aim (1 Cor 14:1). I had to change the person (you to they) and the tense (make to should make). What Paul wrote is now part of what I am saying. This is a paraphrase, but still needs a reference. As you make quotations fit smoothly into your writing, be especially careful with the person and the tense. Above all, be faithful to your source; use brackets to show any addition or modification.

Quoting Bible texts presents unique problems. We often hear: "First Samuel 3:10 says" (at least the sentence begins with a written number!). Obviously, the passage cannot speak. We need to look for another way to quote it. "In 1 Sam 3:10 we read" would be appropriate. Or I could write, "The story reads: 'And the LORD came and stood forth' (1 Sam 3:10)." In the Pauline letters, it is appropriate to write: "Paul wrote." When quoting from Chronicles, I would have to speak of the chronicler or the author of Chronicles.

The quotation of longer passages has its own rules. When you quote eight or more lines, in which there are two separate sentences, you have a "block quotation."[8] You will indent the quotation, at least from the left and preferably from both right and left margins (half as much as the paragraph indentation), and you will single space. Naturally, you still need to introduce the quotation. See chapter 12 for details of format.

Still on the use of quotations: Be careful to include all the necessary quotation marks and footnotes (or endnotes) to avoid being labeled a plagiarist. Even if you paraphrase, give the reference. The origin of a borrowed phrase or idea must be acknowledged by a footnote.

The Writing Process

Writing a paper is a process to be achieved in stages: writing, correcting, and rewriting. Two drafts and a final copy may be enough to produce a good paper; often three or four drafts are needed. If your language is not English, or if the subject is complex, writing and rewriting become even more necessary. Some students may need to find editorial assistance, since ghost-writing papers is not part of the professor's job description.

First Draft: Write and Rewrite

Writing cannot be done effectively in small segments of time. Set aside enough time to write one complete section of the paper in one sitting. If you have to stop and start too many times, you will waste time rereading what you wrote before in order to "get the feel of things" again.

In bygone days, teachers always recommended a first, hand-written draft, to be typed later. Today computers make typing the first draft directly a good idea. You can "cut and paste" and edit to your heart's content, all the while working from a rough draft. If typing is not one of your skills, take the time and make the effort to learn to type. And while you are learning typing, learn a word processing program. If you must write your first draft by hand, leave an empty space between lines so you can make legible corrections.

With the notes in hand, you write, one section at a time, following the order of the sorted cards. The wording of the cards suggests the wording for the paper. When you come to a quotation, you may paraphrase it, copy it from your note card (if it is short), or attach it to the paper without copying it (if it is long). If you are working at the computer, you can cut and paste it from the note file to

---

[8]So says Kate L. Turabian, *A Manual for Writers*, 6th ed., revised by John Grossman and Alice Bennett (Chicago: University of Chicago Press, 1996), 5.4. Earlier editions said two sentences and four lines.

your paper (numbered cards make this easy). In any case, you will need to reference the quotation, citation, or allusion.

If you are using a word processing program that makes automatic footnotes, you are spared tears and sweat. Simply create a footnote (or endnote) and type in all the information for the note. (I work with three files at once: one has the bibliography, one the notes, and one the chapter I am writing. I can import from either of the first two at any time.) If you are typing or writing by hand, simply put the number of the footnote into the text and make a list of the contents of your notes on a separate sheet of paper. This list at first may only include the information on the note card; during the rewriting process, the list must be completed to match the instructions given on footnotes and endnotes in chapter 8.

Once the first writing is completed, allow the draft to rest for a day or so. Then reread and rewrite, making the necessary corrections. Rewriting includes deleting, adding, rearranging, checking spelling and punctuation, completing footnotes, and general editorial work.

Second Draft: Rewrite and Type

After you have corrected the first draft, even you may have trouble reading through the red marks. Rewrite, retype, or—better by far—enter the corrections on the document already in your word processor. This becomes the second draft.

Now is a good time to read the whole paper again, this time aloud or to someone else. Another person who hears or reads the paper usually notices problems you cannot see. Many students find spouses to be excellent critics of their literary work. Students who do not write well in English may need an editor to make corrections.

Whether you input the paper on the computer or hire a typist, you are totally responsible for any mistakes, either in format or typing. Advertisements around schools tout "low prices" for typists. Saving money is not wise here. You need a typist who knows the required format and gives you a perfectly typed paper because you assume final responsibility for the contents, language, and presentation of the paper.

Revising

In the revision process, the writer needs to look for wrong spellings, bad punctuation, unclear sentences, and anything else that mars the reading. The following is a list of specific areas that may cause problems. Pay special attention to them.

1. Flow of ideas—there should be a natural continuity from one idea and one sentence to the next.

2. Coherence—there should be cohesion (a "sticking together") of ideas and sentences. In order to have coherence, there must be some organizing principle.

3. Bridges—there should be natural bridges from one topic to another; over these the reader may walk from one part of the paper to the next. There should be no abrupt transitions or changes of thought.

4. Logic of organization—there must be a reasonable explanation for the way the ideas and topics are organized. The ideas must also be expressed in logical sentences.

5. Weak spots or omissions—there should be no places where it appears there has been insufficient research or something has been left out. If you discover such a spot, go back to the library and look for something to enrich the poor portion of the paper.

6. Awkward sentences—there is usually a better way to say something. If the sentence does not sound right, change it! The best possible syntax and grammar should be used.

7. Unnecessary words—there should be no more words than needed. Such words as "pretty," "rather," "very," are useless and must be eliminated. The best way to say something is the simplest way.

These seven items provide a good basis for examining and revising the paper. Obviously, this kind of rewriting takes time. But high marks and the satisfaction of having done excellent work should repay your effort.

Help for the Novice Writer

The following books from the University of Chicago Guides to Writing, Editing, and Publishing series provide a wealth of material to help you write better:

Booth, Wayne C., Gregory G. Colomb, and Joseph M. Williams. *The Craft of Research.* 1995.

Chicago Manual of Style. 14th ed. 1993.

Turabian, Kate L. *A Manual for Writers.* 6th ed. 1996.

Williams, Joseph M. *Style: Toward Clarity and Grace.* 1990.

Many books on writing could be listed. I have found the following particularly helpful:

Hacker, Diana. *A Writer's Reference.* 3d ed. Boston: Bedford, 1995.

Henson, Kenneth T. *The Art of Writing for Publication.* Boston: Allyn and Bacon, 1995.

Hudson, Bob, and Shelley Townsend. *A Christian Writer's Manual of Style.* Grand Rapids: Zondervan, 1988.

Lederer, Richard, and Richard Dowis. *The Write Way: The S.P.E.L.L. Guide to Real-life Writing.* New York: Pocket, 1995.

Maggio, Rosalie. *The Nonsexist Word Finder: A Dictionary of Gender-free Usage.* Boston: Beacon, 1988.

Strunk, William, Jr., and E. B. White. *The Elements of Style.* 3d ed. New York: Macmillan, 1979.

This chapter describes English research writing style. Chapter 12 will deal with the format required for research papers and dissertations.

XII | FORMATTING THE PAPER

So far, this book on writing research papers has discussed the research process, shown how to make bibliographical and note cards, explained ways of organizing the paper, and described English research language. Now it turns to the matter of format, for a paper, thesis, or dissertation must (1) demonstrate careful research, (2) show logical organization, and (3) be presented in perfect format.

There are different systems for formatting a paper. Of necessity, an arbitrary choice of one system rather than another must be made. Because the Turabian style is widely used for academic writing in the field of religion and theology, this book follows *A Manual for Writers*, both for references and for typing format.[1]

Chapter 12 gives basic guidelines for formatting the page and specific instructions for typing different parts of the paper. The instructions assume that you are using a computer or word processor, probably Microsoft Word™ or WordPerfect™, of which any version will work. "Tips for the Typist," in appendix D, summarizes format instructions.

Page Format

Set up the page format *before* you start typing. You will save yourself untold grief. Measurements are given in inches, but you can use the centimeter equivalent if you prefer (calculate 2.54 cm for each inch). Your word processing program can work with either inches or centimeters.

Body Text

Here are the basic settings for the body text. The page should be letter size (unless you live where A4 is the norm and this size is accepted by your school) and the orientation, portrait. Set the margins at 1 inch on top, bottom, and right (this is default, and does not need changing), and 1.5 inches on the left (for

---

[1]Kate L. Turabian, *A Manual for Writers*, 6th ed., revised by John Grossman and Alice Bennett (Chicago: University of Chicago Press, 1996).

proper binding). Set the line spacing for double spacing. Set the justification on left. Set one tab for the body of the paper at .6 inches from the left margin (2.1 inches from the left edge of the page).

Choose a serif font, either the traditional typewriter kind (Courier) or one that looks like printing (Garamond or Times Roman).[2] Some schools have a rule against a sans serif type such as Arial. Be sure you find out the rules. Evidently, fancy types are out. Usually you can choose the size, within limits: no larger than 12 points and no smaller than 10 points.

Page Numbers

Set the page number for the top center of the page. Use the same font as the body text. The first page of a chapter or major section needs to have the page number at the bottom of the page. In WordPerfect™, use the following command on these pages: format, page, suppress, print number at bottom of page. In Microsoft Word™, you will have to change the placement of the number on that page.

The first page of the INTRODUCTION is page 1 (Arabic numeral), with the number at the bottom of the page. In a dissertation, the preliminary pages are numbered in lowercase Roman numerals, at the bottom center of the page, beginning with the title page. Do not type the number, however, on that page.

Titles and Headings

The number of the chapter or title of major headings, such as the introduction, bibliography, or appendixes, is typed at 2 inches from the top edge of the paper. The chapter title is typed centered, one double space below the number (some schools want a triple space!). If the title is longer than 4.75 inches, it must be divided, with the longer part on the first line, the shorter part on the second line, and a double space between. If the title takes three lines, these are single spaced. Place the first line of text three single spaces below the chapter title. Major headings, such as INTRODUCTION or BIBLIOGRAPHY, are typed at 2 inches (13th line) from the top edge of the page, just as the chapter numbers.

Triple spaces are used before any heading, from level one through level five. (Review headings in chapter 10, under "Visible Organization.") To get the right spacing, you will have to do a hard return (the one that completes your paragraph), change from double to single space, do one hard return, and change back to double space. Write yourself a macro or a style that will do this in one simple stroke.

---

[2]On this page "Page Number's" and "Titles and Headings" are in sans serif type. The text is a serif font.

Titles for appendixes are similar to those of chapters. For example, APPEN-DIX A appears 2 inches from the top of the page (or is centered on the page, APA citation style), with the title one double space below. These are the *only* two items on the page. The appendix material appears on the following page.

Preliminary Pages

Tables of contents should follow the model provided. When the table is more than one page long, it begins with the phrase TABLE OF CONTENTS at 2 inches from the top of the page. If the table is shorter than one page, it may be centered on the page as it is in the example.

Chapter titles are in caps. A double space goes between chapter title and the first heading, which is done in caps and lowercase bold. The table of contents usually includes only the first three levels of subheadings.

The indention for each subheading level is 0.25 inches or three empty spaces. If a title is longer than one line, the second line is indented.

Each heading must have at least one dot leader before the page number. The dots should align vertically and end on the same imaginary vertical line. Your word processing program can automatically insert the appropriate dot leaders. What has been said about the table of contents applies also to the lists of illustrations, tables, and figures.

If you have a title page and one page of table of contents, you need not number them. If you have more pages (a longer table of contents, lists, acknowledgements, etc.), they should be numbered with roman numerals at the bottom center of the page.

Footnotes and Quotations

The appearance of a paper is easily marred by incorrectly placed notes and quotations. The suggestions given here should help you do it perfectly.

Footnotes

Technology has made footnoting simple. You would not even want to hear about how it used to be done! Instructions here fit Microsoft Word™ and WordPerfect™. To avoid an irregular gap between the last line of text and the separator line, place notes below the text. You do this under Insert, Footnote, Options. If your school requires footnote numbers to start with 1 on each page, you can change this in the same place. However, do so only at the end of your work, just before turning your paper in. Having footnotes in numerical sequence while you do revising and editing is helpful.

The word processing program will pick up the indentation from the page setup for the body text. You should have no problems if you set up the page first. If the footnote does not look like those on the model pages, you may have to fiddle until you get exactly what you want.

When you need to insert a footnote, simply place your cursor at the end of the phrase or sentence, after the punctuation marks, and insert a footnote. Your word processor takes it from there.

Quotations

Short quotations—one sentence or less—are easily worked into the paragraph. *Double* quotation marks are mandatory for quotations. In American usage, single quotations marks are used only for a quotation within a quotation. Additionally, closing quotation marks are placed *outside* the comma or the period after the word.

Longer quotations—usually two sentences on eight lines or more—are typed as "block quotations." These quotations are single spaced and indented .3 inches from each margin. For both Microsoft Word™ and WordPerfect™ you need to set up a paragraph style that is single spaced, with indentations at 2.1 and 7.2 inches from the left edge of the paper, hard indent from both sides, and single spacing. You may also make the quotation one point smaller than the body text (11 instead of 12 point, for example). When you complete a paragraph in body text with a hard return, click on the style you have created to make the block quotation look like it does in the model page.

No quotation marks are used for block quotations. When the quotation starts at the beginning of the original paragraph, there is an additional indentation, so that the indentation is identical to that of the regular paragraph. If the quotation comes from the middle of the paragraph, there is no further indentation. To emphasize a quotation, even if it is not eight lines long, set it off in a block quotation.

You may italicize (or underline) words or phrases in a quotation in order to show emphasis. Do so sparingly lest you overdo your point. Always make clear to your reader what was italicized by the author and what you italicized. Normally you will indicate this in the footnote, where you will give the reference and the phrase "italics mine" or "emphasis added" in parentheses after the page number: Jones, 37 (italics mine). If you put the phrase *within* the quotation, place it in brackets.

A quotation is followed by its appropriate reference, usually a footnote. However, a Bible quotation may have the reference in parentheses, followed by the period. In the case of block quotations followed by a reference in parentheses, the period precedes the parentheses.

I appeal to you therefore, brethren, by the mercies of God, to present your bodies as a living sacrifice, holy and acceptable to God, which is your spiritual worship. Do not be conformed to this world but be transformed by the renewal of your mind, that you may prove what is the will of God, what is good and acceptable and perfect. (Rom 12:1–2)

Tables, Figures, and Illustrations

Tables, figures, and illustrations may be used to enhance a paper, thesis, or dissertation. They should be well made, clear, and large enough to be easily read. Colored ink cannot be used for dissertations that are photocopied in black and white. Use instead different kinds of lines or crosshatching. The making of tables is described in chapter 18, which also includes a number of figures to be used as models. Each figure or table must have a number, a title, and a source, if it is not the result of the research being reported.

When the tables or figures are small enough to fit on the page, they may be placed between paragraphs, as near as possible to the text in which they are discussed. It is wise to make a reference to the figure or table in the text: "Figure 4 shows the outline of the walls of Jerusalem in the days of Hezekiah." Leave three empty lines above and below so that tables and figures do not look crowded.

Larger tables and figures are often placed on separate pages, as soon as possible after the text that mentions them. Computer typing often makes this kind of insertion mandatory. Neat appearance and ease of reading are the criteria for designing the pages on which tables and figures are included.

Titles of tables are typed in capital letters, centered, above the table. Titles of figures are typed in sentence style (first word capitalized, the rest lowercase) below the figure. If these titles are short, they are centered; if they are long, they begin at the left margin. Again, examples are given in chapter 18.

Spelling, Punctuation, and Other Details

Needless to say, spelling, punctuation, and other small details are important in a research paper. Professors judge by what their eyes see! You, the student, are responsible for all details. You must carefully read the paper, mark any mistakes, and retype or request your typist to make needed corrections. When the paper is handed to the professor, it should be perfect. The professor should not be expected to correct spelling or point out typographical errors.

Spelling

Depending on your school, the spelling will be either British (Saviour, centre, etc.) or American (Savior, center, etc.). Both are correct, but most American schools prefer American spelling. Of course, your quotations will keep their original spelling. Whichever spelling you and your adviser select must be used consistently.

The spelling of foreign words, whether in titles of books and journals or in the text, must be accurate. That means using all the accents and diacritical marks in the original. WordPerfect™ and Word™ include multinational characters such as ç, ø, and é. Of course, foreign words that do not appear in the English dictionary should be italicized or underlined. An apparent contradiction to this is the allowance for you to insert a *quotation* in another language without italicizing. If you translate a word, give the English in brackets, as you do with any interpolation to a quotation. For non-Latin scripts follow standard transliteration patterns, such as the ones for biblical languages in appendix B. (Note that a reference to parts of the paper does not capitalize the name of the part, chapter, appendix, bibliography.)

Abbreviations appear in notes rather than in the text. Use standard ones, as given in your dictionary, in Turabian (2.26), or the *Chicago Manual of Style* (14.33). One abbreviation unique to biblical studies is "v." for "verse" and "vv." for "verses." Abbreviations other than the initials of an author (E. A. Jones) have no space after the period included in them (e.g., A.D.).

Computer programs that check the spelling and automatically divide words save time and are a definite asset to scholarship. If you do not have access to such programs, use a dictionary.

Punctuation

If there is doubt about the punctuation rules of the English language, review them! An English grammar is an important tool for writing research papers.

Besides causing problems by putting periods and commas before the final quotation marks, English punctuation has other idiosyncracies. In English research language, an enumeration needs a comma before the word "and." For example: We like bananas, mangoes, and papaya. At the same time, the tendency to eliminate commas, except as needed for clarity, is evident. An author whose name includes "Jr." or a Roman numeral is written John Jones Jr.—without a comma. When you invert the name, as in the bibliography, you will use commas: Jones, John, Jr.

Lines, short and long, can also cause problems. A hyphen has no space on either side of it: twenty-two. The printed dash must be typed as two hyphens, with no space on either side of them. For example: We saw someone--who it was, we have no idea--leaving the house. If your computer program turns the double dash into an em dash—so be it! However, use one or the other consistently. Distinguish between a line in the middle of the type (a hyphen or em dash) and a line below the letters (underlining). Use the second for the eight-space line used in a bibliography when an author has more than one book.

Current usage puts only one space after the period or full stop. In fact, all punctuation marks are followed by one space, with one exception. When a colon or a period is used to separate parts of books, there is no space after it. For example: *TWOT*, 1:112 means volume 1, page 112; Irenaeus *Against Heresies* 2.2.3 refers to book 2, chapter 2, paragraph 3.

Other Details

Among these details is the use of numbers. In a scientific paper, Arabic numbers are always used. In reporting statistics, Arabic numbers are always used: for example, 23 percent of the 345 respondents (notice the use of "percent" rather than the symbol) said they preferred bananas. Numbers larger than one thousand have a comma: 4,567. Arabic numbers cannot be used at the beginning of a sentence. Use Arabic numbers for volumes of books or journals. Use Roman numerals only when transcribing a quotation or as page numbers for the preliminary pages (lower case at the bottom of the page).

Ordinal numbers below ten and round numbers should be written out in the text: eighth, one hundredth. In the documentation, however, they are given as numerals: 1st, 2d, 3d, 4th. Note the correct form for second and third! You may use the superscript if you so desire: 1st, 2^d, 3^d, 4th. Be consistent, whichever you choose.

According to Turabian (2.30) numbers under one hundred are written out. Likewise, round numbers, such as "five thousand," are written. Fractions are written out: one-half. However, Bible references and page numbers, as well as dates, decimal numbers, percentages, and sums of money are never written out.

These important details are covered in English grammar books and very specifically in Turabian's *Manual for Writers*. Use these works to produce an A paper. However, always take into account your school's rules.[2]

---

[2]The next few pages show examples in correct format for what a paper should look like. If you wish to see these pages in 8½ by 11 paper, you should be able to access them and run them off at www.zondervan.com\academic\quality research papers. Be sure to check with your professor to see if these pages conform to your school's rules.

[2.5 in]

Andrews University
Theological Seminary

[4 in]

THE IMPACT OF *HEILSGESCHICHTE* ON THE
UNDERSTANDING OF THE BIBLICAL
DOCTRINE OF CREATION

[6 in]

A Report

Presented in Partial Fulfillment

of the Requirements for the Course

GSEM 920 Religious Studies Seminar

[8 in]

by

Karen K. Abrahamson

June 2000

TABLE OF CONTENTS

INTRODUCTION

The term *Heilsgeschichte* was coined by Johann Albrecht Bengel (1687-1752). It came to be used to describe "the nature of the Bible as an account of God's working out divine salvation in human history." Proponents of *Heilsgeschichte* or salvation history "rejected the idea that the Bible is a collection of divine 'proof texts' for constructing doctrine in favor of seeing it as a history of God's redemptive plan."[1]

The formal development of the concept in the nineteenth century, according to A. Josef Greig, came in response to the skepticism that emerged in Christianity as a reaction to "the aims of rationalism and pietism, and the results of the historical-critical method."[2] Hans W. Frei points out that for *Heilsgeschichte*, the "saving facts" of the Bible are "real and historical but not in an ordinary way that would open them up to religiously neutral verification."[3]

The concept of *Heilsgeschichte* allows for the reinterpretation of an event from a historical understanding in time to a nonhistorical and experiential interpretation. This hermeneutical concept suggests the question: What impact does this theory have upon biblical doctrine, in particular, the doctrine of Creation?

In order to answer this question, this paper will examine the historical development of *Heilsgeschichte* and analyze its presuppositions and hermeneutical approaches.

---

[1]Stanley J. Grenz, David Guretzki, and Cherith Fee Nordling, *Pocket Dictionary of Theological Terms* (Downers Grove, IL: InterVarsity, 1999), s.v. *"Heilsgeschichte."*

[2]A. Josef Greig, "Some Formative Aspects in the Development of Gerhard von Rad's Idea of History," *AUSS* 16 (1978): 314.

[3]Hans W. Frei, *The Eclipse of Biblical Narrative: A Study in Eighteenth and Nineteenth Century Hermeneutics* (New Haven: Yale University Press, 1974), 180.

CHAPTER I

HISTORICAL DEVELOPMENT OF

HEILSGESCHICHTE

Several factors played important roles in shaping the *Heilsgeschichte* concept: (1) rationalism, (2) experiential and inward-turning elements within Christianity, and (3) the implementation of the historical-critical method. These factors later came together to form the basis of Liberal Protestantism.

Rationalism

Immanuel Kant rose from obscurity to provide the "theological watershed between [the] classical and modern (liberal) systems" that would, if accepted, make "the classical view impossible."[4] Kant accomplished this task by reinterpreting reason. His philosophy included two aspects: the timeless nature of God and truth, and the limitation of human reason to the spatio-temporal. Fernando Canale notes that such divergences between God and humanity do not allow for cognitive contact between God, as a "timeless or supernatural object," and human reason.[5] Therefore, the need for some other means of communication arises.

Because Kantian understanding leaned heavily toward the intuitive, rationalism brought uncertainty in regard to history. Since certainty could only be attained through reason, "rationalism stimulated a search for a theology of immediacy and inwardness."[6]

---

[4]Fernando Canale, *Principles and Methods of Theology: Student Notes* (Berrien Springs, MI: Andrews University, 1997), 90.

[5]Fernando Canale, "Revelation and Inspiration: The Liberal Model," *AUSS* 32 (1994): 170-171.

[6]Greig, 314.

Speaking of religious theory after Kant, Frei stated:

Religious theory after Kant focused more and more on faith as a distinctive and self-
conscious human stance which is reducible to no other. *And faith in this sense qualifies whatever 'reality' it is properly in touch with,* analogous to the way in which for Kant the structure
of reason qualifies the transcendental ego's contact with the objects of the
sensible world, turning them from things-in-themselves into phenomena for human
consciousness.[7]

Experiential and Inward-turning Elements
within Christianity

Thomas Aquinas desired to introduce Aristotle into Christianity in order to lessen the tension

between faith and reason. To achieve this, he attempted to differentiate theology from philosophy.[8]

Aquinas's views provided the basis for classical scholasticism.

Lutheran Protestantism, though claiming to follow *sola Scriptura*, accepted the hermeneutical

presuppositions of classical scholasticism. After the death of Luther, Protestant theologians began the

process of rational systematization of doctrine "that often included natural theology, Aristotelian logic

and extreme fine-tuning and hairsplitting with regard to doctrinal formulations."[9]

As scholasticism resulted in an increasingly dry and rigid form of religion, nominalism created a

new interest in humanity and came to see the human being as more real than the institution. In addition

nominalism denied the objective reality of universal principles, which were considered to be "mere

concepts with no reality apart from their existence in the mind of the individual."[10] Maintaining the

existence of two realms of truth (scientific and theological) led some nominalists to exalt the experimental

method as the main path to truth, while others began to move in the direction of mysticism "as a way by

---

[7]Frei, 32 (emphasis supplied).

[8]John W. Baldwin, *The Scholastic Culture of the Middle Ages: 1000-1300* (Lexington, MA: D. C. Heath, 1971), 93.

[9]Roger E. Olson, *The Story of Christian Theology: Twenty Centuries of Tradition and Reform* (Downers Grove, IL: InterVarsity, 1999), 475.

[10]Grenz, Guretzki, and Nordling, s.v. "nominalism."

which the individual could come directly into the presence of God."[11] In Greig's words, "The failure of rationalism to attain its theological goals tended to turn the theologian's attitude inwards, toward religious experience." This resulted in the development of the Pietistic movement within German Lutheranism.[12]

German Pietism

Pietism stood "between the controversies of orthodoxy and the more innovative approaches to theology."[13] Olson defined Pietism as "a renewal movement that aimed at a completion of the Protestant Reformation begun by Martin Luther."[14]

Through Pietism Lutheranism was refreshed and revived as three elements in the life of the believer were emphasized: the study and application to daily life of the Bible and the development of a pious life. An additional emphasis on missionary activity caused some, however, to develop an indifference to biblical doctrine and led them into idealism.[15] This idealism found the nature of reality "more in terms of spirit or mind than matter or material."[16] It attempted to "retain the comprehensiveness of vision in Romanticism and Transcendentalism while avoiding their subjectivism. . . . At the same time, it retained an allure for philosophy by attempting to build on rationality rather than intuition."[17]

---

[11]Earle E. Cairns, *Christianity through the Centuries: A History of the Christian Church*, rev. and enl. ed. (Grand Rapids: Zondervan, Academie Books, 1981), 239-240.

[12]Greig, 315.

[13]Ibid., 314.

[14]Olson, 473.

[15]Cairns, 381.

[16]Grenz, Guretzk, and Nordling, s.v. "idealism."

[17]Steve Wilkens and Alan Padgett, *Faith and Reason in the 19th Century*, Christianity and Western Thought, vol. 2 (Downers Grove, IL: InterVarsity, 2000), 63.

SUMMARY AND CONCLUSIONS

Heilsgeschichte has been defined in this paper as a hermeneutical principle within the historical-critical method. Its development was simultaneous with the growth of the Liberal Protestant movement and came about as a result of the need to bridge the gap between the historical veracity of the Bible and the new theologically oriented method of interpretation.

Several factors played roles in bringing about the concept of *Heilsgeschichte*: (1) rationalism, as developed by Immanuel Kant; (2) experiential and inward-turning elements within Christianity, such as German Pietism, Schleiermacher's concept of *Gefühl*, and Hegel's dialectical philosophy; and the historical-critical method.

The paper began with the hypothesis that the Liberal Protestant concept of *Heilsgeschichte* impacts the doctrine of creation by allowing for the reinterpretation of the event from a historical understanding of the event in time to one of nonhistorical and experiential interpretation. This allows for the rejection of the first eleven chapters of the book of Genesis as historical documentation, while preserving the theological integrity of those passages.

An examination of the presuppositions upon which the *Heilsgeschichte* concept is built shows that this hypothesis is true. Furthermore, the nonhistorical and experiential interpretation is problematic on five counts: (1) It uses subjective methods of interpretation, (2) it dissects Scripture, (3) it denigrates the concept of propositional truth, (4) it questions faith, and (5) it does not use consistently its own hermeneutical method—the scientific method.

BIBLIOGRAPHY

Baldwin, John W. *The Scholastic Culture of the Middle Ages: 1000-1300*. Lexington, MA: D. C. Heath, 1971.

Cairns, Earle E. *Christianity through the Centuries: A History of the Christian Church*. Revised and enlarged edition. Grand Rapids: Zondervan, Academie Books, 1981.

Canale, Fernando. *Principles and Methods of Theology: Student Notes*. Berrien Springs, MI: Andrews University, 1997.

_____. "Revelation and Inspiration: The Liberal Model." *Andrews University Seminary Studies* 32 (1994): 169-195.

Frei, Hans W. *The Eclipse of Biblical Narrative: A Study in Eighteenth and Nineteenth Century Hermeneutics*. New Haven: Yale University Press, 1974.

Fretheim, Terence E. *Creation, Fall, and Flood: Studies in Genesis 1-11*. Minneapolis: Augsburg, 1969.

Greig, A. Josef. "A Critical Note on the Origin of the Term *Heilsgeschichte*." *The Expository Times* 87 (1975-1976): 118-119.

_____. "Some Formative Aspects in the Development of Gerhard von Rad's Idea of History." *Andrews University Seminary Studies* 16 (1978): 313-331.

Grenz, Stanley J., David Guretzki, and Cherith Fee Nordling. *Pocket Dictionary of Theological Terms*. Downers Grove, IL: InterVarsity, 1999.

Grenz, Stanley J., and Roger E. Olson. *Twentieth Century Theology: God and the World in a Transitional Age*. Downers Grove, IL: InterVarsity, 1992.

Hasel, Gerhard. *Old Testament Theology: Basic Issues in the Current Debate*. Revised edition. Grand Rapid Eerdmans, 1972.

Hegel, G. W. F. *The Phenomenology of Mind*. 2 vols. Translated by J. B. Baillie. New York: Macmillan, 1910.

Lichtenberger, F. *History of German Theology in the Nineteenth Century*. Translated and edited by W. Hastie. Edinburgh: T. & T. Clark, 1889.

Lundin, Roger, Clarence Walhout, and Anthony C. Thiselton. *The Promise of Hermeneutics*. Grand Rapids: Eerdmans, 1999.

XIII BIBLICAL EXEGESIS AS RESEARCH

Biblical exegesis is not usually listed as a type of research; it is, however, a study that uses research methods. You must think carefully, develop a bibliography, read books and journals, take notes, organize the topic, and write the paper.

This chapter describes a research-oriented exegetical process at an intermediate level. It also lists commonly used sources and describes an acceptable final form for the exegetical paper.

Steps in the Exegetical Process

Many different schemes of exegesis exist. The one described here starts with the biblical text in its canonical context.[1] It assumes the authority and unity of Scripture and seeks to ascertain the meaning of the Bible, both for its original readers or hearers and for my life today.

Step 1: Determine the Canonical Context

Read in its canonical setting the passage you want to study. Find out what it is a part of and how it functions within that setting. Look for the markers that indicate its limits, as well as its relation to what precedes and what follows. Outline your passage within the context of the genre and structure of the section of the book or even of the whole book.

After you have studied the Bible text—your passage and its context—you may want to see how other authors have understood the organization of the chapter and of the book of which it is a part. This information is part of what is given

---

[1]See Grant R. Osborne, *The Hermeneutical Spiral* (Downers Grove, IL: InterVarsity, 1993), 19–40; Lee J. Gugliotto also begins with the context; see his massive *Handbook for Bible Study* (Hagerstown, MD: Review and Herald, 1996). An older, yet excellent guide for NT exegesis is Gordon Fee, *New Testament Exegesis: A Handbook for Students and Pastors* (Philadelphia: Westminster, 1983). An Asian book on exegesis for preaching is Ng Kah Seng, *SEARCH: An Exegetical Process for Preaching* (Silang, Cavite, Philippines: AIIAS Publications, 1989). See also George H. Guthrie and J. Scott Duvall, *Biblical Greek Exegesis: A Graded Approach to Learning Intermediate and Advanced Greek* (Grand Rapids: Zondervan, 1998).

in an introduction (used in the technical sense of a work that tells *about* a Bible book) or in a Bible commentary. However, because authors' presuppositions may cause them to see things in a particular light, you need to be careful about accepting their explanation at face value. Read with care and thought. At this point, do not read interpretations of your passage—only gather information on the canonical context.

The following introductions may be valuable:

Arnold, Bill T., and Bryan E. Beyer. *Encountering the Old Testament*. Grand Rapids: Baker, 1999.

Carson, D. A., Douglas Moo, and Leon Morris. *Introduction to the New Testament*. Grand Rapids: Zondervan, 1992.

Elwell, Walter, and Robert W. Yarbrough. *Encountering the New Testament*. Grand Rapids: Baker, 1998.

Guthrie, Donald. *New Testament Introduction*. 3d ed. Downers Grove, IL: InterVarsity Press, 1970.

Harrison, R. K. *Introduction to the Old Testament*. Grand Rapids: Eerdmans, 1969.

Step 2: Establish the Text

After demarcating the passage to be studied, that is determining its beginning and ending, establish the text. This means determining as accurately as possible, by means of textual criticism, the original text. No variant reading in the whole of Scripture changes the basic biblical message. However, there are textual variants of significance. An example of these is the *Comma Johanneum* (1 John 5:7, 8), used for generations as a New Testament proof of the doctrine of the Trinity, which has now been shown to be a late addition (eleventh century) to the Bible text. There is no point in doing exegesis on a doubtful variant.

In order to find the oldest form of a Bible text—or at least locate the most trustworthy one—the original languages must be used. For the Hebrew Bible, the following are reliable texts:

Biblia Stuttgartensia. Stuttgart: Deutsche Bibelstiftung, 1990.

Rahlfs, A., ed. *Septuaginta*. 8th ed. 2 vols. Stuttgart: Württembergische Bibelanstalt, 1965.

Two editions of the Greek New Testament are recommended. The first is easy to read and use, but its restricted textual apparatus only includes problems that could affect Bible translation. The second has an exhaustive, yet difficult-to-use, textual apparatus.

Greek New Testament. 4th rev. ed. Stuttgart: Deutsche Bibelgesellschaft, 1994.

Nestle, Erwin, and Kurt Aland, eds. *Novum Testamentum Graece*. 27th ed. Stuttgart: Württembergische Bibelanstalt, 1993.

A companion to the United Bible Societies *Greek New Testament, A Textual Commentary* clarifies the decisions on textual criticism made by the Committee of New Testament Scholars. The certainty attributed to the authenticity of a phrase or word is designated by the letters A, B, C, and D. Reasons for the choice are given for each passage. The volume is a useful tool for determining New Testament text:

Metzger, Bruce. *A Textual Commentary on the Greek New Testament.* New York: United Bible Society, 1971.

For those whose biblical languages are poor, a comparison of different Bible versions can help. This comparison—together with a study of notes to the text—will suggest which is considered the most authentic text. Naturally, serious Bible translations, rather than popular ones, should be used for this comparative study. Modern versions constitute an improvement over the King James Version (prepared in 1611), because they use manuscripts not available at that time. The following English versions are suggested:

> *New American Standard Bible.* Published in 1971, revised in 1996, the NASB uses formal but clear English. There are abundant notes and references.
>
> *New International Version.* Published in 1978, the NIV uses clear and simple English. Although it may oversimplify some text problems, the NIV is a sound, modern translation.
>
> *Revised Standard Version.* First published in 1952, the RSV has come to occupy an important place among scholarly modern Bible translations.
>
> *New Revised Standard Version.* This revision of the RSV by a committee of scholars was completed in 1989. It incorporates later discoveries and research and uses inclusive language.

Reading the text in other modern languages is useful if the version you read was translated from the original languages. If it was not, it is one additional step removed from the original.

Step 3: Establish the Translation

Now you ask: What does the original text say? To establish the translation, take into account vocabulary and grammar.

Some reliable dictionaries and lexicons are the following:

Bauer, Walter. *A Greek-English Lexicon of the New Testament and Other Early Christian Literature.* 3d ed. Revised and edited by Frederick W. Danker. Chicago: University of Chicago Press, 2000.

Brown, Francis, S. R. Driver, and C. A. Briggs. *The New Brown, Driver and Briggs Hebrew and English Lexicon of the Old Testament*. Grand Rapids: Baker, 1987.

Holladay, William L. *A Concise Hebrew and Aramaic Lexicon of the Old Testament*. Grand Rapids: Eerdmans, 1993.

Koehler, L., and W. Baumgartner. *Hebrew and Aramaic Lexicon of the Old Testament*. 2d ed. Leiden: Brill, 1994.

Liddell, Hengry George, and Robert Scott. *A Greek-English Lexicon*. Oxford: Clarendon, reprint, 1996.

Some helpful grammars are:

Blass, Friedrich, and Albert Debrunner. *A Greek Grammar of the New Testament and Other Early Christian Literature*. Chicago: University of Chicago Press, 1961.

Gesenius, W., and E. Kautsch. *Gesenius' Hebrew Grammar*. 2d English ed. Revised by A. E. Cowley. Oxford: Clarendon Press, 1970.

Joüon, Paul. *A Grammar of Biblical Hebrew*. Translated and revised by T. Muraoka. 2 vols. Subsidia Biblica. Rome: Pontificio Istituto Biblico, 1996.

Moulton, James Hope, Wilbert Howard, and Nigel Turner. *A Grammar of New Testament Greek*. 4 vols. Edinburgh: T. and T. Clark, 1906–1970.

The Greek and Hebrew grammars you have used in class can also help you. You may also use electronic tools, such as Logos Research Systems and Hermeneutika. Try the Internet, at www.biblestudytools.com, for other study tools.

Step 4: Establish the Meaning

Establishing the meaning goes beyond the simple translation of the text. Now the question is asked: What does the passage mean? In order to determine the meaning of a text, study the syntax of the sentences. In addition, investigate the meaning of important words.

Syntax

In studying the syntax of a passage, look at the structure of the sentence and the function of the words. Look for idiomatic phrases and hard-to-translate prepositions. In Hebrew, look for constructs showing possession or other relations. In short, look for any element that might modify the first, direct, and obvious translation of the passage. For step 4, the following books are useful:

Brooks, James A., and Carlton L. Winberry. *Syntax of New Testament Greek*. Washington, D.C.: University Press of America, 1988.

Moule, C. F. D. *An Idiom-book of the New Testament Greek*. 2d ed. Cambridge: Cambridge University Press, 1978.

Wallace, Daniel. *Greek Grammar beyond the Basics: An Exegetical Syntax of the New Testament*. Grand Rapids: Zondervan, 1996.

Waltke, Bruce K. *An Introduction to Biblical Hebrew Syntax*. Winona Lake, IN: Eisenbrauns, 1990.

Word Study

Look up important nouns and verbs in a concordance to see how they are used in other passages. Start with other occurrences of these words in the same book, then in other passages by the same author, then in other authors of the same period. Afterwards, study these same words in theological dictionaries.

Concordances

Using a concordance in English is not as effective as using one in Hebrew or Greek. English concordances list the words that appear in a given English version; Young and Strong work from the King James Version. Young's *Concordance* does show for each English word what the original language word is, but a given Greek or Hebrew word is not always translated in the same way. To find all the uses of a certain word, you need to use a Greek or Hebrew concordance, either in book form or in one of the Bible software programs.

Even-Shoshan, Abraham, ed. *A New Concordance of the Bible.* Jerusalem: Kiryat Sefer, 1983.

Hatch, Edwin, and Henry Redpath. *A Concordance to the Septuagint and Other Greek Versions of the Old Testament.* Graz: Akademische Druck, 1954.

Kohlenberger, John R., Edward Goodrick, and James Swanson. *The Exhaustive Concordance to the Greek New Testament.* Grand Rapids: Zondervan, 1997.

Wigram, George. *The Englishman's Greek Concordance of the New Testament.* Peabody, MA: Hendrickson, 1996.

_____. *The Englishman's Hebrew Concordance of the Old Testament.* Peabody, MA: Hendrickson, 1996.

Theological dictionaries

Theological dictionaries and books containing word studies are useful to the process of exegesis. However, their authors—as well as their users—have certain presuppositions that must be taken into account.

The following are good for the Old Testament:

Botterweck, G. J., and H. Ringren. *Theological Dictionary of the Old Testament* (*TDOT*). Grand Rapids: Eerdmans, 1974–. (As of 2001, only 11 volumes are available.)

Harris, R. Laird, Gleason L. Archer, and Bruce K. Waltke. *Theological Wordbook of the Old Testament* (*TWOT*). 2 vols. Chicago: Moody Press, 1981.

VanGemeren, Willem A., gen. ed. *New International Dictionary of Old Testament Theology and Exegesis* (*NIDOTTE*). 5 vols. Grand Rapids: Zondervan, 1997.

TDOT is being translated from the German, at a very slow pace. *TWOT* is a condensation and conservative adaptation of the German on which *TDOT* is based. It keys the words to Strong's *Concordance* numbers, thus permitting someone who knows little or no Hebrew to benefit from its contents. *NIDOTTE* has a Scripture index and an English topical index that allow those who may not be strong in Hebrew to take advantage of a wealth of information.

For the New Testament:

Balz, Horst, and Gerhard Schneider. 3 vols. *Exegetical Dictionary of the New Testament.* Grand Rapids: Eerdmans, 1990.

Brown, Colin, ed. *The New International Dictionary of New Testament Theology* (*NIDNTT*). 4 vols. Grand Rapids: Zondervan, 1978–1986.

Kittel, G., and G. Friedrich, eds. *Theological Dictionary of the New Testament* (*TDNT*). 10 vols. Grand Rapids: Eerdmans, 1964–1976.

Verbrugge, Verlyn D., ed. *The NIV Theological Dictionary of New Testament Words.* Grand Rapids: Zondervan, 2000. (Abridgment and reorganization of *NIDNTT*.)

TDNT is a classic, indispensable to biblical scholars. The single most important book of the set, volume 10, contains indexes by Greek, Hebrew, and English words, and also by texts commented. *TDNT* comments on families of words and on words of theological importance. *NIDNTT* is to *TDNT* what *NIDOTTE* is to *TDOT* (see above): less complicated, more conservative, and easier to handle. It also contains much less information.

At the end of this step, you should have a clear, accurate, and smooth translation of the passage—the cumulative result of the first four steps. On the basis of this translation—which should be arrived at quite independently of any existing Bible translation—the next three steps should be undertaken.

Step 5: Establish the Historical and Geographical Context

This step of exegesis considers the historical and geographical context of the passage. It asks: What was happening at the time this passage was written that might explain the text?

Historical information is needed to clarify the text and suggests explanations for what was said or happened. A knowledge of the socio-political and economic situation of the time is important to understanding the passage. Also, knowledge of the geography and climate of the region, as well as of the customs of the people, helps bring the biblical text to life.

For historical and geographical information, the following sources are useful:

Aharoni, Yohanan. *The Land of the Bible: A Historical Geography.* 2d ed. Philadelphia: Westminster, 1979.

Aharoni, Yohanan, and Michael Avi-Yonah. *The Macmillan Bible Atlas.* Rev. 3d ed. Toronto: Maxwell Macmillan, 1993.

Bromiley, Geoffrey, ed. *International Standard Bible Encyclopedia.* 4 vols. Rev. ed. Grand Rapids: Eerdmans, 1979–1988.

Freedman, David Noel. *Anchor Bible Dictionary.* 6 vols. New York: Doubleday, 1992.

See also the two *Encountering* books from step 1.

A related type of information is obtained from biblical archaeology. The excavations and their interpretation provide interesting data on the way people lived. Information concerning ancient languages has also come from archaeological discoveries. Some material on biblical archaeology is found in the dictionaries listed above. Many books have been written on the topic; these three are among the most useful. Your professor may have additional suggestions.

Baker Encyclopedia of Bible Places: Towns and Cities, Countries and States, Archaeology and Topography. Grand Rapids: Baker, 1995.

Blaiklock, Edward M., and R. K. Harrison, eds. *The New Dictionary of Biblical Archaeology*. Grand Rapids: Zondervan, 1983.

Stern, Ephraim, ed. *The New Encyclopedia of Archaeological Excavations in the Holy Land*. 4 vols. New York: Simon and Schuster, 1993.

Step 6: Establish the Original Theological Meaning

In this step of exegesis the question is: What did the passage mean to those who first heard or read it? On the basis of the previous steps and informed by your own biblical and theological understanding, bring out the deeper meaning.

Once you have established a clear understanding of the theological meaning of the passage, you can read what commentators say, to check or confirm your conclusions. Now you should be ready to read others' opinions without danger of being carried away by the postures of scholars. To read commentaries before could prejudice the outcome of your research. Reading them now gives the opportunity of corroborating what you already know, of broadening your knowledge, or even of defending your position against that of other authors who do not see things as you do.

Step 7: Establish the Application for Today

Once the meaning for the people who received the message or sang the psalm or heard the prophecy has been determined, the basic biblical meaning can be extracted. The last step of exegesis applies theological meaning to today's church or individual Christian. This application forms the basis of preaching and teaching.

This step is difficult but necessary if Scripture is to speak to our times. This step of exegesis may not be required in a theoretical paper, but it is an integral part of biblical interpretation, especially for preaching.

By carefully following these seven steps of exegesis I can be reasonably sure of coming to a correct interpretation of Scripture. Naturally, biases and presuppositions can lead me astray. However, careful study of the Bible, starting from the text itself, allows the Bible to speak for itself, to tell me what it wants to say (exegesis), without having me read into it (eisegesis) what I would like it to say.

Presentation of Exegesis

Not all of the search and study undertaken in these seven steps of exegesis is reported. Much of what you do is important to your research but irrelevant to the reader. The written report will not contain the parsing of the verbs or a list of all 144 occurrences of *dechomai* in the New Testament.

In any exegetical study there must be sufficient detail to make clear to the reader how I came to certain conclusions. To ask the reader to accept by faith that I know what I am saying falls short of the rigor demanded of research. If the tense of the verb is important to the interpretation of the verse, the study must point that out and give a clear explanation of why it is important. If knowing Jewish marriage customs clarifies the passage, I must describe and document those customs. If an aspect of the climate explains something in the text, I must note it.

The written presentation may be made in seven parts: one for each of the steps. However, there may be little to say about some of these steps. Another possibility is to do a phrase-by-phrase commentary. It is easier to work in small units than to deal with a whole passage. A weakness of this system, however, is that it tends to blur the unity of the passage. A strength of this system is that it gives equal importance to all details in the passage being exegeted.

A better solution might be to divide the study into three sections. The first would be the introduction, stating the purpose of the research and giving the context of the text studied. The next section would provide a translation of the passage, with notes explaining how I arrived at that translation. The third would interpret the text, giving the theological meaning of the passage and its present application. I must present evidence of having answered all seven questions. The following outline, given as a model to Intermediate Greek students, illustrates this approach.

INTRODUCTION
Passage selected
Reasons for choosing this passage
Setting of the passage
Author
Date
Audience
Literary interrelations
Historical/geographical/socio-economic context

THE TEXT
    Translation of the passage with extensive information on:
    Textual problems
    Grammar and syntax
    Important words
INTERPRETATION
    Meaning for original readers
    Application for today's Christians
  BIBLIOGRAPHY

When we write exegetical papers we often need to quote Greek or Hebrew words. These may be transliterated (see a reasonable transliteration scheme in appendix B) or typed in the original language. WordPerfect™ and Microsoft Word™ have Greek and Hebrew fonts. You may also use the fonts that come with Bible software or download fonts from the Internet.

As was noted at the beginning of the chapter, exegesis as a form of research may be frowned on by some who think of research in terms of surveys, experiments, or archival searching. Nevertheless, an exegesis paper following the seven steps outlined in this chapter allows the exegete to show excellent research techniques and style. It also contributes to the fund of biblical knowledge. And if that is not research, what is?

Another special form of research is descriptive research. It will be discussed in chapter 14.

XIV | DESCRIPTIVE RESEARCH

Descriptive research does exactly what its name says: it describes, usually one or more characteristics of a group of people, technically called a population. This is not a literary or poetical description, but a concrete and concise depiction of reality. Sometimes the information gathered is strictly quantitative—numbers and percentages; other times it is qualitative, including the "why" along with the "how many." This chapter presents the steps of descriptive research, as well as techniques for conducting surveys and interviews.

Within the pastoral setting, descriptive research could portray a congregation: How many members there are, what age groups they belong to, what their professions and occupations are, whether they live in apartments or houses, how often they attend church, if they tithe, and so on. Descriptive research could also be employed to study the population of an area where a church is to be planted or the way pastors perceive the usefulness of their seminary training.

The purpose of descriptive research is to make reality known. On the basis of the description, conclusions may be reached and decisions made. In the times of the Roman Empire, the census was not merely intended to let Rome know how many citizens there were. On the basis of a census, taxes were levied and armies were organized. Today, descriptive research is used to find out how many people watch a certain television program in order to decide what the best airing time is. A marketing company of a particular soap product surveys a large group of teenagers to discover not only how many are washing their face with their product, but to determine the best way to get more of them to use this particular soap. Descriptive research on the preschool children in a certain town may be useful in deciding whether or not the school needs to add another classroom in the next three years.

Descriptive research may have first been used to document need for change by John Howard, who began to fret in 1773 over the inhumane conditions of the prisons in Bedford, England. In order to prove what he was saying, he traveled all over England, visiting jails and noting the exact number of prisoners, what crimes they had committed, the conditions under which they were held, and other matters concerning the prison system. After completing his descriptive study, he stood before the House of Commons and gave a detailed and precise report that became the basis for important prison reforms. Howard later compared English prisons with jails in other European countries. His book *The State of Prisons* (1777) was one of the first comparative-descriptive studies. After studying the prisons of the land, he went on to investigate the conditions in hospitals. In one of these places he contracted an illness and died, a martyr for research.

This interesting story aside, it is evident that the report Howard prepared did not resolve any problem. It only provided the information necessary to set change in motion. This is the usefulness of descriptive research.

In technical language, the purpose of descriptive research is to:

1. Collect detailed factual information that describes existing phenomena
2. Identify problems or justify conditions and practices
3. Make comparisons and evaluations
4. Determine what others are doing with similar problems or situations and benefit from their experience in making future plans and decisions[1]

Obtaining precise data is not always easy. A little boy, asked if he loves his mother, will normally answer: Yes! Human beings want to please the people who ask them questions. Personal observations may not provide accurate data either; what you see may be tainted by your personal bias. If neither respondent nor observer are trustworthy, how can you be sure you are really seeing all there is to see? Use as many different methods as possible to get information. To describe a congregation, get information from the church membership records, the church treasurer's records, the Sabbath or Sunday school attendance records, the lay ministries records, and any other records that may be appropriate. In addition, survey the members, getting specific information from them. Interview former pastors or other persons who might have important information. Finally, add personal observations. The secret for obtaining a complete and accurate description lies in using several approaches, tapping into different sources.

Descriptive research usually studies a situation at a given moment in time. A specialized type of descriptive research studies a person, case, or situation over time. A study of the growth of a church over ten years would be an example. Some descriptions over time may prove difficult or impossible for theology students, except as dissertations. See chapter 20 on D.Min. projects.

---

[1] Stephen Isaac and William B. Michael, *Handbook in Research Evaluation* (San Diego: EDITS, 1971), 18.

Steps in Descriptive Research

The descriptive research process may be divided into four steps: defining the objectives, designing the approach, collecting the data, and writing the results. Usually the first two steps take most of the time.

Defining the Objectives

Within the framework of the purpose of the study, what is the information to be obtained? And from whom is it to be obtained? What facts and characteristics are to be uncovered? These questions must be answered in order to accomplish the first step.

In research on the function of deacons in a church, the objective of the survey might be to discover who the deacons are—how old they are, where they live, where they work, how long they have been church members. One might also wish to find out what they do in the church—visit members, take care of the church property, keep order during services, etc.—and how they consider their responsibilities—whether they feel needed, adequately prepared, or satisfied. Knowing exactly what you need to find out is the foundation of good descriptive research.

Designing the Approach

Once you know what you need to know, the second step is to decide on the best way to obtain the different kinds of information. Personal interviews may be appropriate to gather some data. Other information is best obtained by using a questionnaire. Still other data can be obtained from records. Personal observation is valid as well.

For each of these different approaches a strategy must be developed. Will all of the deacons be interviewed? If not, how will I choose the ones who will be interviewed? When and where will I do the interviews? Will the survey of church members' impressions of the deacons' work be anonymous? How can I get the greatest number of members to reply to my survey? Techniques for surveying, sampling, and interviewing are important enough to be considered under separate headings.

Before designing my own instruments, strategies, and procedures, I must read widely, both on the topic or situation to be studied and on possible methodologies to use. For example, if I am planning to survey the personal devotional habits of young people, I should read everything written about the topic and especially look for studies already done about the devotional habits of young Christians. The *ATLA Index* (*Religion Index One*) is an excellent place to look for this information.

After extensive reading on the theory, the methodology, and the situation to be studied, consultation with the professor guiding the study is in order. Since some of the techniques of descriptive research are foreign to theological education, students should look for professors in education, sociology, or psychology who may be willing to assist in the process.

If at all possible, find instruments (collective name for surveys, questionnaires, interview outlines, etc.) that have already been prepared by a credible researcher. Finding them may take time, but preparing good ones will probably take longer. D.Min. projects, reported in *Research in Ministry* (part of the *ATLA Index*), should provide some examples.

Once the instruments have been designed, some form of validation is appropriate. A pilot study, using a small number of respondents, may be used to find out if the questions are well worded, clearly understandable, and easy to answer. A panel of experts might also be used to study the instruments and advise on their appropriateness. Even better, both methods can be employed.

Collecting the Data

Collecting the data is the exciting part of the research. After all the hard work of preparing, it is fun to send out questionnaires and get them back. It is interesting to go through the interview process. It is satisfying to finally be nearing the goal.

This elation, however, brings with it a major danger. You may trust your memory and not write down precisely and accurately the findings. It then becomes impossible to reconstruct the information obtained. The only antidote to this problem is to set up the easiest possible way to record in an organized and orderly fashion every piece of data. The importance of clear notes or recordings cannot be overemphasized.

Writing the Results

As in all other research papers, there must be an introduction. This gives the background, the definition of the problem, the purpose, the limitations and delimitations, and the definition of terms.

Following the introduction, a descriptive research paper or thesis needs to have what is termed a "review of literature." This section or chapter reports on the preparatory reading, both on the topic or population investigated (youth, deacons, women administrators, etc.), the methodology used (surveys, scales, ranking, etc.), and the theoretical framework, if appropriate.

The review of literature is followed by a section or chapter on the research method employed: How the questionnaire was developed, tested, and applied;

how the sampling was done; how the interview was designed and carried out. This description of the method explains to the reader how the research was accomplished. It helps the reader judge the quality of the study and may assist in future research design.

Then comes the description of the results. What was discovered? The topics are organized in some logical way and described in turn. Often the questions of the survey are taken one after another, or, if the questionnaire is long, by related groups of questions.

Finally, the whole process is summarized. On the basis of this summary, conclusions are drawn. Pastoral research usually ends with recommendations for action. Recommendations for further study may also be made.

The language of the report must be clear and precise. Generalities have no place. The following examples give precise data: how many, what percent. They also use language that only affirms what the subjects said—not what they are assumed to have done or believed.

> Nearly half of the 140 pastors surveyed (48.5 percent) said they had completed a four-year theology course, while 42 (30 percent) responded that they had taken a three-year course. Seventeen individuals (12 percent) reported completing a two-year course, while 13 of those surveyed (9.5 percent) stated that they had no college training before entering the ministry.
>
> In response to a question on their perception of the pastor's sharing of administrative responsibilities with the lay leaders, the largest group of elders (12, or 40 percent of the total of 30 elders) noted that the pastor shared well. The smallest group (4 elders, or 13.3 percent) stated that he did not share at all. Eight elders (26.6 percent) checked the answer "Undecided." Six elders (20 percent) did not reply. If one takes those who did not answer as being undecided, the number of elders who did not feel qualified to answer the question, or who had doubts about their pastor's sharing of responsibilities, was 14 (46.3 percent).

Sampling

When Gallup Polls wants to know which candidate the citizens are going to elect, they do not ask each one of the registered voters. They sample the population. That is, they poll a representative group. Regardless of the kind of instrument used to get information—survey, interview, checklist—sampling is a way to get a lot of information from not so many people.

When a seamstress wants to buy thread for a sewing project, she takes to the store a small piece of the cloth she needs to sew. That sample only shows the color. It does not show the pattern or the design of the material. For a sample to represent the total population—not just the color of the cloth—it must have all the characteristics of that population. A sample must be large enough to represent the population and it must contain the same types of people in the same proportion in which they appear in the total population. Representative, random, and cluster sampling are ways to get the information you need.

Representative Sampling

To represent the population, the sample must include all the different kinds of people in the group. And it must include them in the proportion in which they are found. Thus, a representative sample (often called stratified sample) will include men and women, old and young, rich and poor, black and white, and whatever other kinds of people are in the larger group. If there are more women than men in the church, the sample must contain more women. If there are more old ladies than young ladies, the sample must also represent this characteristic of the total group.

Random Sampling

Random sampling is a technique used to ensure—as far as possible—an unbiased representation of a population. Here "random" does not mean "chance." The researcher designs ways to achieve this by polling every tenth name on the list or interviewing every fourth candidate. However, before random sampling is applied, the population must be studied to ascertain that the method used guarantees, as nearly as possible, a representative sampling.

Random sampling can be applied to the total population. For example, every sixth member of the church—regardless of age, sex, or other factors—receives a questionnaire. Random sampling may also be used with predefined segments of the population, especially if the demographics of the population are important to the results of the study. Perhaps every sixth man between 20 and 40, every sixth woman between 41 and 60, and every sixth unmarried female receives a questionnaire. Random sampling avoids the possibility of choosing only one's friends (or enemies) to answer the questions. It can be a safeguard for the research and the researcher.

Statistical theory indicates the correct size of samples. You will find information on this in a statistics textbook. You can also get help from a statistician or professor of statistics. The rule of thumb is that the larger the population, the smaller the percentage of people who must be surveyed.

Cluster Sampling

Cluster sampling selects sample clusters or groups out of the population and studies all members of those groups. For example, Betty wants to study third-grade children in her city. She finds that there are 56 third-grade classes, of which 40 are in public schools, 10 are in church-related schools, and 6 are in private schools. She also notes that 25 have between 20 and 30 children, 15 have fewer than 15 children, 10 have between 31 and 40 children, and 6 have more than 40 third graders. Once the classrooms are divided into categories, she can randomly choose one room from each category. Betty will then study all the third graders in the clusters (classrooms) chosen.

This approach to sampling could be appropriate for studying churches, Bible classes, or young people's groups. Proximity of the subject makes the study easy to conduct. The dynamics of group interaction, the sharing in the study, may also enrich the study.

Surveys

Surveys have become increasingly popular in recent years. People are asked what kind of toothpaste they use, for which political candidate they will vote, or how they feel about interracial marriage. Some surveys are done orally—the poll on the street before elections. Some use questionnaires to which a person must respond in writing. All share the same intention: to obtain information. While information obtained from a questionnaire is extensive, it tends to be shallow. Many people are polled, but not at great depth. This type of research is called quantitative and depends to a great extent on numbers.

A well-prepared questionnaire can obtain data that describes reality. A poorly prepared one may be useless or, even worse, give distorted information. Preparing questionnaires that will elicit the information needed is difficult. Preparing questionnaires takes time and expertise. The tips given below can help you, but if you are serious about your research, please get help from a professional.

Tips for Preparing a Questionnaire

1. Know exactly what information you want to obtain. Know also what you are going to do with the information you get.
2. Make the questionnaire as short as possible. No one wants to take any more time than is absolutely necessary to answer questions. The chances of a questionnaire's being thrown in the waste basket increase in direct proportion to its length and complexity.
3. Ask only for information not available elsewhere. For example, do not ask members to give their address or date of baptism if the church clerk has that information. Ask only for what you need.
4. Be sure the topic of the survey is important enough to justify the respondents' time and effort to complete it. A survey on the local

church school will be more important to a mother of small children than a questionnaire about retirement homes.

5. Ask questions so that they elicit precise, factual data, rather than impressions or opinions. A question such as "How many hours a week do you read?" will get better information on reading habits than "Do you like to read?"

6. Formulate the questions in a clear, straightforward manner, with little possibility for misunderstanding. This will mean writing the questions, trying them out on people of similar background to those who will be surveyed, and rewriting until they are clear. Use language familiar to those who will be surveyed.

7. Put the items in a logical order. Make one thing naturally follow the other. People asked to answer a survey get frustrated when the questionnaire does not make sense to them. And frustrated people may throw the paper away or answer carelessly, rendering the results useless.

8. Make the format simple and convenient to answer. Doing this enhances the chances that respondents will complete the questionnaire accurately and promptly. Consideration for the respondent translates into better data for the researcher.

9. Give clear instructions for filling out the form. Start out the page with instructions on how to answer correctly. An example may be helpful to the respondents.

Survey Questions

Many kinds of questions appear in questionnaires. However, they can all be classified as open or closed.

Open Questions

An open question allows respondents to answer, without prompting, however they wish. Because answers vary so greatly, the tabulating of open answers is long and involved. However, if the survey is attempting to discover the favorite hymns of a congregation or the lay training most needed by the elders, the question has to be open, in order to allow real freedom.

For example, in a survey on theological education, respondents were asked: "What course or courses, which you did not study as part of your ministerial training, do you now wish you could have taken?" The responses were tabulated and ranked to provide the overall answer to the question.

Closed Questions

In a closed question, the answers are given; from these the respondent must choose. These questions are easy to answer, easy to correct, but the answers may not be totally accurate. If the options do not include all possibilities on the continuum, the respondent may not be able to give a correct response or may skip the question. An example of a closed question:

On the average, how much time do you spend each day in personal, private Bible study and reading? Do not count time spent in family worship or studying the children's Bible lesson.

( ) More than one hour a day
( ) From 45 minutes to one hour a day
( ) From 30 to 45 minutes a day
( ) From 15 to 30 minutes a day
( ) Less than 15 minutes a day

This question is worded in such a way that it is impossible to discover how many church members are not studying the Bible at all. To find that out—embarrassing as it may be to the members—one needs to add another category: ( ) No study at all.

Another form of closed question is the scale, which reduces the answer to a numerical value. For example, a question seeking to evaluate a certain aspect of a training program could offer these three options:

1= Very valuable
2= Of some value
3= Of little value

Respondents may be asked to agree or disagree with a statement. To the assertion "Deacons should give a good example by paying a faithful tithe," the options could be: (1) Disagree; (2) Not Sure; (3) Agree. Asked about the preparation of elders to lead the congregation, the options might be: (1) Not prepared; (2) Little prepared; (3) Acceptably prepared; (4) Well prepared; (5) Very well prepared. Usually these scales are prepared with an uneven number of options. The gradation must be clear and the continuum obvious.

Survey Returns

The ideal would be to have a 100 percent return, that is, to have every one of the questionnaires completed and returned in time for the tabulation. This rarely happens. Either a letter gets lost, or a respondent fails to return the paper, or a questionnaire is not correctly filled out—and the survey results give information on a limited part of the population.

A researcher must plan well and work hard in order to get maximum coop- eration. If the questionnaire is prepared according to the tips given above, if anonymity is guaranteed, if there is some type of follow-up, the possibility of reaching a fairly high level of response is good.

In most areas of the world, anonymity is an important factor in obtaining responses. People want their opinions to be known, but do not want others to know what they think. In one survey on a sensitive issue, respondents mailed their returns from other cities so that not even the postmark could give them away! Even in a small survey, it is wise to make provision for anonymity, thus providing respondents the chance to speak up without having to sign their name.

Student researchers may have difficulty getting responses to their surveys and questionnaires. For this reason, a cover letter written by their faculty sponsor— especially if he or she is well known—can be very helpful. This letter points out the importance of the study and urges people to participate. It can definitely raise the percentage of return.

Making it easy to return the survey is important. A sheet of paper given out to the congregation during the church service should be picked up as soon as it is filled out. If the people are merely asked to leave the papers on a table on the way out of church, they may forget. Pencils or pens should be provided. If the questionnaire is mailed, a stamped, self-addressed envelope encourages respon- dents to answer and mail the survey. (This, of course, functions only within the same country.)

Follow-up is not easy; it takes time and (sometimes) money. Insistence may be the only way to get a complete picture of reality. It is well known that the first ones to answer are those who are totally for or against something. Those who are moderate in their views may need to be prodded to divulge their opinions. Without a fair representation, the results could be skewed.

The second request for answers to a questionnaire may be general—"to all those church members who did not turn in the form last week"—but this system is not very accurate. Some could have forgotten what they did and turn in a sec- ond form! To be more precise, you need to know to whom the questionnaires were given and who did not respond. Using a code number on the form sent out will permit resending the survey to those who did not answer, without compro- mising anonymity. Consult with a statistician on how to accomplish this.

Using the best techniques should assure a good return—perhaps not 100 percent, but certainly well above 60 percent. Make an effort to achieve as high a percentage as possible. A student's advisor or thesis committee often determines the minimum percentage acceptable.

Interviews

Interviews permit a deeper and fuller understanding of the attitudes of a respondent. Whereas the survey may have room only for "agree" and "disagree" answers, an interview can tell the researcher why the person disagrees or agrees. Interviewing takes time but provides information not available through a survey.

In order for an interview to afford the most information possible, the interviewer should record the conversation. A cassette recorder may be used, but only with the express permission of the person interviewed. Usually, the person interviewed will be happier to have the conversation recorded than to risk distortion.

The interviewer should explain clearly what information is needed and why. Ethical behavior demands that the interviewer obtain permission to use materials from the interview in the research report. If the name of the interviewed person is given in the thesis, the person has the right to see and approve these portions before they are published. If the person interviewed is unhappy, far better to modify a quotation or remove it from the paper than to anger one who has cooperated in the study.

Go to the interview with a written outline of the questions to be asked. The conversation may depart from this outline, but at least you will have a framework for your interview. If several people are being interviewed, prepare a sheet of questions for each interview—with space for the answers. This will make it easy to organize the information obtained.

Interviews with a purpose, an outline, and a recording system will give good information. They should be interesting as well. For in-depth information on opinions and attitudes, interviews are superior to surveys. Because of the depth and volume of information obtained in an interview, the number of persons interviewed is much smaller than the number of those surveyed. This kind of research is called qualitative research.

Descriptive methods are often used in pastoral research. Knowing how to obtain and report information is vital to the process. Tables and graphs can enhance your report. See chapter 18 for information on how to create and use them.

Another kind of pastoral research is program development. It is described in chapter 15.

XV | PROGRAM DEVELOPMENT AS RESEARCH

Program development, also called product or curriculum development, is another specialized form of research. This chapter explains the application of this type of research to the pastoral setting.

In program development research, the researcher determines the need for a program, establishes its theoretical basis, sets its objectives, designs the program or curriculum, implements it, and evaluates the results. For example, Pastor Bill might see a need for a new series of Bible lessons for young people coming to church from a well-to-do, secular background. He will first document the need for this type of special approach and study the young people involved. Then he will consult educational theory concerning the learning process. Pastor Bill must give careful consideration to the content of the series, following the best rules of hermeneutics and biblical interpretation. Once the series of lessons has been prepared, he will use the lessons with his young people. Then he must evaluate the whole process.

Steps in Program Development

For the development of a program, series of lessons, or workshop to be considered as research, specific steps must be followed. The eight steps presented here are designed especially for pastors.

1. Define the Problem

Define the problem. What is wrong or needs fixing? Describe the group that needs help, for whom you are preparing the program. Pastor Bill needs to know how many well-to-do, secular youth are in this group he wishes to reach, how old they are, where they attend school, how many have any church connection, and what their home situation is. Even more specifically, what evidence does he have that this class is needed?

Documenting a need involves descriptive research. Techniques described in chapter 14 can be used to obtain this kind of information. If a program is to fit the needs of a church, the place to begin could be a church assessment.[1]

2. Set Goals and Objectives

The first step describes reality. This second step describes the ideal. The goals show the final destination, without which there can be no progress. Goals also serve as a norm against which to measure performance.

Objectives—the smaller and measurable goals along the way—must be expressed as outcomes. The pastor's objective is not to teach the young people something, but to have them demonstrate they have learned something. They may acquire knowledge, understanding, skills, attitudes, or appreciation. The question becomes: What will these young people know, feel, and do because of having followed this series? How will they show the knowledge, understanding, skills, and attitudes they have acquired?

The setting of goals and objectives is done in consultation with experts and with those involved. Thus, the young people themselves, as well as the pastor and local church officers will need to participate in determining what the result of the series of lessons—in the thinking, feeling, and doing of the young people—should be. The first step in setting objectives is for the people involved to write down all the possible desirable outcomes, regardless of importance. Once this brainstorming is done, the objectives may be prioritized, that is, ranked according to perceived importance.

Although they do express positive outcomes, objectives such as the following are very general and not helpful to measure achievement:

The young people will know the doctrines of the church.

The young people will be integrated into the life of the church.

Questions arise: How will I know that the young people know the doctrines? How will I know they are integrated? How will this be visible? More measurable objectives would read somewhat as follows:

Young people will evidence knowledge of the doctrines of the church by passing an examination (or by preparing an outline, or by making a presentation).

Young people will evidence integration into the life of the church by participating in at least two activities every month.

Once set by the group, the objectives should be validated by the pastor (researcher) and other experts, such as experienced youth pastors of another church or seminary professors. One could determine that objectives considered acceptable by four of the five consulted would be retained.

---

[1]See Christian Schwarz, *Natural Church Development: A Guide to Eight Essential Qualities of Healthy Churches* (Carol Stream, IL: ChurchSmart Resources, 1996). ChurchSmart publishes a variety of materials for church assessment.

3. Review the Literature

In this step the researcher must establish the theoretical basis for the project. The review of literature should generally include three aspects: (a) a theoretical basis for the program; (b) a study of other, similar programs; (c) an examination of the content of the program.

Theoretical Basis

A study of the theoretical basis and parameters for the program assures that the series of lessons or workshop will meet the needs of the group involved. In the case of the program designed for the young people, the theoretical basis might include information on the specific type of young people to be reached, the emotional needs of people of that age, and the learning styles of young people. This information is mostly drawn from sociological, psychological, and educational research.

Similar Programs

Books do not yield as much information on the development and implementation of programs as does the periodical literature. Examine *Religion Index One*, *Research in Ministry*, *ATLA Index*, and ERIC for sources. If the program being developed is entirely new, there may be little information on what others have already tried. Although little may be found, the search must be made and documented.

Content of the Program

The educational, psychological, and sociological dimensions only enhance the content. Careful study must be made of the content of the series or workshop. Other curricula or programs need to be examined. A series of Bible lessons demands a biblical-theological study. A workshop in interpersonal relations must be based on the literature of that discipline. A course in home nutrition must be based on the latest and best materials in that field. Whatever the area, the content must be carefully studied.

4. Design the Program

Once the contents of the program have been determined—on the basis of the objectives chosen and the theoretical literature studied—the program can be designed. The nature of the learners, the material to be presented, and the setting in which the learning experience will take place must be taken into consideration in the design. Since program development is being done as research, all of these aspects must be documented.

Designing the program includes deciding on the length and frequency of the meetings, the audiovisuals, the handouts, as well as the speakers or presenters. The program designer determines the steps to be taken in preparation for the meetings—such as obtaining permission from the church board, advertising, and making physical arrangements for the meetings. Even the evaluation, which will take place after the program is completed, must be designed at this time. Nothing is left to chance. Everything is planned, organized, and written down.

5. Prepare Materials and Resources

Write out lectures or talks, even if you are used to preaching with only a brief outline before you. The written version of the presentations will become part of the research. Prepare the visual aids and handouts; they, too, will go into the paper, usually in the appendix. A good rule to follow is to include in the written paper everything someone else would need to replicate the program. Make all necessary arrangements for additional resources, human or material. Get a second opinion from a trusted mentor.

6. Implement the Program

After going through all the preparatory steps—permission from the church board, presentation to the church members, advertising, etc.—present the program according to your plan. Usually it is wise to make a first presentation on a reduced scale, in a small church, or with a small group. Keep a journal, complete with dates, times, and names, as well as impressions. Take note of everything that happens during the sessions. This information will be useful in evaluating the program and in presenting the written report.

7. Evaluate the Program

The evaluation must be multifaceted: several kinds of evaluation made by different kinds of people. For example, the young people involved in the Bible-lesson program could be surveyed to find out how they feel about the program. A doctrinal test given before and after the program could give objective information on acquisition of knowledge. The church officers can be interviewed. The attendance of young people at church meetings and functions can be monitored to see if the program made any difference. Finally, Pastor Bill is entitled to make a subjective evaluation of what has happened.

Successful evaluation must be planned early and with care. Questions must be asked thoughtfully. If people think the pastor wants to hear that the program was successful, they may say exactly that, regardless of how they perceive what happened. Design evaluation questions that minimize this danger. For example,

rather than asking whether they liked the program or not, ask what the participants liked most and least, or what should be added or deleted the next time the
program is presented.

Program development demands weeks and months of reading, planning,
preparation, presentation, and evaluation. It is, therefore, difficult to do for a class
paper. Program development is more appropriate for a thesis or major project,
planned to take a longer period and under the direct supervision of a thesis or dissertation adviser.

After the program has been produced, presented, and evaluated, it must be
written up in a formal report. The next section deals with the writing and organization of the project or dissertation.

Organizing and Writing the Report

The organization of the paper will closely parallel the steps of the research.
Yet, a conventional report of program development research has five chapters.

The first chapter—the introduction—should contain the same elements as
any other introduction: the background, the statement of the problem, the purpose of the paper, the methodology (or overview of the paper), and items such as
the definition of terms, limitations, and delimitations. The need and the objectives, as expressed in steps 1 and 2, must also be included. (In a short paper, this
section may be called INTRODUCTION and not have the status of a chapter.)

Chapter 2 is a review of literature that includes the material in step 3. The
books and articles mentioned in this chapter will not include all of those consulted. Report only those items most closely related to the topic. If the program
has an extensive biblical or theological basis, this may need to be written up in a
separate chapter. On the other hand, if the biblical and/or theological basis is very
evident in the talks or sermons of the program itself, and footnoting is done there,
the supervising professor may consider its exposition in that part of the paper to
be sufficient.

Chapter 3 describes the group for whom the program was designed.

The development of the program is presented in chapter 4. This includes a
report of everything from setting the goals, through obtaining the church board's
permission, to the presentation of the program. Actual dates and places are
reported. People participating are usually not mentioned by name but by position. The outline of events for the program is given. The program is evaluated.
Reference is made to the items to be presented in the appendixes. This section is
a complete history of the entire program and could be divided into three parts:
preparation, presentation, and evaluation.

Chapter 5 contains the summary and conclusions. It may also provide suggestions for future implementation of such a program or for further research. Should the introduction not be given chapter status, the summary and conclusions will not have a chapter number either.

The appendixes present a variety of materials, each in its own section. For example, there will be correspondence, invitations and publicity, the content of the presentations, illustrations (including PowerPoint and overheads), handouts, and evaluation questionnaires. Because the material in the appendixes is vital to replicating the project, they must be complete, well organized, and carefully labeled.

The bibliography is the last item in the paper. However, last is not least; the bibliography may be the first thing a reader peruses.

Program development can be very useful in pastoral work for preparing workshops, special weeks, weekend programs, and lessons series. The techniques described in this chapter are helpful in preparing materials for many different groups within the church. Naturally, in the church setting they may not be followed as precisely as these steps for a research project. However, following the suggestions given here will enhance the pastor's presentation of special programs in the church.

Chapters 13 through 15 have dealt with special forms of research: exegesis, descriptive research, and program development. Chapter 16 deals with the case-study method of research, an alternative form of research often used in practical or applied theology.

XVI | THE CASE STUDY AS RESEARCH

Another method of research, often used in law and the social sciences, is the case study. This kind of research study is also prominent in advanced levels of pastoral studies, especially in pastoral care and counseling classes. This chapter contains a minimal description of the social science case study method and a detailed explanation of the pastoral-theological case study.

The Case Study in the Social Sciences

A case study in social science research involves an intensive study of the background, current status, and environmental interaction of a given social unit: an individual, a group, an institution, or a community. An example of this kind of study would be a school counselor's in-depth research on a pupil with a learning disability or the study of a family unit undergoing counseling.

The in-depth investigation of the case study results in a complete, well-organized picture of the person or group studied. The scope of the investigation may be limited in time, or it may follow the development of the person or group studied for weeks or even years. It may concentrate on specific factors, or it may cover all elements and events. In comparison with the survey, which usually examines a small number of variables in a large group of people, the case study examines a large number of variables in one person or one small group.

Case studies are useful as background information in planning for investigations: They bring to light variables that need further study. Case studies often provide hypotheses that guide additional research. They also provide useful anecdotes to illustrate generalized statistical findings. However, as case studies deal with individuals or small groups, they may not be representative of the total population. They do not lend themselves to generalization. In addition, case studies are often vulnerable to subjectivity. This happens because the cases chosen may be dramatic or highly emotional, or the researcher may become personally involved with the subject or subjects being described, thus failing to view the whole process in an objective manner.[1]

---

[1]The section on the case study in the social sciences is based on Stephen Isaac and William Michael, *Handbook in Research and Evaluation* (San Diego: Knapp, 1971), 20; see also Robert K. Yin, *Case Study Research: Design and Method*, rev. ed. (Newbury Park, CA: Sage Publications, 1989).

The Case Study in Pastoral Research

In pastoral research, the case study is similar to what was described above. It studies one situation, the activities of one group, or one incident. Naturally, a pastor's case study looks at an event or person or situation related to ministry. It must analyze the background of the incident, all of the factors that contribute to the interplay and interaction, and what actually happens.

A pastoral case study is different in that it brings into the study a biblical-theological point of view. Such a case study begins with a narration and ends in a theological understanding of how such an event should be handled. It is a tool for reflection. Since the case is usually taken from the pastoral researcher's own ministry, it leads to self-analysis and assists in establishing theological guidelines for handling future episodes of the same nature.

The case-study method for pastoral-theological reflection described in this chapter is used extensively in doctoral programs in ministry. The version here described owes much to the Doctor of Pastoral Studies Program (DPS) of the South East Asia Graduate School of Theology (SEAGST).[2]

Definition of Terms

Some terms are used in a technical or specific sense. Definition of these words or phrases is important.

Case

A case is an objective description of a pastoral situation or relationship about which theological reflection will be done. The written case is the basis of a case study. "Fructuoso" (in this chapter) is an example of a written case.

Case Study

A case study is the process of pastoral-theological reflection about a given case. Based on the original case, it analyzes, reflects, theologizes, and prescribes action. As far as this book is concerned, the case study is a written paper, the length of which is determined by the complexity of the case, the level of the student, and the demands of the professor. The fact that the word "study" is used to describe this way of thinking suggests method, effort, and discipline in reflection.

Case-Study Method

The case-study method is a way of doing pastoral-theological reflection. Such a method normally starts from a case and proceeds, via critical analysis of the data,

---

[2]Special thanks to Tjaard Hommes, former director of the DPS program for SEAGST. The case-study method is the only one accepted by SEAGST for the DPS dissertation (*Handbook* [Manila: Association for Theological Education in South East Asia, 2000], 123).

to a constructive interpretation of the pastoral-theological issues implied in the case. It culminates in guidelines for action.

Purpose of the Case-Study Method

The case-study method is used in pastoral education to enable pastors to enhance their critical and creative ability for doing theology. Being able to *do* theology in ministry helps answer the nagging question "Why?" Why do I direct worship in this particular way? Why do I handle a broken relationship in the congregation in the way I do? Why do I preach in a certain way? It also helps answer the question "How?" How should I do this better?

The method helps pastors (and student pastors) learn from a situation, either their own or someone else's. The case-study method is a tool to enhance awareness of the individuals involved, of the situation, of the message of Scripture, of the pastor's own religious tradition. Doing a case study is doing theology—applying God's word to everyday life.

This way of doing theology, of thinking theologically, is not simply a tool. It is an experience. However, it is a disciplined experience. Re-living and re-thinking a case brings theology out of experience. The result is a theologically sound, contextually viable, pastoral action.

Parts of a Case Study

The case study for pastoral theology is divided into four major areas: observation, analysis, interpretation, and action. In a case study, these areas will be chapters; in a dissertation, they will be parts, divided into chapters.

Observation

The first activity involved in developing a case study is careful observation of the case. This demands effort to listen, to see, to hear, and even to experience. Everything that is said and done in relation with the incident or case must be noted. Close observation is the basis for understanding.

Once a case has been observed, it should be written down. Simple sentences that clearly tell the story must be used. The words, activities, and gestures of the people involved are written into the case. What a person *said* should be recorded; not how the researcher thinks the person felt. Body language—a raised eyebrow, a frown—is also recorded for later analysis and interpretation. Observable facts and activities are written into the case; they will form the basis of the study.

Details are important in so far as they are related to the incident. If a detail does not appear in the case, the feelings it suggests cannot be analyzed; the theology it calls for cannot be interpreted. On the other hand, irrelevant items cloud the picture. For example, a lady's wearing a red dress may not be essential—unless the case deals with the elder's feelings about a woman who wears a red dress the day she has the Scripture reading in church! The rule is to include all details necessary to the case and exclude all those that do not explain what people do or think.

To protect the privacy of the individuals involved in the case, personal names are usually changed. No one should be hurt or embarrassed by the contents of a case study. The precise town where the case took place may not be mentioned, but the general location must be given because of the importance of socio-cultural factors involved in the case.

An introductory section containing important background information often precedes the written case. Of special interest is the writer's relation to the case. Other matters, such as location and time, may also be included.

In a paper or thesis, the case is presented in double-space format, with numbered lines. The following example comes from Mindanao, in the southern Philippines.[3]

FRUCTUOSO

1   Fructuoso did not receive much of an education. His parents were poor and
2   his home *barrio* was far from a town where a government high school operated.
3   But he could read and write. He used to say that this was almost enough to sat-
4   isfy his hunger for knowledge and truth.
5   When the second world war broke out, Fructuoso joined the guerilla resist-
6   ance movement. Since most of the guerillas had only bolo-knives for weapons,
7   many of them, Fructuoso included, relied heavily on *anting-anting*[4] for protec-
8   tion, defense, and survival. Fructuoso testified that these amulets, claimed to have
9   originated from the spirits, were powerful and effective. He claimed that he sur-
10   vived the war largely because of their power. He often expressed his belief in these
11   supernatural beings.
12   After the war Fructuoso became a Seventh-day Adventist Christian. The
13   American pastor, who instructed him in preparation for baptism, told Fructuoso
14   that although the Bible speaks of devils and demons, the spirits he feared were
15   mostly a product of human imagination and animistic influences. So, when
16   Fructuoso decided to be baptized, he abandoned his amulets by throwing them into
17   the sea. He ended his allegiance to his *abyan*[5] and devoted his loyalty to Jesus Christ.

[3]Reuel Almocera, "Christianity Encounters Filipino Spirit-world Beliefs: A Case Study" (D.P.S. dissertation, SEAGST, 1990). This dissertation is available at the library of the Adventist International Institute of Advanced Studies, Silang, Cavite, Philippines, or from the James White Library, Andrews University, Berrien Springs, MI.

[4]*Anting-anting* is a talisman, usually a piece of paper soaked in "holy oil" inside a small bottle. This is tied to the user's body and is carried by the individual most of the time. For a more extensive treatment of the subject, see Ben E. Garcia, *Diwata ng Anting-Anting* (Cebu City: Sto. Rosario Parish, 1982).

[5]An *abyan* is believed to be the patron spirit or the supernatural being that gives magical powers to the *anting-anting*.

18 Fructuoso's economic life flourished after his baptism. He transformed a
19 choice piece of land into a coconut plantation and, by a moderate standard, he
20 was rich. He became influential in the community and in the church. In fact, he
21 was a church elder for twenty years.
22 At sixty years of age Fructuoso contracted a strange disease. He went to the
23 best hospitals and secured the services of notable physicians. He submitted
24 himself to modern diagnostic tests. He was declared normal and healthy.
25 Fructuoso knew, however, that something was wrong. More than once his
26 stomach bloated when the tide was high. Besides, his stool looked like mud,
27 smelled like rotten fish, and yielded unidentifiable creeping creatures.
28
29 Unsatisfied with the physicians' diagnosis, Fructuoso consulted a *man-*
30 *anambal* [6] who explained that an unidentified sorcerer had cast a spell on
31 Fructuoso, causing his disease. The *mananambal* suggested that the spirits
32 must be appeased or Fructuoso would die. He prescribed a ritual that included
33 the sacrifice of three pigs.
34 Fructuoso solicited some counsel from his fellow church members regarding
35 the prescription of the *mananambal*. Some encouraged him not to submit to such
36 a ritual. But some of the older church members urged him to go ahead; however,
37 they counseled him to first resign from his eldership.
38 Finally, Fructuoso went through the ritual. Soon after, he got well. After
39 attending church services in other places far from his home for some months, he
40 resumed regular church attendance despite the accusing looks of some members.

Analysis

Once the case has been written out, the next step is to carefully analyze the
events, interactions, and reactions of the person or persons involved in the case.
Of special importance are the views expressed about issues or conflicts. Obviously,
the work done at this stage presupposes a well-written case that includes all the
elements on which to base an analysis.

The task of analysis is to understand, not to make judgments regarding the
rightness or wrongness of anyone's actions. Analysis and understanding must be
achieved through critical thinking and perceptiveness. Key questions to be asked
in the analysis of the case are:

- What kind of dynamics affect the way people think and feel, about
  themselves, about others, about life?
- What kind of views, feelings, relationships, interactions, reactions,
  expectations, and priorities seem to motivate the persons involved?

---

[6]A *mananambal* is a practitioner of the spirit world for healing and casting out spirits. He is believed
to be able to heal because of his own powerful contact with the spirit world.

- What kind of power plays, external influences, likes or dislikes, self-understandings or misunderstandings seem to color the case?
- What kind of psychological, social, cultural, political, economic, spiritual, and theological factors seem to play a role in the case?

The analysis is a description of the factors that make people think and act the way they do. The analysis must be done critically, yet with imagination. It must look behind the words used to the feelings expressed. The analysis must be aided by disciplines such as sociology and psychology. The analysis takes into account those local, cultural values that shape life and give it structure. It also values the theological understanding of the people involved in the case.

The research for the analysis of the case is done in the areas of local history, sociology, psychology, religion, values, and more. Some of the information may be obtained from one's own experience as well as the experience of others who know the situation where the case took place. However, a great deal of research must be done in the library. One must investigate what others have thought and written about the dynamics seen in the case. At this point, the research procedure is the same as that described throughout this book.

In Fructuoso's case, the most obvious societal factors had to do with beliefs regarding the spirit world, illness, and healing. Also important was the American pastor's worldview that clashed with the local understanding.

Interpretation

The third activity, called interpretation, has a vertical dimension—it involves interpreting the case in the light of theology. The key question is: What do the Bible, theology, and the church's tradition and doctrine say about the case? Of prime importance in the interpretation is the theology of the case: What is biblically, theologically right or wrong about the issue?

The interpretation must be based on Scripture and informed by the study of the Christian faith and tradition. The writings of theologians, the church's teachings, and the church's practice must be taken into account. In addition, the insight of pastoral counselors, the research of psychologists or sociologists of religion, and the comments of students of relationships between church and culture should be explored as sources of materials contributing to the interpretation.

In Fructuoso's case the theological issue was evil spirits. Do they exist? What or who are they? How powerful are they? What does the Bible say about them? How do Christians relate to the evil powers?

Some cases are very complex and bring up many theological issues. To deal with all of them may force the writer to be superficial. To choose the most important and to focus on it is the better part of valor and intelligence. The questions asked in narrowing and delimiting a research topic may well be applied here.

Action

The fourth activity is that of action planning. Here one evaluates any action already taken and outlines appropriate future pastoral strategies for responding to the case.

The strategy should include not only what one proposes to do but also the rationale for choosing that strategy. The strategy planned must be realistic, contextual, and appropriate to the local situation. Furthermore, it must be correct in the light of principles derived from the research of the interpretation section.

The key questions to ask are: Which action is most appropriate and creative in the light of Scriptures, Christian faith and tradition, and the local situation? Why is this course of action best? These questions must be answered with great pastoral creativity based on theologically sound principles.

In a real-life situation involving a complex case, more than one action plan might be possible—or even desirable. However, a case-study writer should resist the temptation to deal with all likely action strategies. In the normal case study a student should pursue only one action plan in response to the key issue or problem of the case. Alternative suggestions could be mentioned, but need not be developed. If the case describes pastoral action already accomplished, what has been done might be discussed and evaluated.

The Fructuoso case concluded with a plan for giving biblically sound teaching on the spirit world, with emphasis on their reality and Christ's power over them. The action proposed a Christian exorcism ceremony, in which lay leaders and pastors would participate to show Christ's triumph over evil spirits.

Writing the Case Study

Writing a case study is much the same as writing a research paper. The normal methodology for research is used. The format for research papers, as described in this book, is employed. While following academic rigor, the case study provides some room for creativity and imagination.

The four activities described above form the outline for the written case study. Class papers and doctoral theses do, however, have differences between them.

Case-Study Papers

The written case—the product of *observation*—together with the introduction (purpose, background, etc.) become the first chapter in the case study. The case will probably be no more than two pages (double spaced). Each line is numbered, to facilitate reference to it in later parts of the paper. Names of places and people must be disguised to preserve the confidentiality of those involved.

The *analysis*, a study of the horizontal dimensions of the case—socio-cultural, psychological, economic, and political factors involved—constitutes the second chapter of the case study. It is written as a research paper, with subheadings as needed to organize the material. Footnotes are also used to document information brought in from sources other than the case itself or the imagination of the researcher. For example, the case from the Philippines might require an explanation of a Filipino value. Information on that way of thinking might be gleaned from the journal *Philippine Values Digest* and would need to be footnoted.

The format of the *interpretation*, which is chapter 3, is similar to that of the second chapter. Its content is different, in that it looks at the vertical dimensions—the theological, biblical, church-related aspect of the question. Again, footnoting should be used to reference biblical, theological, or church polity sources.

The final section of the case study is the *action*. It is prefaced by a synthesis/summary of the analysis and interpretation, which serves as the basis for the action. This summary brings into focus the factors affecting the case and establishes the appropriate theological response. It is also useful for those who only read introduction, summary, and conclusions of research work. The action plan uses an essay format and describes pastoral action already accomplished and yet to be done. An outline format (see chapter 4) may be used if a procedure is outlined.

The bibliography presents a list of materials consulted, whether quotations or citations from the items were used or not. The purpose of this list is not only to impress the professors and free one's self from charges of plagiarism, but also to provide future researchers with a starting point for their endeavors.

Case-Study Dissertations

When a case study is developed into a dissertation for a professional doctorate in theology, the parts can be outlined as follows.

Part One: Presentation

Chapter 1. Introductory remarks and the written case—the product of *observation*—become the first chapter in the case study. The case will probably be no more than two pages (double space). Each line is numbered, to facilitate reference to it in later parts of the paper.

Chapter 2. Introduction, containing pastoral theological issues, methodology, delimitations, significance, definition of terms (if needed), and descriptive outline.

Part Two: Analysis

The *analysis*, a study of the socio-cultural, psychological, economic, and political factors involved in the case, may have as many chapters as needed to discuss the different problems. "Fructuoso" had two chapters: socio-cultural and psychosocial dynamics, and religious dynamics.

Part Three: Interpretation

The *interpretation* studies the theological, biblical, church-related aspect of the question. The number of chapters depends on the number of issues investigated. No more than three chapters should be allowed. "Fructuoso" had a chapter on spirits and demons in the Bible and a chapter on healing rituals.

Part Four: Action

The *action* section of the study is prefaced by a synthesis/summary of the analysis and interpretation, which serves as the rationale for the action. This summary brings into focus the factors affecting the case and establishes the appropriate theological response. This section usually has two chapters.

Bibliography and appendixes (as needed) close the study.

To summarize, the case-study method requires observation of a situation, analysis of what is happening, interpretation of the dynamics of the case in the light of the Bible and Christian faith-tradition, and a plan for action, dealing with the key issue or problem. When all of these parts are carefully put together, this practical way of doing theology becomes a method of research.

Chapters 1 through 12 gave general instructions concerning research thinking and writing. Chapters 13 through 16 presented specific—and slightly different—research methods, especially designed for pastors and theology students. Chapter 17 deals with two more variations on the theme of research in religion.

XVII | MISCELLANEOUS THEOLOGICAL WRITING

In addition to the research and exegesis papers that are required as part of theological education, professors may request papers that relate theology to the practice of ministry. These are often called papers on theological issues in ministry. In addition, professors commonly assign critical reviews of books or articles. This chapter deals with these types of writing.

Papers on Theological Issues in Ministry

A paper on a theological issue in ministry is in some ways similar to a research paper in theology. There is, however, one important difference. A theological research paper is generally theoretical. A theological issue in ministry study, on the other hand, applies the results of the study of the theological issue to a human reality, usually to a situation in the pastor's own ministry. It is research applied to ministry.

The Usefulness of Papers on Issues in Ministry

Throughout theological training, papers on theological issues in ministry are helpful to students. Writing them helps you gain a broader and deeper knowledge of theology. The exercise equips you for better, more thoughtful, and more creative ministry. In addition, the information and insights gathered can be useful to help other pastors and churches minister more effectively. The study of theological issues in ministry is designed to help writers develop skills in: (a) accurate and objective observation, (b) imaginative analysis, (c) theological reflection, (d) statement of a pastoral-theological point of view, (e) planning effective pastoral strategies, and (f) writing all of the above.

A major study of the theological and practical implications of an issue in ministry can become a dissertation for a professional degree in theology (D.Min. or D.P.Th). See chapter 20.

Writing a Paper on a Theological Issue in Ministry

The basic rules on researching, organizing, and writing papers, as they appear in this book, are followed. All aspects of format and documentation must also be respected. The parts of the paper are the same: preliminary pages, introduction, chapters of the body, summary and conclusion, and bibliography.

The study of a theological issue in ministry is a careful analysis of a particular aspect or problem encountered in a specific situation. For example, in a certain church, some members may find it offensive to have laypersons preach because, they say, the pulpit is sacred and only an ordained minister should occupy it. The issue is practical, but since the reason given is theological, the concern takes on theological dimensions. To solve the dilemma, you will need to carefully study the biblical passages bearing on the topic. You will also want to examine the history of lay preaching, especially in your own denomination, and the writings of church leaders on the topic. You will also take into account the cultural situation of the specific church. After careful consideration of the theoretical bases for what should or should not be done, you will come to a Bible-based, theologically informed conclusion. After that, you will draw conclusions and suggest an action plan. In some ways this type of study is similar to a case study, but the case is not spelled out in detail.

Parts of a Study on a Theological Issue in Ministry

The introduction must include the background of the problem, with an identification of the theological issue involved. Do not give the names of people involved, although they might be at the center of the predicament. If the issue discussed is very sensitive, it may be best not even to specifically identify the church. People must be protected by proper anonymity.

The body of the paper will contain the theoretical foundation for the application to ministry. The number of sections or chapters will depend on the topic. Areas to be researched are normally the biblical and theological. In addition, there may be sections on the history of a doctrine or idea, and on the church's stance on it. If psychological or sociological factors need to be taken into account, they must also be discussed.

The final section of the paper, corresponding to the "Summary and Conclusions" of a regular research paper, is called "Application to Ministry" and should be made up of three parts: (a) a brief summary or synthesis of the theological discussion, (b) the writer's own conclusion on the topic, and, based on these, (c) a suggested course of pastoral action to apply the conclusion to a real situation in ministry. Depending on the length, these parts may be sections in a chapter or separate chapters.

Individual professors may give further information regarding their own requirements for pastoral theology papers. In any case, they are the final authority on your work.

The Critical Review

In today's world, so many books are written and published that I cannot hope to read everything, even in my own field. In order to have an idea of what the others are about, I can read book reviews. They give the thrust of the work, an evaluation of its contents, and an assessment of its importance.

Professors often assign critical book reviews to force students to read carefully and write thoughtfully. In some seminars, students read different books, then report on them in class, so the group benefits, almost as if each had read every item.

Questions to Be Answered

By critical review we mean, not a destructive criticism of the author and his or her ideas, but a careful analysis of the work. A critical review attempts to answer at least seven different questions:

1. **What** is the basic thrust of the author's work?
2. **Why** does the author say what he or she says?
3. **To whom** is the writing directed and for what purpose?
4. **For whom or what** (or against whom or what) does the author stand?
5. **How well** has the author met his or her own objectives?
6. **How** does this work compare with other writings?
7. **What** is the reviewer's opinion of the work?

Writing the Review

Preparing a book review entails reading, taking notes, evaluating what has been read, and writing out a summary, assessment, and comments concerning the book or article.

A student's book review should contain four main parts: (1) a complete bibliographical entry; (2) information regarding the author, his or her academic training, position, and other books authored; (3) a summary of the book which, depending on the length of the review, should be not shorter than one paragraph or longer than two hundred words; and (4) an evaluation of the book.

The format of the bibliographical entry is the same as is used in a bibliography. Complete instructions on preparing this entry appear in chapter 5.

Information on the author may be obtained from the book itself, from biographical files many libraries keep, and from other sources, such as those mentioned in chapter 7. *Religion Index One* or *ATLA Index* is also a good source of information. Search by author to bring up the articles the person has written, as well as reviews of books he or she has published. These listings let you know how much he or she has written, on what topics, and how his or her books have been received.

The summary should synthesize the thrust of the book and its main arguments. Take care not to distort the emphasis given by the author. The length of the summary will depend, not only on the length of the material, but on the complexity of its contents. Try to keep the summary to three or four paragraphs.

Evaluation

The evaluation of the book should be made first of all on the basis of the author's own objectives, as stated in the introduction. This mandates a careful reading of the introduction or preface. If the author said this book was a "simple sketch of the doctrine of the immortality of the soul," he should not be faulted for omitting a record of the theological controversies of the Middle Ages on the subject. Likewise, if an author states that the book deals with New Testament Christology, she will not be expected to deal with the topic in the subapostolic era.

The evaluation is often based on comparison. The content of a religious work may rightfully be evaluated by the Bible. It is correct to point out agreements with biblical teaching and deviations therefrom. However, this must be done carefully, with due documentation, and recognizing that the differences may be in matters of interpretation and presuppositions. At times it is appropriate to compare the book or article with another item written by the same author. This comparison points out differences, similarities, and changes over time. A book or article review may compare the work of one author to that of another on the same topic. When making comparisons, one must describe the two concepts or items, then compare them. It is not enough to merely note that they are different.

A critique must document the author's statements, giving the page where the item was found. Sometimes a review quotes paragraphs that show the author's position. Be sure to keep in mind the author's context in order not to distort the ideas.

Although one may disagree with the author and with the position he or she espouses, the language of a book or article review must be courteous. A well-documented analysis will be more convincing than a heated, emotional tirade. The language of a review written for a class assignment should be similar to that of research—cool, calm, and collected. Think of meeting the author of the book at a professional meeting and having him say in dismay, "So are you the reviewer who hit me so hard?"

Questions to Guide Evaluation

In addition to the broad questions suggested at the beginning of this section, the ten queries listed below may guide critical reading of books and articles, as well as papers, for which the list was originally prepared.[1]

1. Is the subject vital? If so, to whom? What difference will it make ten years from now?
2. Is the subject too broad or too broad for the author? Is it too shallow, too restricted?
3. Is the author straightforward? Does he announce his bias? His limitations? His intentions?
4. In the introduction, are the purpose of the study and the statement of the problem clear?
5. Is the presentation clear and logical? Is the sequence natural? Are there missing points? Are the sections clear and self-contained?
6. Is the research reliable? Does anything indicate you cannot fully trust this paper? Do you feel the author really looked everywhere she possibly could and reported accurately and without bias?
7. What does the use of footnotes show? Are there too many notes? Too few? Are they from old sources? All from similar sources? Or from the same sources? Is the form clear and consistently used?
8. Does the bibliography tell you something additional about the paper? What type of sources are used? Scholarly or not? Is the form correct? Can you tell whether the author is using primary sources? General sources? Or authorities in the field?
9. Is the language clear and concise, or wordy and unnecessarily difficult? Does the choice of words show carelessness? Conceit?
10. Does the paper show a sincere desire to search out truth or is it a defense of a position?

These questions are designed to help you analyze and evaluate the thinking and writing. To evaluate content, you must be conversant with the topic. Perhaps professors assign reviews to motivate students, not only to read, but to study the topic under consideration.

---

[1]Adapted from Shirley Welch Mulkern, Teacher's Notebook for Teaching GREL 610, Methods in Research, Andrews University, Berrien Springs, MI, 1979.

Usually the last item in your evaluation is mention of what group will profit from reading this book. You may also want to suggest how useful the book will be for this certain group.

A Sample Review

Since "a picture is worth a thousand words," an example of a critical review may be more useful than an explanation. While this review provides a model to follow, the evaluation-critique section of your review could be very different. No one scheme is mandatory nor always desirable. In a review you can show creativity and imagination.

This review shows a good summary and an excellent evaluation. Harper gives no information on the editors of the book but he tells us that the book comes from presentations made at a seminar. Obviously, this review is more interested in the content than in the authors.

The bibliographic entry for this review, which has been used with permission, is the following:

Harper, Brian W. Review of *Citizen Christians: The Rights and Responsibilities of Dual Citizenship*, ed. Richard D. Land and Louis A. Moore. *Andrews University Seminary Studies* 33 (1995): 129–130.

The review appears as follows:

Land, Richard D., and Louis A. Moore, eds. *Citizen Christians: The Rights and Responsibilities of Dual Citizenship*. Nashville: Broadman & Holman Publishers, 1994. 176 pp.

Citizen Christians is a collection of essays from the 25th Annual Seminar of the Southern Baptist Christian Life Commission held in Washington, DC, in March 1992. The purpose of the book is to help Christians understand what it means to be citizens of two realms—the earthly and the spiritual. According to the authors, the spiritual realm includes the Church and the Kingdom of God, while the earthly realm refers to the sociopolitical, economic, and cultural context of the United States of America. The essays are grouped into four sections that address issues such as: What does it mean for Christians to be citizens of both America and the Church? What does the term "separation of church and state" mean in contemporary American culture? What is the appropriate relationship between American culture and the Church? How can Christians, both as individuals and as a collective force, shape the moral fabric of culture and influence government?

This book is worth reading if you want to understand how fundamentalists and conservative evangelicals define the Church and its mission. Its authors bring three important issues to our attention. First, they emphasize that the moral fabric of American culture is disintegrating, and Christians have a responsibility to help make repairs. Second, they argue against the notion that Christians ought to remain silent on public issues due to the private nature of religious convictions. In fact, the authors, especially Richard Land and Carl F. H. Henry, contend that the mission of the Church makes it impossible for Christians to ignore public issues and government. The third important issue that Beverly LaHaye, H. Robert Showers Jr., and Jay Strack emphasize is the need for an increase in Christian involvement in local communities and the democratic process.

Despite the importance of these three issues, the authors make the general mistake of basing their understanding of the Church and its mission on three faulty presuppositions. All of these presuppositions fall under the general claim that America was and should be a Christian nation, at least in terms of its moral values and principles. The introduction claims that "we believe many of the guiding principles on which our nation was formed were derived from the Bible. . . . The *Declaration of Independence* particularly reflects an understanding of God's principles found in the Bible" (2). The authors argue that secular humanism has been allowed to permeate American culture, replacing the traditional Christian values and principles upon which our authors assume America was founded. The decay of American sociopolitical, economic, and cultural life is blamed on this loss (78–85). Though there may be some truth to this interpretation of American history, it should by no means be thought of as the best or only interpretation.

A second questionable presupposition is the idea that those who seek to engage public issues must agree to a universal set of values. Of course, this book assumes that traditional Christian values provide the best context for a public forum. If people agree to abide by these values, we can speak the same moral language and reach practical conclusions. The authors, however, do not discuss the fact that Christian values are not for everybody. Non-Christians cannot and should not subscribe to Christian values, because they do not have any commitment to follow Jesus Christ. Furthermore, the authors do not recognize that within the Christian community there are a number of different faithful positions on moral issues. In fact, the modern idea of a "Christian value" ought to be challenged. Christians do not find "values" in the Bible, but a way of life. The Christian life is one of discipleship maintained within a community of fellow believers—the Church.

A third questionable presupposition is the idea that the Bible underwrites a particular sociopolitical and economic theory. Since this book focuses on the Church in the American context, the authors tend to confuse the mission of the Church—the Kingdom of God—with Western democracy and free-market capitalism. As Carl F. H. Henry claims, "the evangelical mainstream defends a free market and private property in the context of biblical principles, including divine stewardship and the propriety of legitimate profit" (52). The careful student, however, knows that the Bible does not advocate the philosophies of free- market capitalism or democracy. Such notions are modern conceptions, completely foreign to the Bible. The authors seem to identify the Kingdom of God with American democracy too readily. They seem to forget that the Church is called to exist under any state or government. Therefore, in the American context the Church represents at best one community among many communities that struggle to be heard in the public square. If Western democracy fails, it does not signal the demise of the Kingdom of God, as our authors sometimes inadvertently suggest. The Church, under the power of the Spirit of God, will continue to pursue its mission to usher in the Kingdom of God under whatever sociopolitical or economic theory dominates in America or other parts of the world.

Brian W. Harper

XVIII | STATISTICS, TABLES, AND GRAPHS[1]

For many, the word "statistics" brings to mind numbers and more numbers, devoid of all relation to reality, unintelligible to most mortals. Others may imagine vast computers that perform complicated operations, impossible to do by hand and head. This leads to attitudes that range from admiration to skepticism. Statistics are an instrument in the hands of politicians, business people, bankers, and others who must manage large quantities of information. They may also be a tool used by a researcher to turn small bits of information into interesting and reasonable conclusions.

Although many people shy away from statistics, in daily life they are used more than one realizes. For example, Christian Schwarz says that "the factor with the strongest correlation to the overall quality and growth of a church is the readiness to accept help from the outside."[2] This is statistical language, and he used statistical method to reach this conclusion. Or, when Win Arn notes that one year after a Billy Graham crusade, of 100 converts, only 15 percent were active in the church, and 82 percent of those had a friend or relative in the church before joining, he is using statistics.[3] Whether or not you use statistics in your papers, you should be able to read and understand statistical information.

Some Basics of Statistics

Chapter 14 described sampling, one of the techniques of statistics. Here we consider basic ideas such as grouping of data, measures of central tendency, and measures of dispersion, distribution, and correlation.

The first and essential idea of statistics is that of the list or inventory. History tells of the listing of population and economic data for planning wars or levying

---

[1]Thanks to Edward Maiorov, professor of mathematics and statistics, River Plate University, Argentina, for his help with the section on statistics.
[2]Christian A. Schwarz, *Natural Church Development: A Guide to Eight Essential Qualities of Healthy Churches*, 3d ed. (Carol Stream, IL: ChurchSmart Resources, 1998), 23.
[3]Win Arn and Charles Arn, *The Master's Plan for Discipling* (Pasadena: Church Growth, 1982), 134, 135.

taxes. Egyptians and Assyrians recorded systematic and periodical censuses. In the Bible there are records of a census of men older than twenty years (Num 1:18) and of male Levites over one month of age (Num 3:15).

Grouping of Data

Numerical data may be organized from large to small, or vice versa, in ascending or descending order. N is shorthand for the number of persons or entries.

Suppose that the ages of the fifty members of a church are the following: 12, 12, 14, 14, 14, 15, 15, 16, 16, 18, 18, 18, 18, 20, 20, 20, 22, 22, 23, 23, 23, 25, 25, 25, 25, 27, 27, 27, 30, 30, 30, 32, 32, 32, 32, 32, 32, 32, 32, 36, 41, 41, 46, 46, 50, 55, 55, 65, 70, 70. Putting these numbers in order shows the distribution of ages in the membership.

The same information is given below in a frequency chart (where frequency shows how many persons are of a certain age). This step of statistical calculations is not part of the final report and is only done in a rough draft.

Age	Frequency
12	2
14	3
15	2
16	2
18	4
20	3
22	2
23	3
25	4
27	3
30	3
32	8
36	1
41	2
46	2
50	1
55	2
65	1
69	2

Especially when N is very large, the data are grouped by intervals. Generally speaking there should be no fewer than five intervals, no more than twelve. The number of intervals will depend on the size of N. The same information presented above is now grouped by intervals.

Age	Frequency
10-19	13
20-29	15
30-39	12
40-49	4
50-59	3
60-69	3

This kind of statistical treatment may be used by a pastor to divide the church members by age groups: youth, adults, and seniors. Limits must be set for each group; for example: youth, 12–19; adults, 20–59; seniors, 60 and above.

Graphic Representation of a Frequency Distribution

The frequency distribution may be graphically shown by a histogram, a frequency polygon, or a frequency curve. Figures 1–3 give a visual representation of the age of members of X Church..

Histogram

The histogram represents a frequency distribution. The width of its bars (or rectangles) is determined by the intervals. The height of the bars is given by the frequency. The scale need not be exactly the same for both dimensions. The histogram should be a little wider than it is tall.

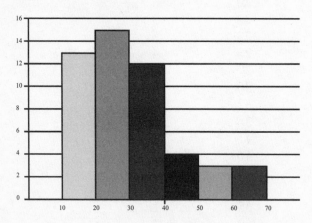

FIG. 1. Members of Church X, by ages

Frequency Polygon

Figure 2 shows the same data as the histogram. The points that shape the frequency polygon are given, on the horizontal axis, by the midpoint of each interval. On the vertical axis the points simply represent the frequency. The line is brought to the horizontal axis at the midpoint of the intervals before and after those used in the graph.

FIG. 2. Members of Church X, by ages

Frequency Curve

When N is very large (for example, if the church had 1,500 members), more intervals are used, and the polygon becomes a curve. If the imaginary church of the previous examples had a similar age distribution, but a much larger member-ship, the graphical representation would be approximately that of Figure 3.

FIG. 3. Members of Church Z, by ages

Measures of Central Tendency

One might ask, How much mission offering does a member give each week? There are three ways of calculating the "average offering." These are called measures of central tendency.

Average or Arithmetic Mean (m)

The mean is the result of dividing the sum (in this case, the total offering) by N (the number of members present). So, if an offering of 200 dollars was given by 40 people, the mean offering was 5 dollars.

If the calculation is made from a frequency chart, using grouped data, these steps must be followed:

1. Find the midpoint of the interval
2. Multiply that midpoint by the frequency of the interval
3. Add all of these
4. Divide by N

Using the example of the fifty-member church, let us calculate the mean age of a church member. This step is merely a rough draft and not part of the final report; it needs no figure number.

Age	Frequency	Midpoint	Frequency x Midpoint
10–19	13	14.5	13 x 14.5 = 88.5
20–29	15	24.5	15 x 24.5 = 367.5
30–39	12	34.5	12 x 34.5 = 414
40–49	4	44.5	4 x 44.5 = 178
50–59	3	54.5	3 x 54.5 = 163.5
60–69	3	64.5	3 x 64.5 = 193.5

TOTAL=1505.0

1505/50 = 30.1 years. The mean age of a church member is a little more than 30 years.

Median

The median is the middle value, halfway from either end of the listing. Consider the mission offerings for one quarter (13 weeks). In order to find the median, the sums must be placed in order: 534, 560, 580, 590, 595, 598, **600**, 602, 605, 610, 612, 620, 630. The median is 600 pesos, because there are six numbers (values) larger than it, and six smaller than it.

If the number of values were even, one would have to average the two middle values in order to determine the median. For example: If the number of persons baptized after studying with six Bible instructors were 20, 22, 24, 30, 32, 38, the median would be halfway between 24 and 30, the two central values. Thus the median would be 27. The arithmetic mean is 26.7 candidates per instructor.

It is possible to obtain a median from grouped data. If you need to do this, see a statistician.

Mode

The mode is the value that appears most often, the one with the greatest frequency. In the imaginary church of fifty members, the mode is 32 years of age. This age was given eight times.

Mean, Median, and Mode

The mean or mathematical average is the most commonly used of the three. However, it is easily affected by extremes. For example, if the salary of five persons were $12,600; $4,500; $4,400; $4,300; and $4,200 a month, the average salary would be $6,000. This would not give a true picture of wages earned, because only one of the five is earning that much. The median would be $4,400 and would give a more accurate picture of the five persons' earnings.

The mode is the least precise of these measures, but it is the easiest to calculate. A book seller is far more interested in the mode than the mean or median. He wants to know which is the most popular book in his store so he can order more copies. To find out, he only needs to count the number of each book sold.

Each of these measurements has its place. However, when you read or present statistics, be careful to note which of the three is being used.

Measures of Dispersion

These measures look not so much at what happens at the middle of the listing as at what happens at the ends. Measures of dispersion focus on differences rather than similarities.

Two church classes have five members each. The ages of the members of Class A are 60, 63, 21, 15, 11. The ages in Class B are 34, 40, 28, 30, 38. The mean (average) age in both classes is 34 years. But in Class A there are two seniors, one young adult, and two adolescents. On the other hand, Class B is more homogeneous, as far as age is concerned. One could say that the ages of the members of Class A are more varied or more disperse.

Range

Range is the simplest measure of dispersion. It is the difference between the highest and lowest values. In Class A, the range is 63–11 = 52; in Class B, the range is 40–28 = 12. The wide range shows that in Class A there is more variance than in class B.

Standard Deviation

Although the range is easier to figure, this measure is not very precise. A more precise measure is the standard deviation or S, which is the square root of the mean of the square of the variances from the arithmetic mean. The formula is:

$$S = \sqrt{\left(\frac{\sum d^2}{N}\right)}$$

$\sum$ is the symbol for sum; d is the difference between a value and its arithmetic mean (x-m). The standard deviation is more easily computed when the numbers are arranged in a table form.

Class A			Class B		
Age	d=x-m	d²	Age	d=x-m	d²
63	63-34= 29	841	40	40-34= 6	36
50	60-34= 26	676	38	38-34= 4	16
21	21-34=-13	169	34	34-34= 0	0
15	15-34=-19	361	30	30-34=-4	16
11	11-34=-23	529	28	28-34=-6	36

$$\sum d^2 = 2576 \qquad\qquad \sum d^2 = 104$$

$$S = \sqrt{\left(\frac{2576}{5}\right)} = \sqrt{515.22} = 22.69 \qquad S = \sqrt{\left(\frac{104}{5}\right)} = \sqrt{20.8} = 4.56$$

The steps for this calculation are:

1. Find the arithmetic mean.
2. Find the variance, subtracting each value from the mean.
3. Square the value of the variance.
4. Add the square of the variances.
5. Divide by N.
6. Obtain the square root.

The larger the S (standard deviation), the greater the range or the variance, and the smaller the homogeneity.

Distribution

Graphic representations have already been used to give a picture of how values are distributed. Figures 2 and 3 show how the church members' ages are distributed. A frequency polygon shows the distribution of a small N (Figure 2), whereas the frequency curve represents a large N (Figure 3).

The distribution of values may be normal or skewed. These concepts are explored in the following section.

Normal Distribution

If we measure the height of a very large number of people, we will find that these measurements form a symmetrical frequency polygon. There are about the same number of very tall individuals as very short ones. The majority are somewhere in the middle. The same happens with the measurement of a large number of leaves from the same tree, or the shoe size of men 25 years old in a given place. The larger the number, the more bell-shaped is the curve, similar to the one in figure 4. Theoretically, in a total population, the distribution of tall and short people should form a perfect curve, such as that in figure 5.

Normal distributions are important to statistics because they represent the ideal—and very close to real—distribution of values in a total population. Samples will usually give symmetrical frequency polygons. From this we deduce that if we could measure the whole population we would have a normal curve. What deviates from the normal curve distribution is considered skewed.

To define a normal curve, we need to know the arithmetic mean and the standard deviation. Curves *A*, *B*, and *C* in Figure 4 have the same mean. The difference among them is that *A* has a larger standard deviation; there is more variance—there are more values farther from the center. Curve *C* has a small standard deviation. In a normal bell-shaped curve, the percentage of values in each portion is mathematically established, as may be seen in Figure 5.

FIG. 4. Normal curves

Fɪɢ. 5. Percentage of area in each standard deviation

In one standard deviation (to either side of the mean), we find about 34 percent of the cases. Approximately another 14 percent fall in the second standard deviation, whereas only some 2 percent fall in the third standard deviation. As an example of this, let us use the measurement of IQs, where the arithmetic mean is 100 and the standard deviation is 13. These figures tell us that approximately 68 percent of the population may be expected to have an IQ between 87 and 113. Only about 2 percent will have an IQ of more than 126 or less than 74.

Skewed Distribution

If a population had a larger percentage than expected of imbeciles or geniuses, the distribution—and hence the curve—would be skewed as the ones in Figure 6. Curve *A* shows a population with more low IQs than normal, while Curve *B* shows more geniuses than expected. A skewed curve shows a distribution of characteristics different from what would normally be expected.

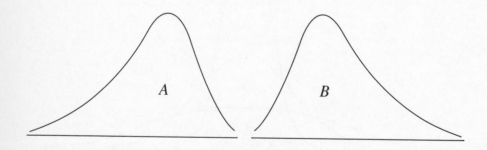

Fɪɢ. 6. Skewed curves

Correlation

An example of correlation is provided by the work of researcher Bert E. Holmes, who counted cricket chirps. Holmes counted the chirps made by 115 crickets in a minute. He also measured the temperature when the crickets were chirping. He discovered that when he counted the chirps for 15 seconds and added 37 to that number, the result was quite close to the Fahrenheit temperature—as long as it was not too cold or too hot, that is between 45 and 80 degrees—at the time of counting.[4]

Without discussing whether the higher temperature caused more chirps or more chirps caused higher temperatures, we can state that there is a positive correlation between the temperature and the number of cricket chirps per second. The higher the temperature, the more chirps. In fact, Holmes found this positive correlation to be very high: 0.9919. A perfect positive correlation is r=+1.00.

In 1975 Mike Scofield studied the relation between the size of a church and the quantity of offerings that entered the treasury per member during the year. He found that when the church grew, the mean per capita offering diminished.[5] This is an example of negative correlation: more members, fewer offerings. A perfect negative correlation is expressed: r=−1.00.

When the correlation coefficient (r) is close to 1.00 (either plus or minus), correlation is said to be high (positive or negative). When the correlation coefficient is close to 0, correlation is low or nonexistent. In fact, a coefficient of less than 0.5 is not very important and may be considered a product of chance.

Used in a regression equation, the correlation coefficient may be employed for predictions. Given the value of one variable, the other may be predicted. Thus, without reading the thermometer, one could tell the temperature by the number of cricket chirps. After years of correlating the scores on entrance tests with students' academic performance, researchers can predict how well students will do. On this basis many universities require a certain score on these examinations.

The correlation coefficient becomes more meaningful as more pairs are studied. If a researcher announced that the correlation between long sermons and member satisfaction is r=−0.80, we would know that the longer the sermon, the lower the satisfaction. But if she also told us that she only consulted four people, we would not pay too much attention. On the other hand, if 100 members were consulted, even if the r=−0.60, we would give credence to the report.

Once again, correlation does not mean causality. The crowing of roosters does not make the sun come out; neither does sunrise make roosters crow. But

---

[4]Bert E. Holmes, "Vocal Thermometers," *Scientific Monthly* 25 (September 1927): 261–267.
[5]Quoted in Gottfried Oosterwal, *Patterns of SDA Church Growth in America* (Berrien Springs, MI: Andrews University Press, 1976), 83–87.

both do happen at approximately the same time. If a high correlation between two items is consistently reported many times, it becomes difficult to doubt a cause-and-effect relationship. Smoking and cancer, notably lung cancer, are a good example. But even in this case, tobacco manufacturers admit correlation, but try to deny causality.

The calculation of r is complicated. If you undertake a correlation study, get help from a statistician. Statistical calculators can do the calculations, but the design of the research demands professional help.

Statistical Tables and Graphs

Statistical information is sometimes written into the text of a research report, often in tables and graphs. Tables contain rows of numbers. Graphs represent the numbers by lines and spaces; they are visually more interesting. Tables and graphs allow much information to be given in an organized manner in little space. The rules governing the presentation of tables and graphs in research writing are explained in the following pages.

Tables

All tables must have a number and a title. They must also be listed in a list of tables, which comes after the table of contents in the preliminary pages. As in this book, if there are only a few tables, these may be listed together with the illustrations.

If the table is too large to fit across the page, it may be placed lengthwise on a following page. If it is too large to fit either way, it may be prepared on a larger page which is then folded to fit into the paper. A smaller font or photographic reduction may be used to make a table small enough to fit on the page.

Reference should be made to the table in the text. This draw the reader's attention to the location and contents of the tables or graphs. A reader should be able to get a clear idea of the results of the research without having to examine every table and graph, even when all details are not in the text. The following example is taken from a description of pastors in South America.

Table 1 shows the contact of pastors with well-educated people. From the pastors' report, it appears that for the entire division the largest group (156, 45.8 percent) has some contact with educated people, and that the next largest group (113, 33.1 percent) reports little contact with them. A comparison between the Spanish-speaking and Portuguese-speaking respondents shows that although a larger group of Portuguese-speaking pastors (38, 23.0 percent) said they have much contact with educated people, more Spanish-speaking pastors than Portuguese-speaking pastors reported some interaction with educated people (Sp.: 94, 54.3 percent; Port.: 61, 37.0 percent).[6]

Tables should be placed as soon as possible after they are mentioned in the text. However, they should not break a paragraph. If a table needs to be on a separate page, it should still appear as soon as possible after the reference to it.

TABLE 1

REPORTED CONTACT OF PASTORS WITH
WELL-EDUCATED PERSONS

Pastor's Contact	Spanish-Speaking Pastors		Portuguese-Speaking Pastors		South American Division	
	N	%	N	%	N	%
No answer	1	0.6	1	0.6	2	0.6
Much	20	11.6	38	23.0	58	17.0
Some	94	54.3	61	37.0	156	45.7
Little	54	31.2	58	35.2	114	33.5
None	4	2.3	7	4.2	11	3.2
	173	100.0	165	100.0	341	100.0

While they are not identical, all three tables are acceptable variations in style. Vertical lines (not allowed in some schools) are used in Table 2. Do not mix different styles in one paper. The titles of the left-hand column are typed flush left. The titles of the other columns are centered over the numbers. Numbers are right aligned. The three dots represent null or zero. The vertical spacing and the font size vary to fit the space available; the vertical spacing should be between one and two lines. The font may be small, but it must still be readable.

You may use the column feature on your word processor. Tables are even easier to format; however, you may have to edit out lines to suit the rules of your school. Be sure to check what the requirements are.

When the information portrayed in the table comes from one's own research, no source is needed. Table 3 shows how to handle the reference to other sources.

Neatness and clarity are hallmarks of well-made tables. Sufficient white space around them sets them off. Normally, three empty lines precede and follow each table and graph. Work until you produce a pleasing effect.

---

[6]Tables 1–3 and Figures 7, 8 come from my dissertation, "Implications of Selected Curricular Determinants for Seventh-day Adventist Graduate Theological Education in the South American Division" (Ed.D., Andrews University, 1978). The South American Division includes countries listed in Table 3.

TABLE 2

TIME SPENT IN SERMON PREPARATION AS REPORTED BY
PRESIDENTS, DEPARTMENTAL DIRECTORS, AND PASTORS

Weekly	Presidents		Departmental Directors		Pastors			
					Graduates		Non-grads	
	N	%	N	%	N	%	N	%
No answer	1	2.8	2	3.3	2	0.9	...	...
No time	...	...	...	...	...	...	2	7.1
0-2 hours	16	44.4	24	40.0	13	6.2	13	46.4
3-5 hours	13	36.1	26	43.3	91	42.7	10	5.8
6-9 hours	6	16.7	4	6.7	76	35.7	2	7.1
10-14 hrs.	...	...	4	6.7	29	13.6	1	3.6
Over 15 h.	...	...	...	...	2	0.9	...	...
Totals	36	100.0	60	100.0	213	100.0	28	100.0

TABLE 3

AGES OF POPULATION IN COUNTRIES OF
THE SOUTH AMERICAN DIVISION

Countries in the South American Division	5–19 %	20–29 %	30–44 %	45–59 %	60–74 %
Argentina	34	17	22	16	11
Bolivia	44	19	20	11	6
Brazil	39	21	22	12	6
Chile	33	21	24	14	8
Ecuador	43	21	20	11	5
Paraguay	42	21	22	10	5
Peru	41	21	20	12	6
Uruguay	29	17	22	18	14

SOURCE: 1991 Demographic Yearbook (New York: United Nations, 1992), 164–167.

Graphs

A simple, attractive, carefully presented graph stands out in the paper. A table may present more information, but a graph is a more effective communicator. The limitations of graphs are evident: (1) they do not show as much data as a table; (2) they represent approximate values; (3) they take time and some artistic talent.

All graphs should be typed or drawn in black ink. Computer-generated graphs are excellent; however, this specialized technology is not indispensable to clear, accurate, and appealing graphs. The most common are bar, line, and circular graphs.

Bar Graphs

These may be simple, compound, or double (sometimes triple).

Simple bars

The bars may be drawn vertically or horizontally; here they are horizontal. Care must be taken to achieve a pleasing appearance while maintaining maximum clarity.

FIG. 7. Percentage of urban population in the countries of the South American Division. Information from Statistical Yearbook 1990/91 (New York: United Nations, 1993), 73–74.

Compound bar graphs

Figure 8 is a compound bar graph showing the same information given in Table 3. It is visually more interesting, but not as precise.

FIG. 8. Age distribution in the countries of the South American Division, according to 1991 Demographic Yearbook, 164–167.

Figure 9, another compound bar graph, compares the tithes and offerings in the Adventist church worldwide from 1988 to 1992. It is visually attractive, but does not give specific sums for each kind of offering. This type of visual aid is very useful in the oral presentation of research. If the graph is shown in colors on an overhead projector it can be particularly eye-catching. Unfortunately, color is not used in graphs in a thesis or dissertation.

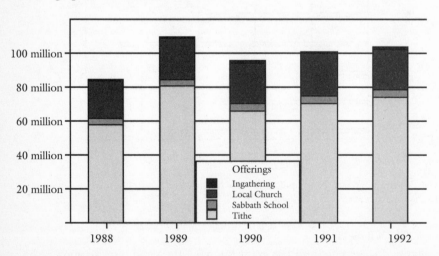

FIG. 9. A comparison of tithes and offerings from 1988 to 1992, according to Annual Statistical Report, 1992 (Silver Spring, MD: General Conference of SDA, 1993), 47.

Double bar graphs

Double bar graphs are used to compare at least two variables. Figure 10 shows the student population from different world regions at Andrews University in 1995 and 2000. The three-dimensional bars are interesting but fail to show the exact numbers of students.

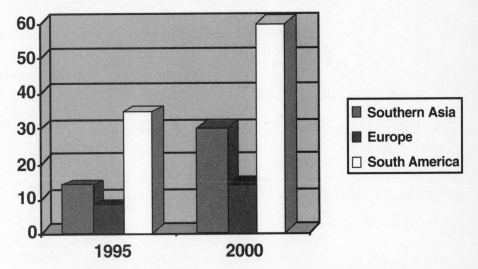

FIG. 10. Student population from southern Asia (India), Euro-Asia (former USSR), and South America, studying at Andrews University, 1995 and 2000, according to the Office of International Students.

Line Graphs

A line graph usually portrays change over time. The horizontal axis represents time; the vertical, another variable, which in Figure 11 is the number of interdivision workers sent out by the Adventist church between 1901 and 1990. Here a computer-generated graphic displays a visually interesting figure.

The scale on each axis does not need to be identical (that is, the same for one missionary as for one year), but care must be taken not to distort the impact of the information. For example, should the year line in Figure 12 be shorter, the increase of institutional workers would appear to be truly astronomical.

Line graphs may compare one phenomenon to another over time. The lines must be different to avoid confusion. Figure 12 shows the number of countries in which the Global Missions Fellowship is working and the number of new churches planted between 1993 and 1999.

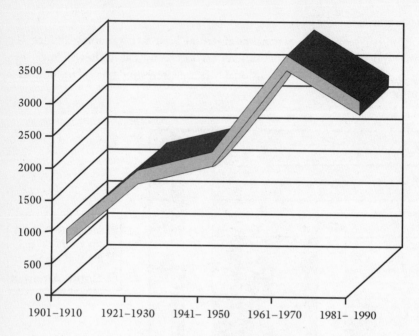

FIG. 11. Adventist interdivision workers sent out by decades, according to the Annual Statistical Report, 1992.

FIG. 12. A comparison of the number of countries where Global Mission Fellowship worked with the number of churches planted between 1993 and 1999, according to "GMF Statistics," http://www.gmt.org/gmt_camp_statistics.html.

Circular Graphs

Also called pie charts, circular graphs represent the total divided into its parts. The figures are usually expressed in percentages, although actual figures may also be given. Figure 13 shows examples of pie graphs. These were made with the WordPerfect™ Presentations program.

If you do not have access to a computer program that makes circular graphs, you may still construct your own. A percentage protractor is useful for this task. It will give you percentages rather than degrees of the circle. However, you can also calculate the areas of your circular graphs. Remember that 180 degrees is the same as 50 percent; 90 degrees is equivalent to 25 percent, and so on.

Divide the circle to represent the percentages. Then label each section with the percentage of the whole and the exact number, if you like. Make the differences between sections show by using different cross hatchings.

As with other graphs, the pie charts are eye catching. However, they do not convey precise information as a table would. You must decide whether you need precision or interest.

Fig. 13. SDA membership by continents, 1970–1990; from Annual Statistical Report, 1970, 1980, 1990.

Statistics and Honesty

Disraeli, the great English statesman, is reported to have quipped that there are three kinds of lies: lies, damned lies, and statistics.[7] On the other hand, H. G. Wells stated that "some day it will be as necessary for an efficient civilization to think statistically as it is to read and write."[8] Both statements may exaggerate, but both contain some truth. Statistics form a part of modern life, but their use demands honesty, not only in telling the truth, but in not stretching facts to suit one's own purposes.

Figures 14 and 15 show how a graphic representation may distort information. The first one shows the growth of the world population between 1950 and 2000. The second uses partial information, which gives a distorted impression of reality.

Fig. 14. Growth of world population, 1950–2000, according to United Nations Statistical Yearbook (New York: United Nations, 1997), 95; and Time Almanac 2000 (New York: Time, 2000), 153.

In Figure 15 the proportion on the X axis (horizontal) has been changed. The growth appears more accelerated, but the distorted world shows that the rapid rise is not real. Were there no world to show the distorted proportions, the visual impact could fool the observer into panic about world overpopulation.

---

[7] D. Huff, *How to Lie with Statistics* (New York: W. W. Norton, 1954), 1.
[8] Ibid.

Fig. 15. A distorted view of the growth of world population, 1950–2000.

Percentages may also be used to convey erroneous information. A physician could state that only three of his patients had died, while someone could argue that the same physician had lost 75 percent of those he had cared for. Both could be telling a half-truth. If there were four patients, three would be 75 percent. A percentage figure should be given along with the total number (N) on which it is based should be stated.

The base number for calculating percentages is important, as may be seen from the following example. If the manager reduces the employee's salary by 20 percent, and the original salary was $100, the employee would now be getting $80. If on this sum the boss gives an employee a 20-percent raise, the unlucky fellow would only be getting $96 (20 times 80 divided by 100 equals 16). What happened? The first calculation was made on the basis of 100; the second on the basis of 80.

When reading statistical reports, do not accept every piece of the data without considering the total picture. All too often authors distort to achieve their own ends. Apply critical thinking even to the numbers you read.

Many ways of lying with statistics could be mentioned. None of them is appropriate to research. Let total honesty prevail! Research reports must be accurate and precise. Pastoral research must be even more ethical and honest.

This chapter has presented some basic notions of statistics and instructions for preparing and presenting different kinds of graphs. Further help in statistical design should be procured from a qualified professional on the subject. The calculation of statistics has become much more simple with the advent of the computer and appropriate software. In fact, tables and graphs may be computer generated from raw data or calculations in a database or spreadsheet. For this type of assistance, look for a computer expert!

To complete the picture of theological-biblical-pastoral research, chapters 19 and 20 turn to theses and dissertations.

XIX | THESES AND DISSERTATIONS

A first theological degree is usually earned by passing courses and examinations. The second culminates with major research, often called a thesis, at the master's level. At the doctoral level, the same kind of work—but longer and more complex—is known as a doctoral thesis or dissertation. Theses and dissertations have many common elements; one of these is the review of literature, important enough to deserve a separate section of the chapter, before the discussion of theses and dissertations.

Review of Literature

A review of literature, which often appears in the first or second chapter of a thesis or dissertation (and sometimes also in the proposal) reports what has already been written, in books and journals, about the topic under research. It provides, so to speak, the background for the painting. In large strokes, the review of literature paints a backdrop against which the research will be done. One professor described the review of related literature as a salute to the past: A recognition of the research and study already done on one's topic. After a gentlemanly tip of the hat, one goes on to further research of the topic. Another description of a review of literature puts it this way: Before inventing a new typewriter, an inventor looks at all existing typewriters—IBM, Smith-Corona, Brothers, Royal, Olivetti, and so on. This survey becomes a starting point for the inventing process.

A review of literature shows your adviser or committee that you have made a thorough investigation of the topic and have read the main works already written on it. It guarantees that there will be no going over the same ground others have covered, no "re-inventing of the wheel." A thorough review of the literature shows you know whereof you speak.

If the proposal has a review of literature, it will reflect extensive reading; however, it certainly will not embody the total reading for the thesis or dissertation. More items that belong in the review of literature will appear in the course of your reading. They may be added later. Conversely, you may decide to remove some item from the final version of the review of related literature.

This summary of the status of research is not a series of book reviews or critiques (see chapter 17). It synthesizes information from many sources about the issue, its background, and previous attempts to resolve the problem. Not only does it review research on the same problem, it also looks at studies that have used a similar methodology to solve a different problem.

The style of writing is descriptive. In this survey, synthesis is the key: putting ideas together to present a big picture. Normally, the review of literature does not include interaction or discussion with the authors reviewed. Evaluation is at a minimum. For example, imagine part of a review of literature on the theological significance (tongue-in-cheek, of course) of the durian, that Asian fruit that has only lovers and haters:

> Professor Adriel Sandoval, in agreement with Yeng Ka Seng and Komarno, states that durian will be the fruit of the tree of life. (References for all three) Sandoval goes so far as to suggest that only the durian could have been tempting enough to Adam and Eve to cause them to disobey God's instructions. (Reference) In clear opposition to his position is that of Vasinee Suvonapong, who claims that durian came into being only after the fall, once decay and decomposition had set in. (Reference)

Students often ask how long the review of literature should be and how many items it should contain. There is no precise answer. Simply put, the full picture should be given: As many items as are needed to show familiarity with the topic of the research should be blended into the review of literature. This aspect of the thesis or dissertation is assessed both qualitatively and quantitatively. Usually, professors tend to be more impressed by quality than by quantity. In spite of that, more is usually better. The omission of an item considered important by an examiner at the thesis defense may force rewriting.

The amount of research already done on the topic will, to a certain extent, determine the scope and breadth of the review. If there is little research on a topic, every item available needs to be included. If much has been written on the topic, the reviewer may take a selective approach.

When a review of literature is selective, rather than comprehensive, a clear rationale for the selection and omission of materials must be given. In a 1990 thesis on preaching, an M.Th. student chose a time limitation; he reviewed "text books written on preaching since 1970." The rationale followed: "This time limitation was chosen because it is unlikely that books written and copyrighted before that date would still be in print and available for use as textbooks." One might also choose to limit the authors by nationality, gender, or approach. At times the literature on a specific aspect of the problem is reviewed. An M.Th. student writing on "Christian Freedom in Colossians 2:6–23" did a comprehensive review (all available commentaries on Colossians and Galatians) of literature but focused only on the question: "From what did Christ's death on the cross free Christians?" The review of literature for a comparative study on soteriology in Theravada Buddhism contained only works that compared Christianity and Buddhism; an appropriate and convincing rationale for this selection was presented.

A review of literature needs to be organized. If there are few studies, one might follow a chronological or alphabetical order for the presentation. This is not usual, however. Most reviews of literature need to be organized topically, with headings and even subheadings. As he read, the student writing on Christian freedom noticed that the answers given by Protestant, Catholic, and Seventh-day Adventist scholars differed significantly, so he divided the review into three parts. The first of these sections was then divided according to what the authors said. Forty-seven items were reviewed under the following organization.

I. Protestant authors
   A. Authors who perceive Christian freedom as freedom from law
      1. Freedom from the moral law
      2. Freedom from the ceremonial law
   B. Authors who understand Christian freedom as freedom from condemnation
II. Roman Catholic authors
III. Seventh-day Adventist authors

A review of literature may be exhaustive or representative. In the first case, every item is described; in the second, only specific items are described. These items are chosen as representative of a larger group, all of which are carefully referenced in the footnotes. When a representative review is written, the student must be sure that the item described does, in fact, accurately represent the others.

You are responsible not only for writing the review of literature, but also for designing the rationale for excluding some materials and including others, and for organizing the review. Yet, your thesis or dissertation committee normally has the final word. Work closely with your adviser or committee to avoid surprises.

In different types of theses or dissertations, the review of literature includes different materials. For example, in descriptive research, the review of literature includes information on other research done on the same topic, on studies using the same methodology, and on the theory that undergirds the research. In product development research, the review of literature includes literature on the group for whom the program is to be developed, on similar programs already developed, and on the method of development. In a dissertation on one aspect of *heilsgeschichte,* the review of literature might contain a history of the concept and evaluations of *heilsgeschichte.*

At times, a thesis advisor or committee may allow alternatives to the review of literature. Two options are the annotated bibliography and the bibliographical essay. The annotated bibliography briefly describes the item, thus showing the researcher has examined it already; an example appears in chapter 5. The bibliographical essay notes what has already been written on the topic and evaluates the usefulness of the sources listed. Some thesis or dissertation committees—especially in Ph.D.-in-religion papers—may prefer to have you put into footnotes a vast amount of information regarding previous studies and opinions on the topic instead of writing a separate review. The thesis or dissertation produced by this method may have as much space dedicated to footnotes as to text. Make sure you know what your adviser and committee want from you before you spend weeks doing what you think is appropriate.

Theses

The Master of Arts in Religion degree often requires a thesis; the Master of Theology degree always does. What is meant by "thesis"? A thesis is generally a long and complex research paper. Instructions given on research methodology in chapters 1 through 12 apply also to the thesis. In fact, the research method must be even more strictly applied to a thesis than to a class paper.

The M.A. thesis is expected to be about 80 pages in length. For an M.A. in Religion, the thesis usually is a bibliographical research paper. The student's thesis adviser or committee may give permission for the student to do a major exegetical paper. Professional master's degree programs may allow descriptive research, program development, or a church-growth study as a thesis.

The M.Th. thesis will normally be from 100 to 150 pages long. The choice of topic will depend on the student's area of concentration. This thesis is a half step between the M.A. and the Ph.D./Th.D.

A thesis—either M.A. or M.Th.—is expected to contribute something new to the fund of general knowledge. It cannot be a mere rehash of old materials. Since the thesis allows more space in which to develop the research, the topic may be more complex than the topic for a term paper. However, you should select a problem that is amenable to treatment within the available time and resources, and within the allotted pages.

Thesis writing is directed by an adviser or supervisor, often with others who form the thesis committee. You must work closely with your adviser in choosing the topic and in writing the thesis proposal, which is then approved by a committee. Each school has its own way of doing theses. Please follow instructions carefully!

The thesis process may be divided into three main segments: proposal, writing, and defense. These three aspects are described in turn.

Proposal

The thesis proposal should contain the same elements as the proposal for a paper (see chapter 4). However, each part must be developed in greater detail. Whereas in a paper proposal, two pages might be sufficient, an M.A. or M.Th. thesis proposal may reach between six and eight pages.

Writing a proposal is not a waste of time. What goes into the proposal eventually goes into the thesis. By the time your proposal is presented and accepted, you will have completed a large part of the reading and research.

A proposal has a title page and a table of contents. It begins much as would any normal research paper; however, the similarities with a regular paper end very soon. The whole of the proposal is dedicated to an explanation of what the thesis will contain.

Your M.A. or M.Th. proposal should begin with a background for the study and the statement of the problem. You should also present the purpose and objectives of the research, as well as its significance. Any delimitations should be explained. (In a thesis, limitations such as lack of time or knowledge are not acceptable; they are considered excuses for poor work and their presence may suggest you need a different topic!) Define any terms that may not be clear to your readers. State your presuppositions. Explain the method you are using. If the study is historical or bibliographical, a description of the methodology is fairly short, yet each step of the procedure must be carefully delineated. Describe the kinds of sources you will use, how you will go about your search for information, and how one part of the research will relate to another. If the thesis follows another form of research, an appropriate description of its steps must be included.

The proposal of descriptive research demands additional information. The instrument or questionnaire forms part of the proposal, and the way in which it will be applied is fully described. Information on the population to be surveyed, sampling techniques, data to be obtained, and the statistical treatment of the data must be provided. In some cases this section will be sufficiently long to merit a place as an independent chapter. The adviser usually makes this decision.

Proposals for other kinds of research have their own introductions. An introduction to an exegetical thesis will state the problem in the text; it will also take into account how others have tried to solve the problem. It will clearly delineate the method to be used. The introduction section in a case-study proposal will give the case, together with its background, the topics that will be examined to explain the dynamics of the case, both sociological/psychological/cultural and theological. In a product development thesis, the steps to be taken must accompany the statement of the problem and the other basics noted in the first paragraph of this section.

Following the methodology section, a detailed tentative outline is presented. This may be done in either format indicated in chapter 4. The outline is prepared in close cooperation with the adviser, who usually makes sure the whole committee (if there is one) agrees on the proposed organization of the thesis. The tentative outline forms part of the proposal.

The last part of the proposal is a working bibliography that lists all items already considered. It will not include all the materials you will eventually use, for it is tentative, and subject to change. However, the committee expects to see a promising list that includes all the best and recognized sources for the research.

A search for sources for a thesis must go beyond the library of the school where you are enrolled. You will get some materials through interlibrary loan; other items, you must find at other libraries. Then, there is the Internet. Learn to use the latest technology. Plan on becoming a library addict before you finish your work.

The student's adviser or thesis committee meets with the student to finalize the proposal. The student presents his or her views, and the professors stipulate their requirements. The proposal is either accepted as it is, accepted subject to certain changes, or rejected. A final copy of the thesis proposal is usually filed with the program director, not only to certify that you have fulfilled this requirement, but to serve as a model for students who will follow you.

The proposal serves you and your adviser or committee as a guide to your writing. It is something of a contract made between the two sides. Departing from the path laid out in the proposal could be dangerous: "There is a way which seems right to man, but its end is the way of death" (Prov 14:12).

Once the proposal has been approved, thesis research and writing begin in earnest. From now until you finish it, the thesis will dominate your life. Some suggestions for the writing and research of a thesis are given in the following section.

Thesis Writing

After your proposal has been accepted, you will continue reading, researching, and taking notes. The greatest part of the time needed to prepare a thesis is dedicated to these activities. Only when you complete this process should you begin to write. There is no point in writing a chapter without having all the information.

Perhaps the most important advice for a thesis writer is to work closely with the thesis adviser and/or committee. Be sure the adviser agrees with any deviation from the original plan. If the work is guided by a committee, make sure you have a committee decision on what you are to do, rather than one member's opinion. If your professor is one who writes out the comments on your work, you are indeed blessed. It is quite acceptable for you to nudge your adviser to give you comments in writing. Suggest that you need to be sure you are doing the right thing. You need not mention that you are trying to make sure the professor does not have a change of heart and mind and ask you to do something different!

Plan time for the adviser and committee members to read all the parts of your thesis. Remember that professors are usually too busy to read your chapter overnight, simply because you have handed it in and are in a hurry to graduate. It is imperative to develop—and follow—a chronogram that allows time for reading and corrections. This goes for both you and the adviser!

Thesis typing is a major enterprise. Finding a thesis typist may be almost as hard as writing the paper. In addition, you are still held responsible for typing and format errors. With today's technology, students usually do their own typing—on the computer. Once more, learning to touch-type and to use a word processor is highly recommended. See additional comments on word processing in chapter 12.

The quality of English required for a thesis demands special attention to editing. You are responsible for getting the necessary editorial help to polish the English. The adviser or committee chairperson may improve the language and style of writing with his or her corrections, but the adviser's main task is to direct in matters of content. The institutional thesis editor will indicate format corrections necessary, but does not have time to rewrite problematic English.

Generally, the thesis must be given to the examiners at least one week—or as much as four weeks—before the defense date. While the examiners read your thesis, you will have time to check for any mistakes in the paper and to prepare the abstract, vita, and any acknowledgments you wish to include.

The preliminary parts of a thesis include an abstract of the thesis and the approval sheet, prepared according to the school's obligatory format. A model used in several schools appears at the end of this chapter. The abstract is a brief summary of the problem studied, the findings of the research, and the conclusions reached. Its normal length is from 150 to 350 words, depending on the degree and the school.

The acknowledgments are a personal note of gratitude to whomever thanks are due. Some theses are dedicated to a special person, but this is not necessary. In any case, wisdom suggests moderation and reserve in the expressions of thanks.

The order of the preliminary pages is fixed by each school. However, the following is considered normal: blank page, abstract title page, abstract, thesis title page, blank page, approval sheet, dedication, table of contents, list of illustrations (or figures), list of tables, list of abbreviations, acknowledgments.

The vita, which gives the student's personal information, as well as academic and professional history, follows the bibliography. This is the last item in the thesis. Check the format customary for your school and degree.

Oral Defense

When all the chapters of the thesis have been written, the conclusions have been drawn, and the bibliography is ready, the thesis adviser sets a date for the defense, if there is one. The student must make complete copies of the thesis for all the members of the committee, including the external examiner, if there is one. Each school has specific guidelines regarding the number of copies needed.

The oral examination or defense usually deals with the thesis and matters related to it. Usually you are given the chance to make a brief presentation of your research. Use visuals to impress the examiners: overhead projection or, even better, PowerPoint computer graphics to add luster to the presentation.

When you come to the oral defense knowing that your thesis is well written, you need not fear. Professors are glad to "show off" a good student! Again, the need for working closely with the adviser and the committee cannot be overemphasized.

Even as late as the oral defense, changes in the thesis may be requested. Once these are completed and certified by the adviser, you are responsible for turning in the original to the dean or program coordinator. From this, as many copies as the school requires are made, always at your expense. These are bound, again at your expense, and kept as a permanent record of your intellectual achievement.

Dissertations

Most of what has been said about theses applies also to dissertations. The main difference is in the scope and length of the required work. A doctoral-quality dissertation takes time, effort, and finances. A student must plan on sufficient time for completing the dissertation—months or years!

A Doctor of Theology or Doctor of Philosophy dissertation is a major research project. It investigates a complex or difficult problem in the area of the candidate's major emphasis. This dissertation will be at least 250 pages long and may be as long as 500 pages.

The writing of a D.Th./Ph.D. dissertation takes for granted that the candidate has the language tools needed to do exhaustive research in the chosen area. A knowledge of biblical languages is presupposed. Normally, the candidate must pass examinations in French and/or German. Other languages may be needed, depending on the topic. For example, a study on early church fathers would demand a knowledge of Latin.

As with the thesis, the main stages of a dissertation are three: proposal, research and writing, and defense.

Proposal

Divergent philosophies guide the proposal process in various schools. Some prefer to have a proposal that contains as many as three chapters of the dissertation. Others want a short and succinct presentation of no more than ten pages. Some schools require students to take a class in which they receive specific instructions on preparing the proposal and writing the dissertation. Be thankful if your school is one of these.

Schools that require a long proposal usually require that the topic be approved before the student is given the green light to write the three chapters. The required three chapters are the introduction, the review of literature, and the methodology. A bibliography is also required. All of this work is done in close association with the adviser and the dissertation committee.

A short proposal shows, in a few pages, that you know exactly what you are going to do and how you are going to do it. The Ph.D. proposal required at Andrews University is an example of the short version. The review of literature is built into the research proposal, especially in the background, justification, viability, and methodology sections. All the essential ideas listed must be present, but may not need their own separate headings. The proposal has three main parts: research proposal, outline, and bibliography. The outline includes chapter titles and two levels of subheadings. It should be no longer than twelve pages, excluding the tentative bibliography.

RESEARCH PROPOSAL
    Background of the Problem (as needed)
    Statement of the Problem
    Purpose of the Research
    Justification for the Research
    Viability of the Research
    Scope/Delimitations
    Methodology
OUTLINE OF THE PROPOSED DISSERTATION
TENTATIVE BIBLIOGRAPHY

Research and Writing

All that has been said about research and writing applies here, when a Ph.D. student lives, breathes, and sleeps dissertation! If meticulous care in taking notes and organizing them was important in a research paper, it is triply so in the dissertation.

The relationship between doctoral candidate and adviser is of paramount importance. After you graduate, you will be your own boss. Until then, you need to practice submission to your adviser's wishes. Writing and defending a dissertation is not only a matter of dogged research and painful writing, it is a political feat as well. In fact, at the termination of the process congratulations for a game well played are often in order.

Each school has its own rules for the interaction of candidate and dissertation adviser and committee. Obtain the handbook from your school and follow it closely, perhaps even blindly. There will be time to celebrate when the process is over.

Defense

What has been said about the defense of a master's thesis holds for the Th.D./Ph.D. dissertation. After having written a masterpiece, you will be confident and your adviser will be thrilled to show you off! The defense will be a joyful exercise in which your achievements are made public. On the other hand, if your work is merely acceptable, and you have had uneasy moments with your adviser, you can expect the defense to be difficult. Given a choice, you will obviously choose the first route.

Specific guidelines for the defense procedure and the handing in of final copies of the dissertation are provided by individual schools. Become familiar with these instructions and follow them closely. You will be spared tears and grief!

At the defense, a Ph.D. candidate usually makes a brief presentation summarizing the research done. Practice this presentation as you did your first sermon! Make the presentation clear yet agile. Touch the high points, what the observers at the defense need to know in order to understand the dissertation without having read it. Use technology if it can make the presentation clearer and more enjoyable.

Asking and answering questions takes up the better part of the defense. Your examiners want to know how well you know the topic and its ramifications. If you are not absolutely clear on the question (or its answer!) ask the examiner to rephrase it. This will give you a few seconds to think. Of course, the ploy cannot be used for every question. Answer the specific question asked, not one you wish the professor had asked. Refer to pages in your dissertation, especially when it is evident that the examiner did not read the document with great care. Whatever you do, do not argue with the examiners or contradict them. It is much better to say with a smile: "You may have a point there; I will be happy to consider it." When the questioning is over and the examiners sit in executive session to decide your fate, they may not remember what you said as much as how you said it.

In conclusion, may your dissertation months be short and your joy at finishing your work be long!

[2 in]   LIBERATION THEOLOGY'S USE OF THE EXODUS

AS A SOTERIOLOGICAL MODEL

[3.5 in]   A thesis presented

in partial fulfillment of the requirements

for the degree

Master of Theology

by

[5 in]   Atilio Rene Dupatonga

APPROVAL BY THE COMMITTEE:

_____   _____

Adviser: Ernesto Ramos   M.Th. coordinator: Samuel Suen

_____   _____

Committee member: Cho Young Mo   Dean, Theological Seminary: Tekito Tumoto

_____

Committee member: Mary Masok

_____   _____

External examiner: Tim Zarate   Date of approval

[Modifications are made to suit the number of signatures needed on the approval sheet. If so desired, the position and/or degree of each person may be added.]

XX | D.MIN. PROJECTS

The D.Min. and D.P.Th. (or Doctor of Pastoral Studies, as it is called in Southeast Asia) are professional programs with an emphasis on practical theology. The variations between the two degrees are more likely to represent the differences between schools than between degrees. Both require theological reflection applied to a pastoral situation. Although D.Min. papers represent doctoral-level work, they are usually called "projects" rather than dissertations. Their aim is not so much to enlarge the fund of knowledge as to solve a problem in ministry and to provide the pastor-researcher an opportunity for personal growth.

The accrediting association to which a seminary belongs has a clear say in defining the form and content of the D.Min. project. Current standards of the Association of Theological Schools point to a "written doctoral-level project that addresses both the nature and the practice of ministry." This "ministry project should demonstrate the candidate's ability to identify a specific theological topic in ministry, organize an effective research model, use appropriate resources, and evaluate the results."[1] The standards for the South East Asia Graduate School of Theology mandate a contextual "thesis-length 'Case Study' on a problem or issue emerging" from the candidate's studies and in his or her "field of specialization."[2]

In a 1999 article in *Theological Education*, Timothy Lincoln reported a survey of D.Min. final papers in schools accredited by the Association of Theological Schools. He found that the D.Min. project constitutes a genre of its own, "an exercise in *phronesis*, practical Christian wisdom." He summarizes: "Written for an audience of persons engaged in ministry, the project should address an issue arising out of ministerial practice, use an appropriate research model informed by the social sciences, and interpret itself from the point of view of a Christian minister."[3]

D.Min. projects are as varied as the ministry of those who write them. Some are more practical; others can be more theoretical. Ministry always figures prominently.

---

[1] *Bulletin of the Association of Theological Schools* 43, part 1 (1998), standard F.3.1.3.
[2] SEAGST, *Handbook*, 123.
[3] Timothy D. Lincoln, "Writing Practical Christian Wisdom: Genre and the Doctor of Ministry Dissertation," *Theological Education* 36 (1999): 171.

A very common model is the "in-ministry" project, described in chapter 15 as program development. In this kind of paper a student develops a program and applies it in his or her ministry setting. Preparation, presentation, and evaluation are all parts of the process and the paper. The program may be as short as a week-end seminar, and as long as a one-year church revitalization program. In the first case, the adviser or the D.Min. committee may require that the program be repeated, possibly at another location. The "in-ministry" project requires hours and hours of thinking and doing; writing it out will take less time and fewer pages than writing other types of projects. Descriptive research may be needed to demonstrate a need for such an intervention (chapter 14). Normally the seminary requires that the adviser or mentor visit the place where the candidate is carrying out the program, often at the candidate's expense. Find out what requirements your school has regarding advising of "in-ministry" projects.

The case study (chapter 16) or the study of a theological issue in ministry (chapter 17) are also acceptable as D.Min. projects. This type of study is more theoretical. There is no actual application or evaluation of a program, but ministry is at the heart of the research. In the same category one could include church growth studies or strategies to reach an unreached people group. Again, descriptive research may be necessary (chapter 14). The application to ministry is clear.

Occasionally a D.Min. project may be even more theoretical than the projects described in the two previous paragraphs. The history of a denomination in a certain country or region may be an acceptable research topic. Biographies of ministers or missionaries could also be done. However, this type of project requires exceptional writing skills and special permission from your school's authorities.

Two important parts complement each other in the project dissertation. There must be theory—the why—and there must be practice—the how to. The proportion of each depends on the topic, the candidate, the doctoral committee, and the school. The theory includes the biblical and theological bases for the practical application, as well as any explanations from the social sciences—sociology, psychology, education, economics, history, geography, culture—that may undergird the intervention. Practice is what you do, on the basis of the theory studied, to solve the problem addressed.

The D.Min. project, just as the thesis or dissertation, is done in stages: proposal, research and writing, and defense.

Proposal

The project proposal can be completed only after many hours of reading, thinking, and observing. Regardless of the shape of the study, the proposal is the initial and required step towards the coveted degree. Its indispensable parts are:

1. Background information on the problem to be addressed to make the proposal clear to the readers and examiners
2. A statement of the problem
3. A statement of the task or purpose of the study
4. The justification for the study: the need for it and the contributions it will make
5. Any presuppositions that might affect the study
6. The methodology to be followed, showing not only the areas to be researched in the library, but practical application of the chosen intervention or program; this part describes the candidate's war plan
7. A detailed tentative outline
8. A preliminary bibliography

Normally a proposal for a D.Min. or D.P.Th. does not exceed ten carefully written pages. Some schools may have different or additional requirements, such as length, a statement of intent, or a vita. Clear the requirements of your school with your adviser or program director.

The Written Paper

The project for a professional degree in theology demonstrates the ability to think creatively and to act decisively. The time spent in carrying out a plan, program, or intervention in ministry is usually not reflected in the number of pages of the project dissertation. How can you translate the hours you spent in evangelism, teaching, or administration into pages? The writing is important, but the doing usually takes precedence.

Most schools set a limit to the number of pages a project dissertation may contain. Usually, the body of the text (excluding appendixes and bibliography) should be under 150 pages. Again, professors are looking for quality rather than quantity. Be sure to follow the guidelines of your seminary or school.

The organization of the paper is similar to that of a dissertation. The first chapter introduces the topic, presenting the problem or issue, the task (or purpose) of the project, the benefits of solving the problem (justification), the approach being followed, definition of terms (if needed), and an overview of the rest of the paper. Chapter 2 normally is theoretical: biblical-theological-sociological-psychological. In fact, there may be two theoretical chapters, if needed. Other chapters depend on the topic. The last chapter is always the same: summary, conclusions, and recommendations. Bear in mind that often only the first and last chapters of a dissertation or project are read. Thus, everything of vital importance must be in those two chapters: where you intended to go and what you found when you arrived there. Appendixes vary according to the project. For a seminar, for example, the outlines of the presentations, together with copies of the handouts and illustrations used belong there. If there were questionnaires, they also belong in the appendix. A bibliography closes the paper.

Each dissertation is to be accompanied by an abstract, which is a 350-word summary of the dissertation. The abstract includes the problem or issue, the findings, and the conclusions. The approval sheet, of which a modifiable model is given at the end of chapter 19, follows the title page.

Procedure

The candidate's dissertation committee is made up of an adviser and at least one reader or second member of the committee (different schools have different rules). Fortunately, the student is usually involved in the selection of the committee. The task of the adviser is to counsel and to supervise the candidate in the preparation of the project. The adviser reads, marks, and returns the material to the candidate, who then rewrites and returns the material to the adviser, who reads, marks, and returns. Normally a candidate rewrites at least three times. The reader usually does not read a chapter until the adviser has approved it. Thus the adviser is far more involved in the preparation of the dissertation than the reader.

In working together, student and adviser should avoid pitfalls that might sour relations or delay the work. One of the dangers is that either party may forget what he or she said. A workable solution to this problem is for you to take notes of what your adviser said and write up a synthesis of the instructions. Give a copy of this summary to your adviser to make sure that you heard correctly. If you do this with a nice spirit, your adviser will probably thank you for making sure you both know what is happening. Another issue that blights the dissertation/project procedure is delays, either by the adviser or the student. Suppose you work hard to complete a chapter, take it to the adviser, only to be informed that he has gone to Outer Slobovia for a series of evangelistic meetings. Likewise, instead of finishing chapter 3 in April, you complete it at the end of May—and the adviser is up to her ears in a major writing project. The solution to this problem is to set up a timetable: when you will turn in your materials and how long you will have to wait for your adviser to read and return them. Obviously, there may still be glitches, but if you two agree, the battle is already won.

Once the dissertation is deemed ready for defense by the adviser and reader(s), a date is set for the oral examination, and copies of the dissertation are made available to the examiners. At the oral examination you will make a presentation of your research. Make it brief and lively. You will then be asked questions about the research, its methodology, its findings, and your own conclusions. The dissertation may be approved as submitted, approved with revisions to be made and certified by the supervisor, or rejected. When the work has been carefully done, there is little danger of rejection!

After the defense, you and your adviser make the necessary adjustments to the paper. Then you will submit the appropriate number of copies to the appropriate office—each seminary has its own rules—at the appropriate time, in preparation for graduation. Most seminaries in North America cooperate with ATLA in the preparation of *Research in Ministry*, an index to D.Min. projects that is part of the *ATLA Index*. You submit your abstract so that future students can refer to your work.

Specific Kinds of D.Min. Papers

This chapter has proposed general directions for D.Min. papers. In addition, specific information appears in other chapters. Chapter 14 has instructions on descriptive research; chapter 15 explains program development; and chapter 16 has information on the case study. In chapter 17 you have materials on the theological issue in ministry. Three other possibilities are given as examples: a church-growth study, a church-planting project, and a strategy for reaching unreached peoples.

Church-Growth Study

A church-growth study may become an appropriate D.Min. project when it carefully studies the growth of a given church over time, analyzes the factors involved in its growth (or lack thereof), and designs appropriate strategies to enhance the church's growth. Occasionally, the study could include a group of churches.

Procedure

1. Become familiar with church-growth literature, both theoretical and narrative. Pay special attention to materials about churches similar to the one you are studying.
2. Investigate the growth patterns of the church over the past ten years. Get information from church records and other sources.
3. Study the climate and activities of the church during the past ten years. Read newsletters and reports; survey and interview as needed.
4. Analyze the community in which the church is located. Find out about its people, its institutions, industry, schools, socio-economic life, and traditions.

5. Come to tentative conclusions regarding the reasons for growth (or non-growth).
6. Applying sound, biblical principles of church growth, design a program for optimum growth for a specific church.

Written Presentation

The following chapters would constitute the study:

Chapter 1: Introduction

This should include a statement of the problem, justification for the study, definition of terms, and methodology used. A bibliographical essay or review of literature on church growth and church growth studies pertinent to the study is appropriate here. This will give the reader the assurance that the candidate is indeed aware of what the literature says. (The scope of the review should be defined. For example, one might set limits on the time of writing or the type of church.)

Chapter 2: History and description of the church

The patterns in growth and finances are described, together with the history of the church during the ten years. Descriptions of current facilities, programs, activities, and membership demographics are also presented.

Chapter 3: Description of the community

This should include demographics, economics, religion, traditions, institutions, etc.

Chapter 4: Analysis of the situation

This chapter analyzes the current church situation and possibilities for growth in light of church-growth theory, the history and statistics of the church, and the characteristics of the community.

Chapter 5: Strategy for growth

This chapter designs a strategy for sustainable growth by applying missiological and church-growth principles to the local situation.

Chapter 6: Summary, conclusions, and reflections

Appendixes

Bibliography

Church Planting

A church-planting project will take the planting of a new church from design through realization. This type of D.Min. project will naturally take much longer than bibliographic research.

Procedure

1. Study the literature on church planting.
2. Choose a location for the new church.
3. In collaboration with the adviser, design the plan and chronogram for the church planting, together for the criteria for evaluating the final result.
4. Obtain support of church administration and members to be involved in the church planting.
5. Carry out the plan.
6. In collaboration with the adviser, evaluate what has been done.
7. Write the dissertation or project.

Written Presentation

The body of the paper (excluding bibliography and appendixes) should be less than 100 pages long. The bulk of the work is in doing, not in reading or writing.

Chapter 1: Introduction
Task, justification, plan, and chronogram, criteria for evaluation (all taken from the proposal)

Chapter 2: Theoretical basis
A discussion of biblical and theological principles and assumptions relevant to the project. Review of literature on church planting under similar circumstances.

Chapter 3: Narrative of the church planting
A careful narrative of the steps taken to plant the church includes dates, activities, programs, and participants. This chapter shows how the objectives described in chapter 1 were met.

Chapter 4: Evaluation of the project
A narration of the evaluation process and the presentation of its results.

Chapter 5: Summary, conclusions, and reflections
The summary is provided for those who read only chapters 1 and 2. The conclusions and reflections give opportunity for subjective evaluation of the process and suggestions for someone who might attempt to plant a similar church.

Strategy to Reach an Unreached People Group

This type of doctoral project is more common for a concentration in mission than for other types of D.Min. programs. It is theoretical rather than practical.

Such a dissertation is especially significant for those whose ministry brings them in contact with non-Christian peoples but are currently studying in areas other than their own.[4]

Procedure

1. Read the literature on reaching unreached peoples.
2. Select a target group.
3. Study this group, its customs, beliefs, and socio-economic situation.
4. Analyze any contacts the group has had with Christians in general and with your particular denomination.
5. Design a strategy for the specific group.
6. Write the project/dissertation.

Written Presentation

Chapter 1: Introduction
Statement of the problem, naming the group and its location, justification for the study, definition of terms, methodology, etc.

Chapter 2: Description of the unreached people
Location, culture, religion, history, socio-economic status, health, education, etc. Description of the people's interaction with Christianity in general and with your denomination in particular.

Chapter 3: Analysis of deterrents and bridges to evangelism
Study of factors that seem to make evangelism difficult. Inquiry into possible natural bridges from the group's culture and religion to Christianity.

Chapter 4: Proposed strategy
An application of sound, biblical, missiological principles to design an implementable strategy for creating a Christian presence among the group.

Chapter 5: Summary, conclusions, and reflections. The summary is provided for those who read only chapters 1 and 5.

Appendixes

Bibliography

Now and then I hear people denigrate the D.Min. project, comparing it unfavorably to a Ph.D. dissertation. Such comments rankle my soul! Rightly done,

---

[4]My thanks to Bruce Bauer for this outline. When he prepared it, he was director of the Andrews University D.Min. in Missions; in 1998 he returned to mission service, this time in Cambodia. Useful to this type of study are the following books: John D. Robb, *Focus! The Power of People Group Thinking: A Practical Manual for Planning Effective Strategies to Reach the Unreached* (Monrovia, CA: MARC, 1989); Bill Stearns and Amy Stearns, *Catch the Vision 2000* (Minneapolis: Bethany, 1991).

this project has all the earmarks of research: It is based on solid theory—biblical, theological, and otherwise—and it contributes to the welfare of God's people as well as to the growth of ministry. May your D.Min. project bring satisfaction to you and glory to God.

CONCLUSION

This book has described several different types of endings for papers and dissertations. There is the summary-conclusion ending or the summary-conclusion-recommendations finale. You have also read about the theological issue in ministry with an "application-to-ministry" ending. The ending for this book does not follow any of these patterns.

In fact, it is not for me to conclude this book. It is for you, the student, to do so. The work you have produced following these guidelines summarizes, concludes, and applies any conclusion that I could have written. Your work will speak for me as well as for you.

May the skills you have honed and the abilities you have developed, to say nothing of the masterpiece you have produced, satisfy you and your professor. May this have been a battle well fought, a victory won with honor.

If you have written a good paper, I shall be content. My motto has long been: ἐκ χαοῦ κόσμος (lit., "out of chaos, order"). If your paper is well done, beauty and order have come out of chaos. I am satisfied.

And as you and I strive to bring order and beauty out of that which is unclear, confused, or unknown, may it be *soli Deo gloria*.

APA CITATION STYLE

Each discipline prefers its own citation style. While history and religion tend to use the Chicago style (Turabian), the social sciences adhere to the style known as APA (American Psychological Association).[1] This style is described in the *Publication Manual*, 1994.[2] Some seminaries use the APA style, especially for Doctor of Ministry projects or dissertations, since they often report information from different social sciences. The APA system has two general formats: the one required for manuscripts presented for publication by the American Psychological Association, the other for student papers and dissertations (*Publication Manual*, 1994, pp. 331–336). This appendix shows the second use; it employs APA style and uses the same examples that appear in Turabian style in chapter 9.

The APA citation style consists of two parts: in-text citations and a reference list (or bibliography). Without the reference list, the citations make absolutely no sense. Yet, the citations must be clear so a reader can easily find an item in the reference list.

In-Text Citations

In-text citations are enclosed in parentheses within the text. The basic format for this note is the surname of the author (or authors) and the date of publication. If you refer to a specific part of the source named or quote, you must also add the page(s) where you found the quotation or idea.

If there are two to five authors, use all surnames: (Smith, Peters, & Jones, 1999) in the first citation; for items with three to five authors use (Smith et al., 1999) in subsequent citations. If there six or more authors, use the first surname

---

[1]In chapter 10, Turabian (6th ed.) presents "Parenthetical References and Reference Lists." In chapters 11 and 12, this system is compared to the regular Turabian. It is similar to APA, yet does not qualify as APA.

[2]The reference list entry for this source is the following: American Psychological Association. (1994). *Publication Manual of the American Psychological Association* (4th ed.). Washington, D.C.: Author.

See also the following websites:

www.bedfordstmartins.com/hacker/resdoc/social_sciences/documenting.htm

owl.english.purdue.edu/handouts/research/r_apa.html

www.apa.org/journals/webref.html

My thanks to Bonnie Proctor, Dissertation Secretary at Andrews University, for sharing her expertise in APA.

plus "et al." in all citations. If the author is a corporate entity, the first note will read (United Nations, 1985); successive notes will say (UN, 1985). The entry in the reference list will have the name spelled out: United Nations. If your paper uses two authors with the same surname, add an initial to distinguish between them: (N. Smith, 1947) and (B. Smith, 1976).

When there is no author, the title (or a shortened form of the title) appears first: (*Education Handbook*, 1987, p. 35); in the reference list this item will be alphabetized under "Education." You may also use the form (Anonymous, 1977), as long as the reference list puts the same item under "Anonymous."

In an in-text citation, as in the text of the paper, you will capitalize the first word and all important nouns in titles as well as the first word after a colon. Articles will be in quotation marks and books or reports in italics or underlined.

The date of publication follows the comma after the author's surname. This date is the year the book or article was published, not the year in which it was written. Thus, you will not need to invent the year Irenaeus wrote *Against Heresies*, but only the year in which it was published in the work you are listing in the reference list.

If you quote, you must provide the exact page at the end of the quotation. The way you introduce the quotation will determine whether author and date are in one set of parentheses and the page in another, or all three are together. For example:

> Speaking of the differences between Acts and Galatians, Johnson (1992) notes that "both sources are partial and tendentious" (p. 270).
> One opinion regarding the differences between Acts and Galatians is that "both sources are partial and tendentious" (Johnson, 1992, p. 270).

A quotation of more than forty words must be treated as a block quotation, which in APA is indented five spaces from the left margin and single spaced. The page number in parentheses follows the final period of the quotation.

Ouro (2000) concludes his discussion of the state of the earth in Gen 1:2 by saying:

> Our study of the OT and ANE literature has found that Gen 1:2 must be interpreted as the description of the earth as it was without vegetation and uninhabited by animals and humans. The concept that appears in Gen 1:2 is an abiotic concept of the earth, with vegetable, animal, and human life appearing in the following verses. (p. 66)

Since APA does not use "ibid.," the author and date are repeated. In this sense, there is no "second note" form.

Letters and other personal communications (such as e-mail and interviews by the author) appear only in the text; they do not appear in the reference list. They are considered unretrievable as sources for other scholars.

APA in-text citations are user-friendly to the writer/researcher. They are, however, often quite unfriendly to a reader who wishes to find a reference. APA style does not require a page number in the in-text citation unless there is a direct quotation. This system works well for citations of a short article; your reader may have to search through only ten pages to certify that the author did indeed say what you said she did. By contrast, if you refer in APA style to an idea on page 270 of Luke Timothy Johnson's 568-page *Acts of the Apostles*, you only need to insert the following: (Johnson, 1992). Finding the page you have in mind may require reading half of the book! To assist your reader, you may insert the number of the page to which you are referring, as if you had used a direct quotation (Johnson, 1992, p. 270). This addition to APA style is permissiblee, highly desirable, and most useful to the reader. Be sure to follow the instructions of your school, and, more specifically, your adviser, on the use of APA style.

Reference List

Proper APA style for submitting articles requires the reference list to be double-spaced with the first line indented. However, the style for student papers allows for the reference list to look almost like a Turabian bibliography, single spaced and with hanging indentation. The important difference is that the date of publication appears in parentheses immediately after the author statement, which ends with a period or full stop.

The names of all authors are inverted. Initials are used instead of first names: Johnson, L. T. Use the ampersand (&) instead of "and" when there are multiple authors. The list is alphabetized by the (first) author's surname, the corporate author, or the title (if there is no author).

The copyright date is placed in parentheses and followed by a full stop. When a particular author has more than one work, the items are ordered chronologically, from oldest to newest. Should there be two or more items published in one year, add a letter to the year: 1993a, 1993b, 1993c. Make sure the in-text notes have the same dates as the reference list.

Titles of books and journals are underlined or written in italics. Only the first word and proper nouns of the title are capitalized. Titles of articles have no quotation marks. The underlining (or italics) goes beyond the title to the volume number of a journal.

Samples

The samples given below for the in-text citation (C) show how to report an allusion or citation. A direct quotation requires a page number, either in the same parentheses with the date or at the end of the quotation. The sample reference list entries (R) are in APA student format.

Books

Authorship

One or two authors

C   (Drummond, 1996)

R   Drummond, L. (1996). *Miss Bertha: Woman of revival.* Nashville: Broadman & Holman.

C   (Aland & Aland, 1989)

R   Aland, K., & Aland, B. (1989). *The text of the New Testament* (Rev. ed.). Leiden: Brill.

Three to five authors

C   (VanGemeren, Bahnsen, Kaiser, Strickland, & Moo, 1993)
       Second reference: (VanGemeren et al., 1993)

R   VanGemeren, W. A., Bahnsen, G. L., Kaiser, W. C., Jr., Strickland, W. G., & Moo, D.
       (1993). *The law, the gospel, and the modern Christian.* Grand Rapids: Zondervan.

Corporate author

C   (Southern Baptist Convention, 1975)

R   Southern Baptist Convention. (1975). *Annual of the Southern Baptist Convention.*
       Nashville: Southern Baptist Convention.

No author, edition other than first, with translator

C   (*Bhagavad-Gita as It Is*, 1972)

R   *Bhagavad-Gita as it is.* (Abridged edition). (1972). (A. C. Bhaktivedanta Swami .
       Prabhupada, Trans.). New York: Bhaktivedanta Book Trust.

Editor instead of author; joint publication

C   (VanderKam & Adler, 1996)

R   VanderKam, J. C., & Adler, W. (Eds.). (1996). *The Jewish apocalyptic heritage in early
       Christianity.* Assen, Netherlands: Van Gorcum; Minneapolis: Fortress.

Component part by one author in a work edited by another

C   (Davidson, 1998)

R   Davidson, R. M. (1998). Headship, submission, and equality in scripture. In N. J.
       Vyhmeister (Ed.), *Women in ministry: Biblical and historical perspectives* (pp. 259–
       295). Berrien Springs, MI: Andrews University Press.

Multivolume Works

One author

C   (González, 1970–1975)
     or
     (González, 1970–1975, 1:176)

[You may also use vol. 1, p. 176, but use the same format throughout your paper.]

R   González, J. (1970–1975). *A history of Christian thought* (Vols. 1–3). Nashville:
       Abingdon.

C   (Latourette, 1970)
R   Latourette, K. S. (1970). *Three centuries of advance: Vol. 3. A history of the expansion of Christianity*. Grand Rapids: Zondervan.

Several authors—independent titles for each volume.

C   (Rapske, 1994)
R   Rapske, B. (1994). *The Book of Acts and Paul in Roman custody*. In B. W. Winter (Gen. Ed.), *The Book of Acts in its first century setting* (Vol. 4). Carlisle, UK: Paternoster, 1994.

Part of a Series

C   (Booth, Colomb, & Williams, 1995)
R   Booth, W. C., Colomb, G. G, & Williams, J. M. (1995). *The craft of research*. Chicago Guides to Writing, Editing and Publishing. Chicago: University of Chicago Press.

Reprint

C   (Nevius, 1894/1968)
R   Nevius, J. L. (1968). *Demon possession*. Grand Rapids: Kregel. (Original work published 1894)
C   (Reynolds, 1913/1977)
R   Reynolds, H. R. (1977). Introduction to the Gospel of St. John. In H. O. M. Spence & J. H. Excell (Eds.), *The pulpit commentary* (Vol. 17, pp. iv-clxi). Grand Rapids: Eerdmans. (Original work published 1913)

Secondary Source

C   In his *Life and Passion of Cyprian,* Pontius the Deacon (as cited in Olson, 1999, p. 116) affirmed . . .
[Give all the information on the primary source that you want your reader to have, as well as the page in the secondary source. The reference list mentions only the secondary source.]
R   Olson, R. E. (1999). *The story of Christian theology*. Downers Grove, IL: InterVarsity.

Periodicals

Magazines

C   (Lemonick & Dorfman, 2000)
R   Lemonick, M. D., & Dorfman, A. (2000, May 8). The amazing Vikings. *Time, 155,* 69–74.

Journals

C   (Shank, 1985)
R   Shank, D. (1985). Mission relations with independent churches in Africa. *Missiology, 13,* 23–44.

When a journal begins each issue from page 1 (rather than continued paging throughout the volume), specify which issue of the volume you have used. Thus you will include the number, month, or season in parentheses after the volume number, though not in italics: *Newsletter, 4* (1), 9.

Specialized Books

Classical Authors and Church Fathers

C   (Irenaeus, *Against Heresies* 2.2.3) or (Irenaeus, *Against Heresies* 2.2.3, *ANF* 1:421)

R   Irenaeus. (1989–1990). *Against heresies.* In A. Roberts & J. Donaldson (Eds.), *The ante-nicene fathers* (Vol. 1:315–567). Grand Rapids: Eerdmans.

C   (Chrysostom, *The Priesthood* 3.17)

R   Chrysostom, J. (1862). *The priesthood.* In J. P. Migne (Ed.), *Patrologia Graeca* (Vol. 48, cols. 623–692). Paris: Apud Garnier Fratres.

C   (Josephus, *Jewish war* 2.14.5)

R   Josephus, F. (1869). *Jewish War.* In W. Whiston (Ed.), *The works of Josephus* (Vol.3, p. 317– Vol. 4, p. 352). New York: Oakley, Mason & Co.

Rabbinical Works

C   (Mishnah *Sanhedrin* 10:3)

R   *The Mishnah.* (1933). (H. Danby, Trans.). London: Oxford University Press.

C   (B. T. *Sanhedrin* 97a) or (B. Talmud *Sanhedrin* 97a)

R   *The Babylonian Talmud.* (1935). (I. Epstein, Ed.). London: Soncino.

Bible Commentaries and Concordances

Commentaries—Author given

C   (Polhill, 1975)

R   Polhill, J. B. (1992). *Acts.* New American Commentary. Nashville: Broadman.

C   (Campbell, 1975)

R   Campbell, E. R. (1975). *Ruth.* Anchor Bible, 7. Garden City, NY: Doubleday.

C   (Delitzsch, 1949)

R   Delitzsch, F. (1949). *Biblical commentary on the book of Job* (Vols. 1–2). Biblical Commentary on the Old Testament. Grand Rapids: Eerdmans.

C   (Craddock, 1998)

R   Craddock, F. B. (1998). The letter to the Hebrews: Introduction, commentary, and reflections. In *New interpreter's Bible* (Vol. 12, pp. 3–173). Nashville: Abingdon.

C (Wright, 1954)

R   Wright, G. E. (1954). Exegesis of the book of Deuteronomy. In G. A. Buttrick (Ed.), *Interpreter's Bible* (Vol. 2, pp. 331–540). New York: Abingdon.

Commentaries—No author given

C   (Hastings, 1971, 17:159)

R   Hastings, E. (Ed.). (1971). *The speaker's Bible* (Vols. 1–18). Grand Rapids: Baker Book House.

Concordances

C   (Young, n.d., 785)

R   Young, R. (n.d.). Analytical concordance to the Bible (22d American ed.). Grand Rapids: Eerdmans.

Dictionaries and Encyclopedias
Dictionaries and encyclopedias with unsigned articles

C   (Webster, 1976)

C   (*Columbia Encyclopedia*, 1976)

Well-known dictionaries and encyclopedias do not appear in the reference list. Dictionaries and encyclopedias in the area of religion do.

C   (Youngblood, 1995)
R   Youngblood, R. F. (Ed.). (1995). *Nelson's new illustrated Bible dictionary* (Rev. ed.). Nashville: Nelson.

C   (*Seventh-day Adventist Encyclopedia*, 1996)
[Later references: (*SDA Encyclopedia*, 1996)]
R   *Seventh-day Adventist Encyclopedia*. (1996). (Vols. 1–2). Hagerstown, MD: Review and Herald.

Dictionaries and encyclopedias with signed articles

C   (Lapin, 1992)
R   Lapin, H. (1992). Rabbi. In *Anchor Bible dictionary* (Vol. 5. pp. 600–602). New York: Doubleday.

C   (Bultmann, 1964–1976, *Aidōs*)
R   Bultmann, R. (1964–1976). *Aidōs*. In *Theological dictionary of the New Testament* (Vol. 1, p. 169). Grand Rapids: Eerdmans.

R   Kittel, G., & Friedrich, G. (Eds). *Theological dictionary of the New Testament* (Vols. 1–10). Grand Rapids: Eerdmans.

C   (Demsky, 1971–1972, 6:384)
R   Demsky, A. (1971–1972). Education: In the biblical period. In *Encyclopaedia Judaica* (Vol. 6, pp. 382–398). Jerusalem: Encyclopaedia Judaica.

Collected Works of Individual Authors

C   (Barth, 1960, III/3, p. 82)
R   Barth, K. (1960). *Church dogmatics* (Vol. III/3). Edinburgh: T. & T. Clark.

C   (Luther, 1955–1976, Vol. 51, p. 259)
or
      (Luther, 1955–1976, 51:259)
R   Luther, M. (1955–1976). *Sermon on the sum of Christian life*. In *Luther's Works* (American ed.,Vol. 51, pp. 259–287). Saint Louis: Concordia.

R   Luther, M. (1955–1976). *Luther's works*. (American ed., Vols. 1–55). Saint Louis: Concordia.

Book Reviews

C   (Meyers, 1999)
R   Meyers, C. (1999). [Review of the book *The Archaeology of Israel: Constructing the past, interpreting the present.*] *Journal of Biblical Literature, 118*, 530–531.

Video and Sound Recordings

C   (Anderson, 1989)

R   Anderson, K. (Producer). (1989). *Hudson Taylor* [Videocassette]. (Available from Ken
       Anderson Films, P.O. Box 618, Winona Lake, IN 46590)

C   (Landriscina, 1985)

R   Landriscina, L. (1985). Judío en el Vaticano. In *Mano a mano con el país* (Vol. 5)
       [Audiocassette No. 64232]. Buenos Aires: Phillips.

Unpublished materials

Academic Sources

Theses and dissertations

C   (Nogueira, 1999)

R   Nogueira, P. C. (1999). *Equipping laity for ministry in multi-church districts in Brazil.*
       Unpublished doctoral dissertation, Andrews University, Berrien Springs, Mil.

APA distinguishes between unpublished dissertations (as given above) and
dissertations accessed by means of *Dissertation Abstracts International*. The format for the second is:

R   Choi, P. R. (1997). Abraham our father: Paul's voice in the covenantal debate of the
       second temple period (Doctoral dissertation, Fuller Theological Seminary, School
       of Theology). *Doctoral Dissertations International, 58*, (05A):1759.

C   (Silitonga, 1988)

R   Silitonga, H. (1988). *Christological implications of Leviticus 16:11–23: A study from an
       Indonesian perspective.* Unpublished master of theology thesis, Adventist
       International Institute of Advanced Studies, Silang, Cavite, Philippines.

APA makes no distinction among different kinds of doctoral dissertations.
The same goes for master's theses. Your school may allow you to specify the type
of dissertation (D.Min., Ed.D., or Ph.D.) or thesis (as in the above example).

Miscellaneous academic papers

C   (Reeve, 1997)

R   Reeve, T. (1997). *The 'Just Man' in the writings of Philo.* Unpublished class paper, THEO
       611 Philo Seminar, University of Notre Dame.

C   (Fanwar, 1999)

R   Fanwar, W. M. (1999). *He who created the heavens and the earth: Contributions of Isaiah to
       Rev 14:7c.* Unpublished seminar paper, GSEM 920 Religious Studies Seminar,
       Theological Seminary, Andrews University, Berrien Springs, MI.

Syllabi

C   (Vyhmeister, 1999)

R   Vyhmeister, Nancy. (1999). *Course outline for GSEM 854 Ph.D. Proposal Seminar.*
       Theological Seminary, Andrews University, Berrien Springs, MI.

Class notes

C   (Program in Language Acquisition Techniques, 1980)

R   Program in Language Acquisition Techniques. (1980). [Class notes]. Missionary Internship, Farmington, MI.

APA insists on postal codes for states; there is no other choice.

Miscellaneous Unpublished Sources

Reports

C   (Seventh-day Adventist Theological Seminary, Far East, 1985)
[In subsequent notes: (SDATSFE, 1985)]

R   Seventh-day Adventist Theological Seminary, Far East. (1985). *Financial statement of graduate apartments, 31 August.* Silang, Cavite, Philippines: Seventh-day Adventist Theological Seminary, Far East.

C   (Association of Theological Institutions in Eastern Africa, 1979)

R   Association of Theological Institutions in Eastern Africa. (1979). *1978/79 Bachelor of Divinity degree syllabus.* Nairobi, Kenya: Association of Theological Institutions in Eastern Africa.

Speeches and presentations

C   (Maxwell, 1976)

R   Maxwell, C. M. (1976). *Which sacrifice, Lord?* [Typescript]. Seminary Chapel sermon. Andrews University, 20 October 1976.

C   (Paulien, 1996)

R   Paulien, J. (1996). *The lion/lamb king: Reading Revelation from popular culture.* Paper presented at the annual meeting of the Society of Biblical Literature, New Orleans.

Manuscripts

C   (Benoit, 1875)

R   Benoit, P. L. (1875). Photocopy of typewritten transcript of Canon Benoit's diary of a trip to America, 6 January to 8 June 1875, including descriptions of Josephite missions among freed slaves. Archives, University of Notre Dame.

C   (White, 1905)

R   White, E. G. (1905). Letter to Dr. Patience Bourdeau, 8 June 1905. Letter 177, 1905. Ellen White Research Center, Newbold College, Bracknell, England.

Personal communications

In APA style, letters, interviews, and e-mail are considered as personal communications. The name of the source appears in the text; the phrase "personal communication" (or "interview") and the precise date are given in the in-text note. Since information from this communication is not available to the reader, nothing appears in the reference list.

C   Bryan Ball, editor of *The Essential Jesus* (personal communication, 13 March 2000), stated that . . .

C   Yeow Choo Lak, Executive Director of the Association for Theological Education in Southeast Asia, agrees with this position (interview, Singapore, 15 July 1985).

Electronic media

CD-ROM

C   (Bunyan, 1998)

R   Bunyan, John. (1998). Pilgrim's Progress, stage 2 [CD-ROM]. Logos Library System 2.1 (Vol. 1). Oak Harbor, WA: Logos Research Systems.

World Wide Web

C   (Hahne, 1997)

R   Hahne, H. (1997). *An annotated bibliography on computer-assisted biblical and theological research*. Retrieved 21 April 1997, from www.epas.utoronto.ca:8080/~hahne/scbibann.html.

For further information on the citation of online materials, see *Electronic Reference Formats Recommended by the American Psychological Association*, www.apa.org/journals/webref.html.

Appendix B | TRANSLITERATION OF BIBLICAL LANGUAGES

The following is an acceptable academic scheme for transliterating biblical Hebrew and Greek. Students in advanced courses or writing dissertations may be required to use additional diacritical marks for the Hebrew. Each student should consult his or her advisor on this matter.

Hebrew

Consonants

א =	ʾ	ט =	ṭ	פ =	p
ב =	b	י =	y	צ =	ṣ
ג =	g	כ =	k	ק =	q
ד =	d	ל =	l	ר =	r
ה =	h	מ =	m	שׂ =	ś
ו =	w	נ =	n	שׁ =	š
ז =	z	ס =	s	ת =	t
ח =	ḥ	ע =	ʿ		

Masoretic Vowel Pointings

= a	(vocal shewa) = ě	= o
= ā	or = ê	= ŏ
= ă	= i	ו = ô
= e	= î	ו = û
= ē	= ō	= u

No distinction is made between soft and hard *begadkepat* letters; *dāgēš forte* is indicated by doubling the consonant.

Koine Greek

A α	=	A a	K κ	=	K k	T τ	=	T t
B β	=	B b	Λ λ	=	L l	Υ υ	=	Y y
Γ γ	=	G g	M μ	=	M m	Φ φ	=	Ph ph
Δ δ	=	D d	N ν	=	N n	X χ	=	Ch ch
E ε	=	E e	Ξ ξ	=	X x	Ψ ψ	=	Ps ps
Z ζ	=	Z z	O o	=	O o	Ω ω	=	Ō ō
H η	=	Ē ē	Π π	=	P p	ʿ	=	H h
Θ θ	=	Th th	P ρ	=	R r			
I ι	=	I i	Σ σ	=	S s			

Before γ, κ, ξ, χ, gamma is transliterated as *n*. In a dipthong, upsilon is transliterated as *u*.

For further details on transliteration of ancient languages, see *SBL Handbook of Style*, 5:1–9.

Appendix C | LIST OF COMMON ABBREVIATIONS

This is a short list of reference works and serials titles in the area of religion.[1] Titles of journals and books are italicized (or underlined), but titles of serials are set in roman characters, as are acronyms of authors' names when they are used as sigla.

These abbreviations are only used in footnotes when a list of abbreviations has been placed before the introduction of the paper. Abbreviations are not used in bibliographical entries.

ASOR	American Schools of Oriental Research	BAR	*Biblical Archaeology Review*
AB	Anchor Bible	BASOR	*Bulletin of the American Schools of Oriental Research*
ABD	*Anchor Bible Dictionary*	BCSR	*Bulletin of the Council on the Study of Religion*
AHR	*American Historical Review*	BDB	Brown, Driver, and Briggs, *Lexicon*, 1907
AJT	*American Journal of Theology*		
ANEP	*Ancient Near East in Pictures*	BDF	Blass, Debrunner, and Funk, *Greek Grammar*
ANET	*Ancient Near Eastern Texts*		
ANF	The Ante-Nicene Fathers	*BHS*	*Biblia hebraica stuttgartensia*
ANRW	*Aufstieg und Niedergang der römischen Welt*	*Bib*	*Biblica*
AThR	*Anglican Theological Review*	BiPa	Biblia Patristica
AusBR	*Australasian Biblical Review*	*BJRL*	*Bulletin of the John Rylands Library*
AUSS	*Andrews University Seminary Studies*	*BK*	*Bibel und Kirche*
BA	*Biblical Archaeologist*	BKAT	Biblischer Kommentar: Altes Testament
BAG	Bauer, Arndt, and Gingrich, *Lexicon*, 1957	*BO*	*Bibliotheca orientalis*
BAGD	Bauer, Arndt, Gingrich, and Danker, *Lexicon*, 1979	*BR*	*Biblical Research*
		Brev	*Bible Review*

[1]For a much longer list of abbreviations, especially in biblical and Near Eastern studies, see *SBL Handbook of Style* (Peabody, MA: Hendrickson, 1999), 89–121. The ultimate list of abbreviations is available in *Theologisches RealencyklopädieAbkurzungsverzeichnis*, 2d ed. (Berlin: De Gruyter, 1993).

BSac	*Bibliotheca Sacra*
BT	*The Bible Translator*
BTB	*Biblical Theology Bulletin*
BZ	*Biblische Zeitschrift*
BZAW	Beihefte zur *ZAW*
BZNW	Beihefte zur *ZNW*
CAD	*Chicago Assyrian Dictionary*
CBQ	*Catholic Biblical Quarterly*
ChrCent	*Christian Century*
CH	*Church History*
CHR	*Catholic Historical Review*
CIG	*Corpus inscriptionum graecarum*
CIJ	*Corpus inscriptionum iudaicarum*
CIL	*Corpus inscriptionum latinarum*
CIS	*Corpus inscriptionum semiticarum*
CJT	*Canadian Journal of Theology*
CQ	*Church Quarterly*
CQR	*Church Quarterly Review*
CT	*Christianity Today*
CTJ	*Calvin Theological Journal*
CTM	*Concordia Theological Monthly*
CurTM	*Currents in Theology and Mission*
DJG	*Dictionary of Jesus and the Gospels*
EDNT	*Exegetical Dictionary of the NT*
EEC	*Encyclopedia of Early Christianity*
EKL	*Evangelisches Kirchenlexikon*
EncIs	*Encyclopedia of Islam*
EncJud	*Encyclopedia Judaica*
ER	Eliade, *Encyclopedia of Religion*, 1987
EvQ	*Evangelical Quarterly*
EvT	*Evangelische Theologie*
ExpTim	*Expository Times*
GRBS	*Greek, Roman, and Byzantine Studies*
GTJ	*Grace Theological Journal*
HALOT	Koehler, Baumgartner, and Stamm, *Lexicon*, 1999
HeyJ	*Heythrop Journal*
HR	*History of Religions*
HTR	*Harvard Theological Review*
HUCA	*Hebrew Union College Annual*
IB	*Interpreter's Bible*
IBC	Interpretation Bible Commentary
ICC	International Critical Commentary
IDB	*Interpreter's Dictionary of the Bible*
IEJ	*Israel Exploration Journal*
Int	*Interpretation*
ISBE	*International Standard Bible Dictionary*
JAAR	*Journal of the American Academy of Religion*
JAOS	*Journal of the American Oriental Society*
JAS	*Journal of Asian Studies*
JBL	*Journal of Biblical Literature*
JBR	*Journal of Bible and Religion*
JCS	*Journal of Cuneiform Studies*
JEA	*Journal of Egyptian Archaeology*
JETS	*Journal of the Evangelical Theological Society*
JEH	*Journal of Ecclesiastical History*
JES	*Journal of Ecumenical Studies*
JJS	*Journal of Jewish Studies*
JMedHist	*Journal of Medieval History*
JMES	*Journal of Middle Eastern Studies*

JMH	Journal of Modern History	NIDNTT	New International Dictionary of NT Theology
JNES	Journal of Near Eastern Studies		
JPOS	Journal of the Palestine Oriental Society	NIGTC	New International Greek Testament Commentary
JQR	Jewish Quarterly Review	NKZ	Neue Kirchliche Zeitschrift
JR	Journal of Religion	NovT	Novum Testamentum
JRAS	Journal of the Royal Asiatic Society	NPNF	Nicene and Post-Nicene Fathers
JRE	Journal of Religious Ethics	NRT	La nouvelle revue théologique
JRelS	Journal of Religious Studies	NTAp	NT Apocrypha, Schneemelcher
JRH	Journal of Religious History	NTS	New Testament Studies
JRT	Journal of Religious Thought	ODCC	Oxford Dictionary of the Christian Church
JSJ	Journal for the Study of Judaism		
JSNT	Journal for the Study of the NT	OLZ	Orientalistische Literaturzeitung
JSOT	Journal for the Study of the OT	Or	Orientalia (Rome)
JSS	Journal of Semitic Studies	OrChr	Oriens christianus
JSSR	Journal for the Scientific Study of Religion	OTP	OT Pseudepigrapha, Charlesworth
JTC	Journal for Theology and the Church	OTS	Old Testament Studies
JTS	Journal of Theological Studies	PEQ	Palestine Exploration Quarterly
K&D	Keil and Delitsch, Commentary	PG	Patrologia Graeca, Migne
KBL	Koehler and Baumgartner, Lexicon, 1958	PL	Patrologia Latina, Migne
L&N	Louw and Nida, Lexicon on Semantic Domains	PW	Pauly-Wissowa, Realencyclopädie
LCC	Library of Christian Classics	RA	Revue d'assyriologie et d'archéologie orientale
LCL	Loeb Classical Library	RAC	Reallexikon für Antike und Christentum
LQ	Lutheran Quarterly		
LW	Luther's Work, American Ed.	RArch	Revue archéologique
MQR	Mennonite Quarterly Review	RB	Revue biblique
Neot	Neotestamentica	RelS	Religious Studies
NHS	Nag Hammadi Studies	RelSoc	Religion and Society
NICNT	New International Commentary, NT	RelSRev	Religious Studies Review
		RevExp	Review and Expositor
NICOT	New International Commentary, OT	RevQ	Revue de Qumrán
		RevScRel	Revue des sciences religieuses
NIDOTTE	New International Dictionary of OT Theology and Exegesis	RevSém	Revue sémitique
		RHE	Revue d'histoire ecclésiastique

RHPR	*Revue d'histoire et de philosophie religieuses*	*TS*	*Theological Studies*
		ThTo	*Theology Today*
RHR	*Revue de l'histoire des religions*	*ThWAT*	*Theologisches Wörterbuch zum AT*
RL	*Religion in Life*	TU	Texte und Untersuchungen
RR	*Review of Religion*	*TWOT*	*Theological Wordbook of the OT*
RRelRes	*Review of Religious Research*	*TZ*	*Theologische Zeitschrift*
RSPT	*Revue des sciences philosophiques et théologiques*	*UF*	*Ugarit-Forschungen*
RSR	*Recherches de science religieuse*	*USQR*	*Union Seminary Quarterly Review*
RTP	*Revue de théologie et de philosophie*	*VC*	*Vigiliae christianae*
SA	*Sociological Analysis*	*Vid*	*Vidyajyoti*
SB	Sources bibliques	*VT*	*Vetus Testamentum*
SBLDS	SBL Dissertation Series	VTSup	Vetus Testamentum, Supplements
SBLMS	SBL Monograph Series	WA	Luther's Works, Weimarer
SBLSBS	SBL Sources for Biblical Study		Ausgabe
SBLTT	SBL Texts and Translations	WBC	Word Biblical Commentary
SBT	Studies in Biblical Theology	*WTJ*	*Westminster Theological Journal*
SC	*Sources chrétiennes*	*ZA*	*Zeitschrift für Assyriologie*
SCJ	*Sixteenth Century Journal*	*ZAW*	*Zeitschrift für die alttesta-mentliche Wissenschaft*
SCR	*Studies in Comparative Religion*	*ZDMG*	*Zeitschrift der deutschen morgenländischen Gesellschaft*
Sem	*Semitica*	*ZDPV*	*Zeitschrift des deutschen Palästina-Vereins*
SJT	*Scottish Journal of Theology*		
SMRT	*Studies in Medieval and Reformation Thought*	*ZEE*	*Zeitschrift für evangelische Ethik*
SSS	Semitic Studies Series	*ZHT*	*Zeitschrift für historische Theologie*
ST	*Studia Theologica*	*ZKG*	*Zeitschrift für Kirchengeschichte*
TD	*Theology Digest*	*ZKT*	*Zeitschrift für katholische Theologie*
TDNT	*Theological Dictionary of the NT*	*ZMR*	*Zeitschrift für Missionskunde und Religionswissenschaft*
TDOT	*Theological Dictionary of the OT*		
TGl	*Theologie und Glaube*	*ZNW*	*Zeitschrift für die neutesta-mentliche Wissenschaft*
TJ	*Trinity Journal*	*ZRGG*	*Zeitschrift für Religions- und Geistegeschichte*
TLZ	*Theologische Literaturzeitung*		
TP	*Theologie und Philosophie*	*ZST*	*Zeitschrift für systematische Theologie*
TQ	*Theologische Quartalschrift*	*ZTK*	*Zeitschrift für Theologie und Kirche*
TRev	*Theologische Revue*	*ZWT*	*Zeitschrift für wissenschaftliche Theologie*
TRu	*Theologische Rundschau*		

Appendix D | TIPS FOR THE TYPIST

In addition to reading this summary, the typist should refer to chapter 12, especially to the model pages given there. Items are listed here in alphabetical order to facilitate finding.

Corrections

Visible corrections are not allowed in the paper that is handed in. If a photocopy is turned in, corrections on the original copy should be made—either with white ink (liquid paper) or with self-adhesive paper strips—so that the copy looks perfect. There is no problem with "cutting and pasting," as long as the copy shows no lines or shadows.

Footnotes

Footnotes begin with a 20-space underline located one line under the last line of text. The footnote number is indented 8 spaces, 1.5 lines below the underline. The text of the footnote follows, 2 lines below the underline. Footnotes must follow the format given in chapters 8 and 9. Automatic footnoting, as done by Microsoft Word™ and WordPerfect™, is highly recommended. The student is responsible for footnote content and format. Model pages including footnotes appear in chapter 12.

Headings

Chapter numbers and titles are typed in uppercase letters, on lines 13 and 15 (2 inches from the top of the page and double space below). Other headings are as follows:

First-Level Heading: Centered, Bold (or Italics)
Second-Level Heading: Centered, Not Italics

Third-Level Heading: Flush Left, Bold (or Italics)
Fourth-level heading: flush left, not underlined; only first word capitalized
Fifth-level heading: indented same as paragraph. Bold or *italics*,
only first word is capitalized. Paragraph continues immediately.

Leave two lines blank before a heading; one line blank after. More information in chapter 12.

Indentation

Indentation is .6 inches for paragraphs and footnotes. Block quotations are indented .3 inches from each margin. If the quotation starts at the beginning of a paragraph, it is indented another .3 inches. Second lines of bibliographical entries are indented .4 inches.

Margins

The left margin should be 1.5 inches. The other three margins should be 1 inch. If pica (10 point) type is used, there will be room for 60 characters on a line. If elite (12 point) is used, there will be 72 characters. Margins must be observed meticulously.

Page Length

Letter-size paper of good quality must be used. In order to fit within the margins indicated above, there must be no more than 54 single spaces or 27 double spaces of text on a normal letter-size page. In areas where A4 paper is the norm, this size paper can be used. The margins should remain the same, giving a slightly narrower and longer area for the text.

Pagination

Page 1 is the first page of the Introduction. Page numbers are centered on the 5th line (at the top of the page) except on the first page of a chapter, introduction, summary, conclusion, or bibliography. Then they are centered at the bottom, on the 61st line of the page. Use the automatic page numbering function of a word processing program.

Pagination of preliminary matters begins on the title page and is typed, centered, at the bottom of the page in small roman numerals.

Photocopying

Photocopying tends to enlarge the text slightly. This makes it imperative to stay within the margins indicated. Generally, good quality photocopies are accepted as originals. There should be no need for making carbon copies.

Punctuation

The spacing required after punctuation marks is one space after period (full stop), comma, colon, or semicolon. For pages of books, there is no space after a colon, 5:66. For pages of journals, there is a space after the colon (1998): 66.

Commas and periods go inside quotation marks, unless these enclose one letter or number: He said "Good-bye." This is Phase "A".

In typing, a dash is represented by two hyphens or a long dash, with no space on either side of them. For example: He said--or wrote, I'm not sure which--that he was coming next week; or, He said—or wrote, I'm not sure which—that he was coming next week,

In an enumeration, a comma follows each item: He asked for a pen, some paper, an envelope, and a stamp.

Quotations

All materials quoted from another source must be enclosed in double quotation marks. Single quotation marks are to be used only for a quotation within a quotation. The comma and the period (full stop) go within the quotations; the colon and the semicolon go outside. If a quotation is a question, the question mark goes inside the quotation marks. If the quotation is part of the question, the question mark goes outside.

Block quotations are used for quotations longer than one sentence and four lines. They must be single spaced and indented .3 inches from both margins. If the beginning of the block quotation coincides with the beginning of a paragraph, the first line is indented another .3 inches.

Spacing

Research papers, theses, and dissertations are double spaced. Block quotations are typed single space. Footnotes and bibliography entries are single spaced, but have a blank line between them. Three lines are left blank above and below a table or figure. Two blank lines precede a heading; one follows it.

Spelling

Either American or British spelling may be used. However, both may not be used in the same paper. The student is responsible for the spelling. The typist is responsible for correct word division.

Table of Contents

Follow the model on page 110 in chapter 12.

Title Page

Follow the model on page 109. For theses or dissertations add the approval page on page 191.

SELECTED BIBLIOGRAPHY

Andrews University Standards for Written Work. 9th ed. Berrien Springs, MI: Andrews University Press, 1996.

Badke, William B. *The Survivor's Guide to Library Research: A Simple, Systematic Approach to Using the Library and Writing Research Papers.* Grand Rapids: Zondervan, 1990.

Bissell, Juanita. *A Guide for Research Writing: AIIAS Theological Seminary.* Silang, Cavite, Philippines: AIIAS Publications, 1996.

Booth, Wayne C., Gregor G. Colomb, and Joseph M. Williams. *The Craft of Research.* Chicago Guides to Writing, Editing, and Publishing. Chicago: University of Chicago Press, 1995.

Davies, Richard E. *Handbook for Doctor of Ministry Projects.* Lanham, MD: University Press of America, 1984.

Davis, Gordon B., and Clyde A. Parker. *Writing the Doctoral Dissertation: A Systematic Approach.* 2d ed. New York: Barron's, 1997.

Durusau, Patrick. *High Places in Cyberspace: A Guide to Biblical and Religious Studies, Classics, and Archaeological Resources on the Internet.* 2d ed. Atlanta: Scholars Press, 1998.

Henson, Kenneth T. *The Art of Writing for Publication.* Boston: Allyn and Bacon, 1995.

Hudson, Bob, and Shelley Townsend. *A Christian Writer's Manual of Style.* Grand Rapids: Zondervan, 1988.

Isaac, Stephen, and William Michael. *Handbook in Research and Evaluation.* San Diego: EDITS, 1971.

Kepple, Robert. *Reference Works for Theological Research.* 3d ed. Lanham, MD: University Press of America, 1992.

Lester, James D. *Writing Research Papers: A Complete Guide.* 9th ed. New York: Longman, 1999.

Madsen, David. *Successful Dissertations and Theses: A Guide to Graduate Student Research from Proposal to Completion.* 2d ed. San Francisco: Jossey-Bass, 1992.

Maggion, Rosalie. *The Nonsexist Word Finder: A Dictionary of Gender-free Usage.* Boston: Beacon, 1987.

Publication Manual for the American Psychological Association. 4th ed. Washington, D.C.: American Psychological Association, 1994.

The SBL Handbook of Style for Ancient Near Eastern, Biblical, and Early Christian Studies. Peabody, MA: Hendrickson, 1999.

Slade, Carole. *Form and Style: Research Papers, Reports, Theses.* 11th ed. Boston: Houghton Mifflin, 2000.

Strunk, William, and E. B. White. *The Elements of Style.* 3d ed. New York: Macmillan, 1979.

Turabian, Kate L. *A Manual for Writers of Term Papers, Theses, and Dissertations.* 6th ed. Revised by John Grossman and Alice Bennett. Chicago: University of Chicago Press, 1996.

University of Chicago. *The Chicago Manual of Style.* 14th ed. Chicago: University of Chicago Press, 1993.

Williams, Joseph M. *Style: Toward Clarity and Grace.* Chicago Guides to Writing, Editing, and Publishing. Chicago: University of Chicago, 1990.

INDEX

We want to hear from you. Please send your comments about this book to us in care of the address below. Thank you.

GRAND RAPIDS, MICHIGAN 49530

www.zondervan.com